D1171949

HD
7105.35
.C2
P72
1993

Pratt, Henry J.,
  1934-

Gray agendas.

$39.50

DATE			

BAKER & TAYLOR

Gray Agendas

Gray Agendas:

Interest Groups and Public Pensions in
Canada, Britain, and the United States

Henry J. Pratt

Ann Arbor

THE UNIVERSITY OF MICHIGAN PRESS

Copyright © by the University of Michigan 1993
All rights reserved
Published in the United States of America by
The University of Michigan Press
Manufactured in the United States of America

1996   1995   1994   1993   4   3   2   1

A CIP catalog record for this book is available from the British Library.

Library of Congress Cataloging-in-Publication Data

Pratt, Henry J., 1934–
    Gray agendas : interest groups and public pensions in Canada,
Britain, and the United States / Henry J. Pratt.
        p.   cm.
    Includes bibliographical references and index.
    ISBN 0-472-10430-6 (alk. paper)
    1. Old age pensions—Government policy—Canada.   2. Old age
pensions—Government policy—Great Britain.   3. Old age pensions—
Government policy—United States.   4. Social security—Canada.
5. Social security—Great Britain.   6. Social security—United
States.   7. Aged—Canada—Political activity.   8. Aged—Great
Britain—Political activity.   9. Aged—United States—Political
activity.   10. Lobbying—Canada.   11. Lobbying—Great Britain.
12. Lobbying—United States.   I. Title.
HD7105.35.C2P72   1994
362.6'0971—dc20   93-23236
                                                              CIP

To Annis

Acknowledgments

Numerous individuals have contributed to this book, and I am grateful for their contribution to whatever merit it may possess. Given the book's cross-national, comparative theme, my sense of obligation extends to persons in each of the three countries.

Friends and colleagues in Canada were of major importance in helping to launch this project and later on move it forward. I am indebted to the government of Canada for its award to me in 1991 of a Senior Fellowship in Canadian Studies to investigate Canadian seniors' organizations. In making application for the grant, I benefited from the support of two scholars, C. G. Gifford of Dalhousie University and Victor W. Marshall of the University of Toronto. In the years that followed, both these individuals maintained their support and continued as sources of insight. C. G. Gifford, especially, has earned my gratitude for agreeing to read and critically comment upon the completed manuscript. In addition, two Canadian embassy/consular officials, Norman London and George Costaris, were helpful at the time of the Senior Fellowship, and remained so in later years. Other Canadians whose generosity is appreciated include Robert and Rheba Adolph, Kenneth Kernaghan, Mary Lynn Becker, and Kenneth Pryke.

I am indebted, also, to colleagues in the United Kingdom. Pat Thane of Goldsmith College, University of London, gave generously of her time during my research in that city and was particularly enlightening in regard to the early history of British pensioner activism. Andrew Blaikie of Aberdeen University drew upon his social gerontology expertise to direct me along several fruitful lines of inquiry. Robin Means of Bristol University spent time with me summarizing the results of his research into the history and development of British age-related organizations and made several worthwhile suggestions. And my research in Britain would have been diminished had it not been for the willing assistance provided by several policy-level civil servants and executives on the staffs of age-active voluntary organizations. I especially want to thank George Dunn (of NFRPA), Sally Greengross (of Age Concern), Jillian Crosby (NPCA), and Mervyn Kohler (Help the Aged) for agreeing to be interviewed for this study. Finally, John Miles has earned my gratitude for making available his M.A. thesis on recent British pensioner activism, and for reading and commenting upon the British portion of my completed manuscript.

In regard to the United States, I must begin by acknowledging the support of colleagues in the Wayne State University Department of Political Science. The late Dale Vinyard, whose untimely death in 1991 represented for me the loss of a friend as well as a professional colleague, fostered my initial involvement in aging studies in the early 1970s, and his interest in my endeavors remained unswerving. Charles D. Elder, in the course of numerous conversations, not only gave me the benefit of his rich insight, but also pointed out to me articles and books that otherwise would have escaped attention. I wish also to acknowledge the interest shown by Harold Wolman, John Strate, and Charles Parrish.

Also deserving of my appreciation is the staff of the Wayne State University Institute of Gerontology. A grant from the institute in 1988, under its Summer Scholars Program, contributed significantly to this project during its early stages.

I am very grateful to the students who have enrolled in my courses, Introduction to Canadian Studies and Public Policy and the Aged, at Wayne State University, and I would like to thank them for their valuable suggestions and contagious enthusiasm.

Beyond the limits of my own university, several individuals extended themselves particularly. John B. Williamson, of Boston College, whose research agenda in certain respects parallels my own, deserves special commendation; John was always "there" for me. Andrew Achenbaum of the University of Michigan read this manuscript when it was under consideration by the University of Michigan Press, and his informed criticisms and suggestions enhanced the final product. Peter Hughes gave generously of his time, on the basis of his years of service in the government relations area at AARP, and was enlightening in regard to the community of U.S. groups active in aging issues. Others who were significant in helping sustain my sense of endeavor were Allan Nettleton, Christine Day, and William Lammers.

Special gratitude is owed to the staff at the University of Michigan Press. Colin Day, the press's director, contributed in ways that exceeded the customary expectations of that role. And Laurie Ham was unfailingly helpful.

Finally, I am deeply grateful to my colleagues in the Wayne State Office of the Provost for their encouragement and interest during the latter stages of this project. My secretary, Cele Michalik, was most helpful as the manuscript was undergoing final revision and being readied for submission. And the personnel at the Wayne State University Word Processing Center, especially David Nelson and Susan Smith, were extremely cooperative.

The dedication of this book to my wife, Annis, expresses a gratitude not easily conveyed in words.

Contents

Abbreviations

AAA	Area Agencies on Aging
AALL	American Association for Labor Legislation
AAOAS	American Association for Old Age Security
AARP	American Association of Retired Persons
AASS	American Association for Social Security
AFL	American Federation of Labor
AFL-CIO	American Federation of Labor and Congress of Industrial Organizations
AOA	Administration on Aging
BPTUAA	British Pensioners Trade Union Action Association
CAG	Canadian Association on Gerontology
CAP	Community Action Program
CARP	Canadian Association of Retired Persons
CIAA	Conference of Interested Agencies in Aging
CPA	Center for Policy on Aging
CPC	Canadian Pensioners Concerned
CPP	Canada/Quebec Pension Plan
DHSS	Department of Health and Social Security
DSS	Department of Social Security
FADOQ	Federation de l'Age d'Or du Quebec
FCCC	Federal Council of Churches of Christ
FSA	Federal Security Agency
GAR	Grand Army of the Republic
GIS	Guaranteed Income Supplement
GSA	Gerontological Society of America
MSRC	Moral and Social Reform Council
NASC	National Alliance of Senior Citizens
NCPSSM	National Committee to Preserve Social Security and Medicare
NCCOP	National Corporation for the Care of Old People

NCOA	National Council on the Aging
NCOAP	National Council on Old Age Pensions
NCSC	National Council of Senior Citizens
NCSS	National Council of Social Services
N4A	National Association of Area Agencies on Aging
NFOAPA	National Federation of Old Age Pensions Associations
NFRPA	National Federation of Retirement Pensions Associations
NOPWC	National Old People's Welfare Council
NP&SCF	National Pensioners and Senior Citizens Federation
NPC	National Pensions Committee
NRTA	National Retired Teachers Association
NTLC	National Trades and Labor Congress
NWRO	National Welfare Rights Organization
OAA	Old Age Assistance
OAI	Old Age Insurance
OAS	Old Age Security
OASDI	Old Age, Survivors, and Disability Insurance
OASI	Old Age and Survivors Insurance
OECD	Organization for Economic Cooperation and Development
OXFAM	Oxford Committee for Famine Relief
SERPS	State Earnings-related Pension Scheme
SOS	Save Our Security
SSA	Social Security Administration
SSB	Social Security Board
TGWU	Transport and General Workers Union
TLC	Trades and Labor Congress
TUC	Trades Union Congress
USCO	United Senior Citizens of Ontario
VCG	Help for Vital Causes Group

CHAPTER 1

Introduction

Over the past quarter century interest groups active on behalf of the elderly in the United States, and likewise in the other industrial democracies, have come to represent a major social phenomenon. As is well known, a handful of such groups have become extremely large, with one of their number, the American Association of Retired Persons (AARP), at thirty-three million members and $300 million in 1990 revenues now the largest, and probably the wealthiest,[1] voluntary organization in the United States, and quite possibly in any country.[2] AARP's approximate counterpart in the United Kingdom, Age Concern, with over a thousand local units, is likewise among that country's larger age-advocacy organizations. Moreover, there has been significant recent growth among smaller, more specialized aging organizations devoted to specific clienteles and particular problem areas.

And it is not only their number and size that account for these groups' high level of social visibility and perceived importance. Another factor has been the public's growing awareness of senior citizens and generalized sympathy toward their needs and aspirations. To a large extent, the public has embraced the compassionate stereotype that seniors are perceived as a group in deserving need—notwithstanding that the stereotype involves a distortion of reality in a manner potentially harmful to the specialized needs of various subsets of the elderly population.[3] Further adding to the importance of seniors' organizations has been population aging. Even though not an entirely new phenomenon—it actually became manifest in some countries, Sweden and France especially, toward the end of the nineteenth century—population aging did not impact the industrialized world generally until well into the twentieth century, and only recently has it become a "worldwide phenomenon that commands immediate attention."[4] Given the increased recognition

---

1. Janet Novack, "Strength from Its Gray Roots," *Forbes Magazine*, November 25, 1991, p. 89.

2. Bruce Jacobs, "Aging and Politics," in Robert Binstock and Linda K. George, eds., *Handbook of Aging and the Social Sciences*, 3d ed. (New York: Academic Press, 1990), p. 324.

3. Robert Binstock, "The Aged as Scapegoat," *Gerontologist* 23 (Summer 1983): 136–43.

4. George C. Myers, "The Demography of Aging," in Robert Binstock and Linda K. George, eds., *Handbook of Aging and the Social Sciences*, 3d ed. (New York: Academic Press, 1990), pp. 19–44 (quotation, p. 20).

accorded this trend, spokespersons for the elderly, including the leaders of voluntary organizations, have achieved enhanced stature and acceptance.

By virtue of their large size and scale of operations, combined with their perceived legitimacy in the eyes of attentive publics, it is reasonable to assume that voluntary organizations on aging can, and do, influence their members' attitudes, values, and aspirations, thereby indirectly influencing the societies of which they are a part.

Aging organizations would therefore qualify as worthy of serious attention even if they were not involved in the governmental process. Yet it is clearly the case that political action undertaken by these organizations has added greatly to their importance, as perceived by both political elites and voting electorates. There was a delay of a decade or more after these groups' initial political involvement before they gained any appreciable measure of scholarly recognition. Yet any disregard of them in the past has now been largely remedied, as social scientists have come to acknowledge their often significant governmental role.[5] Such enhanced interest has been especially apparent in sociology and political science, where several scholars have made the study of age-active interest groups a major part of their research agendas.[6]

Still, interesting and important questions remain to be addressed regarding these organizations, and it is unclear that these can be adequately treated through the single-country approach, which has dominated this field to the virtual exclusion of cross-national comparison.[7] It becomes clear upon reflection that at least two difficulties confront the former of these approaches: first,

---

5. Illustrative of the recognition presently accorded such political organizations by students of government is the current content of college-level American government textbooks. I recently examined the contents of eleven such texts, sent to my department by their publishers, including all the leading books of this type that are currently available. The survey revealed that seven of the eleven reference AARP—well above what could be expected considering that these texts devote but limited space to interest groups, and typically name but a handful. It is likely that a similar collection of American government texts from as recently as the mid-1970s would not have mentioned AARP, or any other aging organization. This surmise cannot be easily tested, since no texts from that or any other earlier period are readily available. Yet three books from the 1970s, all devoted entirely to interest groups, contain not a single reference to AARP or to any other seniors' organization. They are James Q. Wilson, *Political Organizations* (New York: Basic Books, 1973); L. Harmon Zeigler and Wayne Peak, *Interest Groups in American Politics*, 2d ed. (Englewood Cliffs, N.J.: Prentice-Hall, 1972); Carol S. Greenwald, *Group Power: Lobbying and Public Policy* (New York: Praeger, 1977).

6. For the United States such scholars would include (in addition to the present author): Robert Binstock, Christine L. Day, William W. Lammers, Lawrence A. Powell, and John B. Williamson; for Canada: C. G. Gifford; for the United Kingdom: Andrew Blaikie and Pat Thane.

7. An exception to this statement is C. G. Gifford's recent book, *Canada's Fighting Seniors* (Toronto: James Lorimer, 1990). In addition to its highly illuminating comments on aging organizations in Canada, this book contains worthwhile discussions of similar organizations in the United States, Britain, and several continental European countries.

single-nation analyses largely preclude one's controlling for idiosyncracies of place and political setting, and second, the number of cases may fall below the minimum considered necessary from the standpoint of hypothesis testing. The comparative, cross-national approach is appealing as a means of dealing with both these concerns, and that has entered into my decision to adopt it in this book.

Three countries have been selected for attention, namely Canada, Britain, and the United States. The basis for this selection is that seniors' organizations in these settings are believed to stand out to an unusual degree from the wider social landscape. There are data to suggest that in a global perspective it is the exception and not the rule for seniors' organizations, or any type of voluntary organization on aging, to have any very pronounced influence on government. As brought out by John B. Williamson of Boston College and Fred C. Pampel of the University of Colorado, such groups are in a position to achieve such influence only when certain societal preconditions are met. The conditions include a minimal guarantee of civil liberties, especially the rights of freedom of speech and peaceable assembly; some societal tradition of voluntarism; and disposable personal income adequate to permit large-scale citizen support of voluntary organizations. Even though it may be possible to form nongovernmental organizations on aging in the absence of certain of these conditions, groups formed in that manner are less likely to possess much voice or autonomy. These authors observe:

> The analysis presented in our four industrial nation case studies makes extensive use of the interest group pressure thesis . . . [whereas] the evidence in support of the thesis is weaker for the three Third World countries. . . . Well developed democratic structures may be necessary for a fully developed version of interest group pluralism.[8]

The Williamson-Pampel study compares seven countries—four in the developing world (Britain, Sweden, the United States, and Germany) and three in the Third World (Brazil, Nigeria, and India). Although this study is not concerned with seniors' organizations primarily, it does include references to such groups in the section of each chapter devoted to the "neo-pluralism model." Two of its findings are of interest in the present context. Firstly, among the four Third World nations, nongovernmental aging organizations were in no case significant actors in regard to old age security policy. This is reflective of several factors: these countries' authoritarian traditions of government, prevailing low literacy levels, and extreme ethnic and/or tribal di-

---

8. John B. Williamson and Fred C. Pampel, *Old Age Security in Comparative Perspective* (New York: Oxford University Press, 1993), p. 218.

versity, which contributes to low levels of national consensus. Secondly, even though senior citizen mass membership organizations exist in all four of the industrially developed countries covered in the study, they have acted independently, in a highly visible pressure group role, only in the two that are characterized by liberal political cultures, namely, Britain and the United States. In Germany and Sweden, where the prevailing political culture has been more corporatist, pensioner and senior citizen organizations, although routinely consulted by policymakers as the principles of corporatism demand, have not been an important external source of political activism or pressure.

It is apparent, then, that senior citizen organizations represent an independent source of policy input and realized political influence in but a handful of countries, among them Britain and the United States. And given the close similarities, cultural and political, existing between those two countries and Canada, one has every reason to anticipate that it, likewise, will display age-advocacy organizations to a significant extent. It should be stressed that the selection of these three countries for investigation in no way depends on showing that the role that senior organizations have come to play in these countries is necessarily typical of that of their counterparts elsewhere, either among industrial democracies or in the Third World. The selection is based, instead, on evidence suggestive of their being settings highly congenial to interest group activity, and where hypotheses relating to such organizations are likely to be the most readily testable.

My intent as a scholar concerned with the study of political interest groups is threefold: first, to describe how these aging organizations succeeded in initially forming themselves, bearing in mind the odds against successful group formation; second, to describe the changing political settings, or arenas, in which aging policy has been decided in each of the countries; and third, to analyze their political roles in the light of interest group theory.

One point worthy of emphasis in regard to voluntary organizations on aging, or any other field, is the inherently risky nature of group formation and group maintenance. Membership groups represent a hazardous undertaking, confronting as they do various risks: the potential for debilitating member apathy and indifference (compounded by the distracting effects of television and other forms of mass entertainment); the potential for internal factionalism and cleavages; and the threat of displacement of goals (i.e., away from the originally stated objectives toward others not always formally acknowledged or generally agreed upon). And additional risks apply especially to membership groups made up of senior citizens—the limited life expectancy of the typical newly recruited member (only fifteen years more or less beyond age sixty-five), the reluctance to displace one's group affiliations of a lifetime in favor of senior-group status, the fact that membership eligibility often occurs at a time in one's life of declining personal income, and the energy and willingness to take on new commitments, including voluntary organizational membership.

That the risks to age-group survival are real, not just imagined, is apparent from the historical record. The names of numerous organizations have appeared, only later on to disappear, from the listings given in successive editions of encyclopedias of associations published for various countries. While such organizational bankruptcies seem to have been especially common in the United States,[9] the same applies also to Britain and Canada. And it is not merely the smaller, more obviously fragile, organizations that have been at risk. One of the largest retiree or senior citizen organizations ever to arise, namely the U.S.-based Townsend movement, eventually succumbed, notwithstanding its early large base of members—in the hundreds of thousands—and seemingly secure finances.[10] The special difficulties involved in forming a seniors' organization, or indeed any association specific to the concerns of seniors, are implicit in the fact that the greatest wave of interest group formation in U.S. history, namely that occurring in the period 1900–1920, of which it has been said that "there has never been anything like it before or since,"[11] saw no effort to form a national organization on this particular basis. This cannot be attributed to any generalized refusal to acknowledge seniors as a distinct population grouping, since, as W. Andrew Achenbaum points out, as early as the second decade of the twentieth century, on the basis of changing cultural assumptions and statistical realities, "old age [had become] a national problem."[12]

It can be taken as a given, therefore, that powerful external forces may be required in order for viable seniors' organizations to emerge. What might these consist of? A clue may inhere in the tendency for such groups to originate in waves, or clusters, as opposed to random moments over time. This clustering tendency, whose exact dimensions are outlined in the following, appears not to have been remarked on previously, and moreover, is not easily explainable on the basis of existing interest group theory. While political scientists have formulated hypotheses intended to account for the observable wavelike patterns of group formation throughout American history, they

9. Henry J. Pratt, "National Interest Groups among the Elderly: Consolidation and Constraint," in William P. Browne and Laura K. Olson, eds., *Aging and Public Policy: The Politics of Growing Old in America* (Westport, Conn.: Greenwood Press, 1983), p. 147.

10. Abraham Holtzman, *The Townsend Movement* (New York: Bookman Associates, 1963).

11. Wilson, *Political Organizations*, p. 198.

12. W. Andrew Achenbaum, *Old Age in the New Land: The American Experience since 1790* (Baltimore: Johns Hopkins University Press, 1978), chap. 6.

do not entirely square with the observed pattern in aging. Thus, in the course of his classic 1951 analysis of interest groups,[13] David B. Truman develops the theme that the recurrent waves of new group formation are best understood as a response to environmental disturbances of one kind or another, especially technological innovation (resulting in economic disturbance) and war. Thus, in Truman's formulation an initial disturbance, resulting in the coalescence of a given group not previously organized, can easily end up creating a ripple effect, as other latent groups, threatened by the coalescence of the first, now proceed to organize in self-defense and in hopes of restoring the preexisting social balance. Writing some two decades after Truman, another leading political scientist, James Q. Wilson, offers fresh insight on this same point.[14] Wilson observes that the tendency for interest groups to form in clusters often is reflective of a prevailing climate of "moral concern," which from time to time has surfaced throughout the course of American history. Given such an opinion climate, appeals made by organizers ("political entrepreneurs") to both present and potential group members are likely to achieve heightened credibility—above what might be expected in more normal times. The fledgling voluntary organization is thereby better able, in Wilson's view, to survive its most vulnerable, fledgling stage and to evolve into a mature, stable organization.

While the formation of certain voluntary organizations on aging is explainable on the basis of one or the other of the preceding hypotheses, that does not seem to be the case in general. It is true that the Townsend movement could well serve as a textbook case of group formation stemming from a prior disturbance, in this case the Great Depression of the 1930s. And the formation in 1970 of the Gray Panthers—a cross-generational interest group whose policy concerns encompass but are not confined to aging issues—was largely attributable to the heightened moral fervor of the 1960s, which contributed to its formation as it did also to other movement groups of the time. (Indeed, *Gray Panthers* was a modification of *Black Panthers*, the name used by a leading race protest and self-help organization of the time.)

Nevertheless, a survey of aging organizations formed sometime during this century, including ones in Britain and Canada as well as the United States, reveals that the bulk of them were formed, not chiefly in response to some tangible disturbance, or at a time of pronounced moral fervor, but rather under quite different circumstances. Thus, for example, the two largest U.S. age-membership groups, AARP and the National Council of Senior Citizens (NCSC), were both formed over a common three-year period, 1958–1961, as

---

13. David B. Truman, *The Governmental Process* (New York: Knopf, 1951), pp. 54–55.
14. Wilson, *Political Organizations*, chap. 10.

was also the National Council on the Aging (NCOA)—an association of professionals involved in this field. Notwithstanding the minor economic downturns of 1958 and 1960, this was a period of relative prosperity in the United States, and it came before the era of protest and activism that would mark the 1960s. The same point applies to the largest present-day seniors' organizations in Britain and Canada, Age Concern and the National Pensioners and Senior Citizens Federation (NP&SCF), respectively. The former of these coalesced in 1970, and the latter received its federal charter in 1954,[15] neither of them particularly stressful or exceptional moments in British or Canadian history. In short, one is dealing here with interest group coalescence occurring for the most part in periods of relative peace, social order, and economic good times.

Caution is warranted in suggesting that the formation of seniors' organizations over the course of the twentieth century has been chiefly responsive to factors other than those mentioned by Truman and Wilson. Two considerations underlie the need for such caution. Firstly, the motivations that animated the various organizational founders are not readily knowable, and conceivably one or another of their points of emphasis (i.e., a moral concern climate or an external disturbance) may have animated these leaders' thinking to some unsuspected degree. Secondly, in an aging context the dimension of moral concern can never be ruled out entirely as a factor promoting collective action and group formation. All the Western democracies have evolved in their understanding of society's moral obligation toward the poor and the disadvantaged. Thus, a leading British scholar, Richard M. Titmuss, some years ago observed that over the course of the past 150 years Western society has moved through three distinct periods (or models) of social policy: (1) an initial "Residual Welfare" model, characterized by the assumption that individuals naturally meet their needs through the channels of the private market and the family, and where public welfare benefits are offered begrudgingly and only as a last resort; (2) a subsequent "Industrial Achievement-Performance" model, marked by a general acceptance of various types of social welfare institutions (including state-funded), but in which the definition of "need" remains focused on recipients' merit, work performance, and productivity; and, most recently, (3) an "Industrial Redistributive" model, under which social welfare is seen as the major integrating institution in society—"providing universalist services outside the market on the principle of need"—and where redistribution of resources on behalf of the disadvantaged

---

15. The founding year for this federation was 1945. Yet for several years it functioned essentially as a regional movement, its members being drawn entirely from Canada's four western provinces, and with no established presence in Ottawa, the national capital.

becomes a fundamental operative principle.[16] Implicit in all this evolution in moral understanding is a broadening of the sense of entitlement, a more comprehensive and universalistic notion of rights. And one by-product of this evolution has been Western society's enlarged acceptance of voluntary organizations and politically active interest groups—ones capable of giving voice to disadvantaged groupings of various kinds, among them senior citizens.

Nevertheless, while useful to bear in mind as background, this trend cannot directly explain the formation and subsequent evolution of senior organizations. This is so because the trend described was very gradual, encompassing many decades, whereas the voluntary organizations here in question emerged in clusters at discrete historical moments.

It would appear, then, that some other factor, not specified in existing theory, was critically involved in the observed waves of organizational development. It therefore serves as one of this book's basic purposes to identify, if possible, the missing element, and to suggest how it may have affected the politics of aging and age-based political action.

This brings me to the basic thesis of this book. The approach here adopted involves a departure from earlier analyses of aging policy, wherein the emphasis has been commonly placed on the forces that gave rise to various age-policy developments over time, and the perceived impacts of changing policy outputs on nations undergoing population aging. Instead, the message here is that formal legislative enactments by governments have both direct program effects (on eligible beneficiaries) and indirect effects (on the wider political environment of aging). The direct effects are for the most part deliberate and consciously intended, while the indirect are mostly unintended and unconscious. It is the latter, indirect, effects that are chiefly of interest here, especially as they relate to age-active political organizations and interest groups. New aging-related legislative enactments and policy directions will be studied from the standpoint of their potential indirect effect on the political arenas, with special attention paid to (1) the formation of new interest groups and (2) the ability of such groups, assuming their survival, later on to influence the scope and content of subsequent government action on old age security matters. Reversing, in other words, the more usual stress on how pressure groups can help to shape how government chooses to act, the present discussion—while taking that dimension into account—is more fundamentally concerned with public policy change as a factor in political action.

This line of thought is developed for each of the three countries, in a historical sweep beginning with the opening years of the twentieth century and moving to the present time. The working hypothesis is that the designated

---

16. Richard M. Titmuss, *Social Policy: An Introduction* (New York: Pantheon Books, 1974), pp. 30–31.

stages have arrived in the same sequential manner in each of these countries, and with similar consequences for political participation—a commonality in responses that has not been undercut by the marked variations, cross-nationally, in the timing, size, and scope of aging programs.

The discussion considers the possibility that at each successive stage, as the level of mandated state benefits in aging has been enlarged over that of the stage immediately preceding, the number and variety of political interest groups has been increased, and at roughly the same rate of change. A further possibility is that similar patterns of interest group activity have characterized each country at a given stage of age-policy development. The larger the policy stimulus, one can reasonably hypothesize, the greater will be its consequences for political behavior.

The decision to investigate these matters ties into a long-standing intellectual concern of mine. I have been fascinated for a number of years by the social and cultural settings that have proved conducive to interest group formation, and to later reorientations of groups' accustomed modes of social action.[17] It has disturbed me that the interest group literature has mostly seen groups as fixed in their original modes, impervious to change. I have also been intrigued by the possible reciprocal relationships that can develop between interest groups and government, images often obscured in the customary "demand pressure model," which posits a unidirectional pattern (influence is presumed to run from interest groups, viewed as the source of pressure. to government, which is seen as the target). While it would be an exaggeration to suggest that existing theory has entirely disregarded such reciprocity,[18] the tendency remains fairly strong in the literature.

Considerable indirect evidence exists to suggest that the general pattern of interest group and government interactions is more complex than is usually assumed. In an era of "positive government," the state has greatly expanded its private sector role over the course of this century. In response to economic forces and shifting public expectations, governments have acted in a variety of ways: enlarging, contracting, and redirecting their interventions as circumstances appear to warrant. In the process they have shown a capacity first to *shape*, and later to *reshape*, state programs, including ones on aging and social security. The existing literature contains occasional brief references to public

---

17. In *The Liberalization of American Protestantism: A Case Study in Complex Organizations* (Detroit: Wayne State University Press, 1972), I trace the forces giving rise to a fundamental reorientation of political strategy on the part of the National Council of Churches of Christ, under the impact of the civil rights movement.

18. Thus, David B. Truman points out that one of the larger and more influential major American interest groups, namely the American Farm Bureau Federation, was formed directly as a result of insistence on the part of the U.S. secretary of agriculture that the then-scattered farming organizations should coalesce. Truman, *Governmental Process*, pp. 90–93.

policy change as a factor in age-group formation, including the insightful comments on the U.S. case by Robert B. Hudson and John Strate, and on Canada by Kenneth Bryden.[19] But systematic development of these observations has been lacking. Furthermore, there appears to have been no attention given to the possibility that *changing* public policy outputs, involving occasional redefinitions of existing policy arenas on aging, may prompt existing groups to abandon, or greatly modify, traditional strategies in favor of fresh approaches.

These remarks take on added significance in light of a wider intellectual trend in the social and policy sciences that has been apparent over the past decade. The question of how and for what reasons governments come to adopt particular approaches to social welfare, and with what consequences for the larger society, has proved intriguing to a number of policy analysts. Such analysts' differing explanatory models have reflected, in part, their diverse disciplinary backgrounds, and also their varying ideological orientations: liberal, Marxian, conservative, among others. For a number of years, in the 1950s and 1960s especially, the tendency among leading scholars was to stress *social forces* as the major determinants of public policy outcomes. But in the 1970s and early 1980s there occurred a shift in emphasis, involving an increased stress on the state and its potential to shape outcomes. Under this emergent *state-centered* conception, governmental officials came to be viewed as in large part autonomous actors. The shift was evident in both sociology and political science, even though the reasons involved were radically different in the two cases.

In sociology, as Theda Skocpol remarks in a discussion devoted to the problem of accounting for social revolutions, the shift arose as a challenge to both liberal and Marxist varieties of social theory:

> [The traditional assumption was that] political structures and struggles can somehow be reduced (at least in the "last instance") to socioeconomic forces and conflicts. The state is viewed as nothing but *an arena* in which conflict over basic social and economic interests are fought out. What makes the state-as-political-arena special is simply that actors operating within it resort to distinctive means for waging social and economic conflicts—means such as coercion or slogans appealing to the general good.[20]

---

19. Robert B. Hudson and John Strate, "Aging and Political Systems," in Robert Binstock and Ethel P. Shanas, eds., *Handbook of Aging and the Social Sciences*, 2d ed. (New York: Van Nostrand Reinhold, 1985), p. 578; Kenneth Bryden, *Old Age Pensions and Policy-making in Canada* (Montreal and London: McGill-Queens University Press, 1974), p. 194.

20. Theda Skocpol, *States and Social Revolutions: A Comparative Analysis of France, Russia, and China* (Cambridge: Harvard University Press, 1979), p. 25.

The earlier sociological outlook came to be challenged, especially among Marxist-oriented intellectuals, in the course of a renewed interest in the "problem of the state." In contradistinction to the traditional Marxian notion of states as essentially tools to be manipulated in the interests of the dominant social class, an insurgent group of Marxian sociologists now began to explore the degree to which rulers may free themselves, within limits, of class subservience. The rulers are not viewed as entirely autonomous, since they are seen as constrained by various pressures, class among them, whose effect is somewhat to limit the rulers' range of policy options. But their margin of choice is considered as far wider than traditional Marxians had supposed. Such a view was first developed rather tentatively by several sociologists in the late 1960s and early 1970s, and then later more explicitly and radically by three writers of kindred outlook: Theda Skocpol, Ellen Kay Trimberger, and Fred Block. Variously labeled as the "organizational" and the "realist" approach, these theorists have maintained that the state is at least potentially autonomous, "not only over against dominant classes but also vis a vis entire class structures or modes of production."[21]

In the field of political science, the parallel shift represented to some extent a break from the preceding liberal view, which is traceable to the eighteenth-century thinking of James Madison, and more immediately to various twentieth-century authors associated with classical interest group theory, especially Pendleton Herring, David B. Truman, V. O. Key, and Robert Dahl. Parting company with such classicists, and building to some extent on a series of challenges to "group theory," which appeared in the 1960s, this outlook elaborated on what came to be termed an *institutional* or *constitutive* paradigm. These terms denote the view of the state as possessing wide autonomy from outside pressures, interest group and otherwise, and as possessed of the ability to bring otherwise scattered members of the political community into organic relationship with one another. Stephen Elkin develops such a view in the context of a theoretical discussion of American urban politics.[22] Likewise, Eric A. Nordlinger, an American, and Alan Cairns, a Canadian, each develop the same theme in commentaries devoted, respectively, to national and provincial governments.[23] This state-centered approach was found helpful in

---

21. Ibid., pp. 27 and 301 note 73; Ellen Kay Trimberger, "State Power and Modes of Production: The Implications of the Japanese Transition to Capitalism," *Insurgent Sociologist* 7 (Spring 1977): 85–98; Fred Block, "The Ruling Class Does Not Rule: Notes on the Marxist Theory of the State," *Socialist Revolution* 33 (May–June 1977): 6–28.

22. Stephen Elkin, *City and Regime in the American Republic* (Chicago: University of Chicago Press, 1987), pp. 106–9, 199–200.

23. Eric A. Nordlinger, *On the Autonomy of the Democratic State* (Cambridge: Harvard University Press, 1981); Alan Cairns, "The Governments and Societies of Canadian Federalism," *Canadian Journal of Political Science* 10, no. 4 (December 1977): 695–725.

seeking a more adequate understanding of the impact of shifting governmental priorities, as one group of leaders replaces another in office. A recent commentary dealing with the United States, for example, underscores how the decline of the traditional "subgovernments" and "iron triangles" in Washington, and their replacement by emergent patterns of redistributive politics, were traceable in part to the assumption of power by the ideologically conservative Reagan administration.[24]

In addition to those political scientists whose work can be regarded as comprising the larger challenge to traditional liberal thought, others in the same discipline drew inspiration from a reaction against a perceived orthodoxy in comparative studies, under which a sociological view was seen as exerting a dominant, and to their minds baleful, influence. Thus, in a 1979 essay devoted to public welfare provision in Scandinavia, Francis G. Castles and R. D. McKinlay take issue with what they describe as "the sociological view that public policy outcomes are primarily a reflection of what can loosely be described as 'environmental' factors: the demographic structure of the population, the incremental logic of policy programmers, and, most important of all, the level of economic development." In place of this outlook, described by Castles and McKinlay as the "politics does not matter view," evidence is offered to support the view that political factors have been critical in the region's social policy development. Special prominence is given in this essay to development of a more realistic view of the Scandinavian case, with emphasis being placed upon the variation over time in the electoral strength of the major party of the Right and the varying size and internal cohesion of Scandinavia's several labor movements. Both of these political factors are revealed as independently important in fostering policy change in Scandinavia, in regard to the rate and scope of change.[25]

Implicit in this conception of state-as-autonomous-actor is a basis for skepticism regarding the capacity of interest groups to dominate government decision making. While it is true that even the classical interest group theorists, with their strong emphasis on the pervasiveness of group penetration of the political process, never assumed that governmental actions can be accounted for entirely in group terms, it remains the case that it has been the more recent theorists who have been the more explicit in regard to factors that tend to set limits on group political power. Such inhibition is a useful point to keep in mind at the outset of the present investigation into the role of groups

---

24. Randall B. Ripley and Grace A. Franklin, *Congress, the Bureaucracy, and Public Policy*, 4th ed. (Chicago: Dorsey Press, 1987), pp. 147 and 210.

25. Francis G. Castles and R. D. McKinlay, "Public Welfare Provision, Scandinavia, and the Sheer Futility of the Sociological Approach to Politics," *British Journal of Political Science* 9 (1979): 157–71.

active in the aging or state pension field. And, in fact, preliminary investigation does strongly suggest that the major pensioner and age-advocacy organizations in the three countries are regularly reminded of the limits on their political influence, and of governments' capacity to act in ways not always congenial to their own policy preferences. There are data to suggest that the aging organizations have found special difficulty in influencing the momentous legislative changes that have marked the transitions between policy stages.[26]

The present study does not demonstrate the validity of the state-centered or state-as-autonomous conception, notwithstanding that some limited evidence consistent with such a view is offered, especially in chapter 6. Instead, it is taken as a given, useful as a point of departure and as corrective of any suggestion that policy choice is reducable, finally, to factors of an essentially nongovernmental nature. The need for such correction can scarcely be overemphasized. As recently as the 1960s and early 1970s scholars were inclined to regard age-policy development as derivative from wider social forces and mass movements.[27] And while this society-centered view no longer represents the predominant mode of analysis, it has not been altogether absent from recent scholarship.[28]

The potential payoff from applying a state-centered view to the field of aging is implicit in the highly suggestive work of the late Jack L. Walker and his colleagues Mark A. Peterson and Thomas L. Gais at the Institute of Public Policy Studies at the University of Michigan. These investigators produce evidence showing that during the quarter century following World War II in the United States, government-provided patronage served as a major resource upon which interest group leaders were able to draw. The postwar period witnessed a veritable explosion of group formation in American national government, including many new political organizations that, by the accepted

---

26. Given the very high stakes involved, it is perhaps not surprising that Theodore R. Marmor's classic study of the struggle over Medicare legislation in the United States should make no mention whatever of any interest group specific to aging. See Theodore R. Marmor, *The Politics of Medicare* (Chicago: Aldine, 1973).

27. Holtzman, *Townsend Movement*; J. Douglas Brown, *The Genesis of the American Social Security System* (Princeton: Industrial Relations section, Princeton University, 1969); Jackson K. Putnam, *Old-Age Politics in California: From Richardson to Reagan* (Stanford: Stanford University Press, 1970); Francis Fox Piven and Richard A. Cloward, *Regulating the Poor: The Functions of Public Welfare* (New York: Vintage Books, 1971); Harold Wilensky, *The Welfare State and Equality: Structural and Ideological Roots of Public Expenditure* (Berkeley: University of California Press, 1971); David Collier and Richard Messick, "Prerequisites versus Diffusion: Testing Alternative Explanations of Social Security Adoption," *American Political Science Review* 69 (1975): 1299–1315.

28. Jill Quadragno, *The Transformation of Old Age Security: Class and Politics in the American Welfare State* (Chicago: University of Chicago Press, 1988).

"logic of collective action,"[29] could be considered as well-nigh impossible to organize and maintain, in particular, public interest lobbies and citizen groups.[30] Walker, Peterson, and Gais do not point to government as the sole source of such patronage—their data reveal, for example, that private foundations also were an important provider. Yet their findings make it clear that *governmental* patronage was highly significant. Moreover, in a single-authored essay, Walker points out that in no area of public policy was government-provided patronage more critical than in the organizing efforts undertaken among senior citizens and retirees. "More than half of the 46 groups representing the elderly in my study were formed after 1965," he remarks, "the year of the great legislative breakthroughs of Medicare and the Older Americans Act."[31]

Other analysts have elaborated on this same theme, although without specific reference to senior citizen and aging organizations. Thus, Eric A. Nordlinger points out that sponsorship of interest groups by government has frequently come about through governmental officials seizing the initiative, and is not simply a response to interest group prodding—an observation that this author uses to reinforce his larger point about government's capacity for autonomous action.[32] And Theodore Lowi makes it one of the three defining features of his highly influential concept of interest group liberalism that "the role of government is one of ensuring access particularly to the most effectively organized, and of ratifying the agreements and adjustments worked out among the competing leaders and their claims."[33] Lowi then goes on to point out that increasing acceptance of interest group liberalism on the part of policymakers in Washington, especially during the 1960s, led them inevitably to insist that if an interest group is not already organized then government must take steps to ensure that it becomes so. A short time later, Lowi's model was applied to the field of aging by Robert Binstock.[34]

In this book I take these earlier findings and commentaries into account, while seeking to extend their relevance and scope. To do this requires some

---

29. Mancur Olson, *The Logic of Collective Action* (Cambridge: Harvard University Press, 1965).

30. Jack L. Walker, "The Origins and Maintenance of Interest Groups in America," *American Political Science Review* 77 (June 1983): 390–406; Thomas L. Gais, Mark A. Peterson, and Jack L. Walker, "Interest Groups, Iron Triangles, and Representative Institutions in American National Government," *British Journal of Political Science* 14, pt. 2 (April 1984): 161–85.

31. Walker, "Origins and Maintenance of Interest Groups in America," p. 403.

32. Nordlinger, *On the Autonomy of the Democratic State*, p. 161.

33. Theodore Lowi, *The End of Liberalism: Ideology, Policy, and the Crisis of Public Authority* (New York: W. W. Norton, 1969), pp. 71 and 83.

34. Robert Binstock, "Interest-Group Liberalism and the Politics of Aging," *Gerontologist* 12 (1972): 265–80.

shift in emphasis. Instead of emphasizing the capacity of politicians and government officials directly and consciously to promote interest group development, the emphasis here is on government's far more substantial potential, acting indirectly and without necessary conscious intent, to establish the foundations upon which age-group formation can later take place. I argue that this development eventuated in transformations in the arena of public pensions and aging, such that eligible beneficiaries were initially made conscious of their stake in public pensions, and later on in the benefits inherent in governments lending support to age-advocacy organizations of various kinds. In the largest sense, therefore, the emphasis here is on governments' potential to drive politics and political behavior.

One advantage inherent in the historical and cross-national approach employed here consists in its potential for improving one's understanding of how interest groups can form, and later survive, under widely varying social and political circumstances. The comparative approach should prove helpful in explaining why, for example, it was possible for the early interest groups on aging to subsist despite an absence of legitimization from national governments. Obviously, the early gray lobbies in various countries could not look to government for support, direct or indirect, given the absence of positive governmental commitment at that point to meeting old age security needs. On what basis, therefore, were such early interest groups able to become established and to assert a political mandate? And how did those early groups, which originated around the turn of the century, differ from ones established later, when governments had finally entered the field and begun offering public pensions and other aging programs? One of the purposes of this study is finding answers to such questions.

Every field of public policy has certain distinguishing characteristics that taken together justify its separation from other fields. With respect to public policy in aging, the distinguishing features consist of several elements. One has been the vast scale of expenditures involved—eclipsing that for almost any other governmental program, domestic or international. A second has been the tendency for programs in this field to expand linearly throughout the twentieth century, beginning with the first tentative efforts undertaken early in this century and proceeding in stages to the present. At each stage lawmakers have attempted, through the provision of direct state benefits, to meet an existing need among aging and aged individuals. Thirdly, this field has been unique in terms of the special public legitimacy accorded to the clientele: the senior citizen population. Such perceived legitimacy has contributed importantly to governments' willingness to expand benefits in a consistently more generous direction.

And fourthly, while not exactly unique to the field in question, it is worthwhile noting that aging policy has been characterized by a perceived permanency of programs. None of these mandated benefit increases ever entirely realized, perhaps, the larger objectives set forth for them by its legislative sponsors, it being one thing for governments to enact social security measures but quite another to provide genuine security for the mass of their elderly population. And, indeed, the perceived inadequacies of existing social security and state pension programs have been a repeated theme among advocates for the elderly both within government and on the outside. Such criticisms have had their effect in promoting further policy changes and reforms. Nevertheless, criticisms along this line have not entirely undercut the basic perception in the Western democracies—shared in by policy elites within government and by the general public—that these age-benefit programs have broadly proved their value, and that turning back to a laissez-faire state is not feasible. Thus, the programs now anchored in place in this field are considered as essential to the health and stability of a democratic, urban industrial society. The existing legislation in this field, often highly controversial at the time of enactment, has for the most part passed into the realm of the consensual—with the basic statutes having in some cases survived in essentially their original form, and in others having been entirely recast.

As previously made clear, this book's main emphasis is on how new state enactments in aging may have indirectly altered the political setting for age policy in ways not always fully intended or wholly anticipated by the sponsors of the original legislation. The following questions are illustrative of the course to be followed. How and to what extent have the age-benefit schemes in the three countries served as incentives in fostering the mobilization and maintenance of various advocacy organizations for seniors in the three countries? How large must the incentives become if they are to overcome the countervailing tendency for state benefits, often enacted with fanfare and great rhetorical flourish, to negate the perceived need for such mobilization? And, finally, as the number of age-related interest groups has expanded and the arena of aging has become more densely populated, to what extent have those groups found it necessary to negotiate not just with government but also with one another? Given an increasing density of age-group interaction, in other words, how has the character of the present-day age-policy arena been affected?

Some questions may be raised about the heavy stress placed on interest groups in this study, given that they are only one among several actors that collectively comprise the age-political arenas in the three countries. Obviously, any attempt to comprehend totally the context of aging policy would have to give detailed treatment to a variety of actors—some of them within government (e.g., lawmakers and appointive government officials) and others not on the public payroll (e.g., social welfare think tanks, political party elites, the insurance industry, the medical and hospital lobby, and organized labor). Obviously, any comprehensive study of the politics of the elderly would require attention being paid to such policy participants. Yet a primary emphasis on senior citizen groups, and other age-advocacy groups, appears justified on several grounds. Firstly, by virtue of their self-definition as advocates for the aging, such groups are uniquely positioned to benefit from the generalized approval modern society accords upon aging and elderly individuals. Secondly, almost without exception, the existing scholarly literature in the politics of age field devotes substantial space to this particular category of political actor. Evidently, leading students in this field generally share the view that this particular force is one deserving of special emphasis. And thirdly, and perhaps most importantly, pensioner organizations and senior citizen groups typically maintain a consistency of focus on the concerns of aging and aged individuals, in contrast to other types of interest groups—labor unions, medical associations, and war veterans' organizations—whose participation in this field tends to be more episodic. Seniors' organizations have unique potential for becoming an element in the constituency around which age-benefit programs are initially fostered and then later develop. As earlier suggested, they would be important from a societal standpoint even if they were to choose, for some reason, not to involve themselves in the governmental process. Their centrality in the field of aging appears reason enough to accord them a special measure of attention.

The arrangement of material in this book moves in essentially chronological fashion. Chapters 2 and 3 are concerned with the process by which governments in the three countries first confronted, and then eventually overcame, the substantial barriers that initially prevented their taking positive action on the problem of old age insecurity. The former of these chapters begins at the point in the late sixteenth and early seventeenth centuries when the concept of state responsibility for indigent persons was first emerging, but when there was no awareness yet of the possible advantages inherent in approaching the hazards associated with old age, sickness, and unemployment in a comprehensive manner through government. It then considers several factors, among them the English poor law system and its North American counterparts, which collectively thwarted early adoption of national systems of old age pensions. Chapter 3 discusses how this set of barriers finally gave way, paving the way for positive action by the state, and analyzes the role played in that process by various policy disseminators keenly aware of pension developments in foreign countries and prepared to organize in behalf of securing similar legislation domestically.

Chapters 4 and 5 explore the indirect consequences for age-group mobilization of governmental decisions, initially that of entering this field and later that of introducing new programs on an expanding scale. The indirect effect of government programs as a potential source of incentives upon which age-group organizers (entrepreneurs) might capitalize is considered. One of the themes to be explored is that the newly offered benefits must exceed a certain critical level if they are not to end up becoming disincentives from an age-organizational standpoint.

Chapter 6 begins with a recapitulation of the findings of the previous chapters and then proceeds to consider the changes in the wider economic, social, and ideological age policy as possible constraints on government decision making.

Chapters 7, 8, and 9 discuss the present, fourth phase of policy development in each of the countries. In an era of greatly enlarged state benefits in aging, consideration is given to the possible impact of those changes on age-active organizations, both newly formed and preexisting.

A consideration of the findings of this study from a theoretical standpoint occurs in the concluding chapter, chapter 10. Among the topics to be explored is the potential for age-based collective action into the twenty-first century.

CHAPTER 2

First Phase, Part One: Barriers
to Policy Innovation

Later chapters of this book will cover the apparent impacts of early public pension schemes on political arenas in aging. Before beginning that discussion, however, one can usefully consider an earlier stage of policy development during which governments had yet to launch old age security measures, or any large programs aimed broadly at their elderly populations. The theme of both this chapter and the one immediately to follow is that, notwithstanding the absence at this time of government old age security programs, the legislative initiatives that were occurring in foreign countries were viewed by important elites in Canada, Britain, and the United States as attractive and worthy of domestic emulation. Special attention is devoted to the possibility that the foreign models became significant from the standpoint of advocacy group formation. This chapter focuses particularly on the factors that served to delay the early adoption of public pension legislation in any of the three countries here under discussion. Why were these countries not among the pioneers in old age security, and instead fairly laggardly by comparison to certain other Western democracies? Chapter 3 moves beyond this to consider how various policy disseminators—informed about the foreign models and eager to secure their domestic adoption—helped to spearhead the pension cause in the three national settings.

The Elizabethan Poor Law Tradition

The countries here under discussion were initially alike in their reluctance to accept the premise that national government has a positive obligation to address the concerns of needy and economically insecure elderly persons. By the time that even the first of them, Britain, had finally acted on this front, several other nations had already done so. Following the lead of Germany, Europe's leading industrial power, whose adoption of general compulsory old age insurance occurred in 1889, two other European countries soon followed, namely Denmark (1891) and France (1905). In addition, New Zealand and the Australian states of New South Wales and Victoria had all taken similar action before 1900. And by the time the U.S. government had finally acted, in 1935, essentially all of the industrialized world—save only for Switzerland and Japan—had long since done so. The relative tardiness of Britain, Canada, and the United States in this field of public policy is somewhat surprising, considering that in other respects, for example in the area of universal, free, and compulsory public education, they were considered as progressive, and considering their relatively high living standards and levels of industrial development. In seeking to explain this apparent reluctance to take positive action, a useful point of departure is the then-prevailing climate of opinion, as shaped by these countries' shared poor law traditions.

Modern social policy in Britain, Canada, and the United States has a common heritage in the Elizabethan poor laws of England. Enacted originally in successive parliamentary measures in the late 1500s, and then codified in the Poor Relief Act of 1601, the English poor law system decreed that public response to the needs of indigent persons was a responsibility of the local parish, the country's then-prevailing unit of local government. Under the act of 1601, justices of the peace were obliged to appoint an official in the parish charged with giving relief to the poor. (By the nineteenth century this responsibility had devolved upon a set of officials known as the "poor law guardians.") The act of 1601 also empowered the parishes to levy a tax on property for the support of this program. The system was never very popular among its poor law clients, who were obliged, as a condition of qualifying for benefits, to subject themselves to investigation by local officials and otherwise to prove their status as paupers. Severe punishment could be meted out to persons deemed as lazy or unwilling to accept available labor. In addition, residency in the parish was made a requirement for poor law benefits, and loss of residency entailed their cessation. A major side effect of this was Britain's retarded development of a national labor pool and the resulting drag on its economic growth.

Still, despite its inequities and unintended side effects, the poor law system endured. It was relatively cheap, enjoyed strong backing among tax-conscious politicians, and was amenable to modification as changing conditions seemed to warrant. In Britain, its country of origin, the system remained in place for more than three centuries, with its last vestiges only finally eliminated in the 1940s. Contributing to this long continuance was the timely enactment by Parliament of poor law reform legislation, chiefly that of 1834. The 1834 measure mandated a common standard of cash allowances by placing relief under national supervision, and it mandated that all parishes should establish workhouses ("indoor relief") intended to replace the existing eighteenth-century system of home, or "outdoor," relief. In addition it streamlined the existing administrative arrangements. None of these changes, it should be emphasized, ever entirely eliminated the demeaning and unsanitary conditions that existed in many of Britain's workhouses, orphanages, and almshouses—as vividly brought to life in the writings of Charles Dickens and other nineteenth- and early twentieth-century novelists and social critics.

In the seventeenth and eighteenth centuries the poor law system exerted a marked influence upon the English colonies in North America, even though the conditions there never allowed for its full application. Kenneth Bryden sums up as follows the system's influence on Canada:

> The Elizabethan poor law was not accepted in any of the Canadian colonies except New Brunswick and Nova Scotia where it was only indifferently applied. . . . English thinking and experience, however, affected Anglophone Canadians. In the ad hoc expedients devised to deal with welfare problems, one can detect the influence of the principles of both local responsibility (Elizabethan Poor Law) and the efficacy of institutional care (1834 Reform).[1]

Among the Canadian provinces, Quebec in particular applied a system of poor relief that departed markedly from English precedents, with Quebec opting for principles inherent in the social doctrines of the Catholic church.[2]

In the case of the thirteen American colonies, later to become states of the Union, the poor law system was fairly well established in most areas by the early eighteenth century, and from that point persisted following independence. Although lacking the centralized national control of the British model, the American states followed poor law precedents in most respects, including the principle of local responsibility for support of poor and indigent persons. In the nineteenth century, furthermore, the American states paralleled the course of policy development in Britain in providing for the establishment of county poorhouses, almshouses, and other such indoor relief measures.[3]

Classical Liberalism and Social Darwinism

The persistence of at least some poor law elements for over three centuries, despite vast changes occurring in the meantime in each country's social and economic structure, is suggestive of the depth to which that system had penetrated the basic social fabric. The system's long survival was reflective of a public philosophy that comprised several elements: a social doctrine, a theory of human progress, and a set of slogans. These elements were tied

---

1. Kenneth Bryden, *Old Age Pensions and Policy-making in Canada* (Montreal and London: McGill-Queens University Press, 1974), p. 22.

2. Ibid., p. 23.

3. Walter I. Trattner, *From Poor Law to Welfare State: A History of Social Welfare in America* (New York: Free Press, 1974).

together in a manner that succeeded in legitimating the existing order and in deflecting any and all criticisms. Both the doctrine and the theory emerged out of the principles of classical liberalism, which held that personal distress or financial insecurity is essentially a matter requiring a remedy by the individual and by the person's family. Proposals for treating social problems through government were greeted with deep misgiving. Thus, Adam Smith, in his classic work *The Wealth of Nations* (1776), contends that private interest would bring about public welfare; Smith was prepared to acquiesce to governmental provision of social services only under exceptional circumstances and with respect to only certain defined categories of the population. By the nineteenth century, intellectuals of liberal persuasion mostly insisted upon a very narrow conception of state action and preached the social benefits of strict adherence to laissez-faire.

A second doctrine, one especially fashionable in the 1880s and 1890s, but of lingering influence well beyond 1900, went under the name "Social Darwinism." Charles Darwin, the man from whom the doctrine derived its name, was not himself a social philosopher or a reformer, but this did not prevent his books *On the Origin of Species* (1859) and *The Descent of Man* (1871) from being interpreted in a social context. Darwin's writings were seen as having significance, not simply to the fields of biology and paleontology, but to political economy, sociology, and social welfare, where their application was seen as implicit. Two authors especially—Herbert Spencer, an Englishman, and William Graham Sumner, an American—took the lead in shaping social Darwinist thought on each side of the Atlantic in the latter part of the nineteenth century. In reference to Spencer, a recent analyst, Greta Jones, remarks that for him any effort to alleviate poverty through state intervention would gravely endanger social progress. She points out that "Spencer attributed to economic competition the same role which Darwinism had given natural selection. Economic competition weeded out the 'fit' from the 'unfit,' the economic failure from the success. This implied that laissez faire was the best condition under which economic competition and hence social evolution could take place."[4] Spencer's views on the iniquitous effects of social reform, of government intervention, and of collective action generally were ones appealing to many English publicists and intellectuals. Not the least among these was Leslie Stephen, the father of Virginia Woolf and a figure of intellectual prominence in late Victorian England. Stephen argued that there was a class of apparently moral actions that, if applied, would have disastrous social consequences. In particular, he singled out "indiscriminate"

---

4. Greta Jones, *Social Darwinism and English Thought* (Sussex, England: Harvester Press, 1980), p. 56.

charity. "Charity," Stephen proclaimed in 1893, "increases beggary, and so far tends to produce a feebler population; therefore, a 'moral' quality tends to diminish the vigor of a nation."[5]

William Graham Sumner labored to spread the same gospel on the American side of the Atlantic. In the 1880s he launched a series of attacks on reform legislation of all varieties—for example, those limiting convict labor and providing for creation of the Interstate Commerce Commission—and at the same time attacked free silver, poor laws, and eleemosynary institutions and expenditures. He swept aside socialism in all its forms, defining it as "any device whose aim is to save individuals from any of the difficulties or hardships of the struggle for existence and the competition of life by the intervention of the state."[6]

Spencer, Sumner, and their intellectual kindred did not entirely monopolize the field of social welfare thinking and advocacy in America, since other intellectuals and publicists, ones favoring a less individualist, more collective approach, also found an audience. Still, this was a time when science, or what was taken for science, had achieved high esteem, and thus by casting their views in the language of Darwin, possibly the best-known scientist of the nineteenth century, the social Darwinists gained an advantage over their less "scientific" competitors. The effect of all this, obviously, was to shore up opposition to government intervention intended to mitigate the often harsh consequences of marketplace competition. And even though government-funded old age pensions were not among the topics treated in the writings of Spencer and Sumner, any prospect for such legislation could not but suffer from the opinion climate that these authors helped to engender.

It is indicative of the pervasiveness of social Darwinist thought in the late nineteenth century that certain of its tenets were accepted even among social reform advocates, some of them active in the case of old age pensions. Even though they broke with strict social Darwinism in embracing the need for state intervention, these advocates often shared in its individualistic assumptions. As Hugh Heclo points out in regard to the early pension advocacy in Britain, "Industry, temperance, financial prudence—these were the key values shared by the small group of politicians, publicists and voluntary organization leaders who thought about a policy of income maintenance in old age."[7] One must temper, therefore, the usual image of social Darwinists as persons of the political Right so as to take account of its impact on many

---

5. Ibid., p. 50.

6. Richard Hofstadter, *Social Darwinism in American Thought* (New York: George Braziller, 1944), pp. 62–63.

7. Hugh Heclo, *Modern Social Politics in Britain and Sweden* (New Haven: Yale University Press, 1974), p. 158.

persons more leftist in their leanings. For example, no late nineteenth- or early twentieth-century British intellectual was more influential in promoting the welfare state in Britain than Beatrice Webb, one of the founders in 1884 of the left-leaning Fabian Society. During her childhood and adolescence Beatrice Webb lived for a time in the same household as Herbert Spencer, with whom she developed a strong intellectual and emotional affinity. In later years she recalled Spencer as the only person in her childhood who had consistently cared for her. Although in young adulthood Beatrice (along with her husband, Sidney) was to break with her former mentor in choosing to embrace the collectivist creed and the need for a positive state, "nevertheless, the influence of Spencer upon her mental development is difficult to over-estimate."[8] Such influence was apparent, for example, in Webb's insistence on "national efficiency" as an overriding national priority for Britain and her belief in the efficacy of social engineering.[9] Thus, even when circumstances matured to the point that public old age pensions could finally win legislative enactment, they tended to be drafted in a manner reminiscent of the earlier era of rugged individualism.

Constitutional Structure

The opinion climate described in the preceding section represented a major constraint for policymakers in all three countries. Additional factors applied in just one or two of the cases, representing still further limits on the range of available policy alternatives. One such factor, which applied in both Canada and the United States, consisted in the constitutionally mandated federal system, whereby governmental power is divided as between the central government and the provinces or states, with neither jurisdiction being allowed to interfere in the other's defined sphere.

In Canada, a federal system was decreed in the country's basic constitutional document, the British North America Act of 1867. The act, in allocating powers between the federal (or dominion) government and the provinces, stipulated that health and welfare concerns were to be the sole responsibility of the provinces. At the same time, the act granted to the federal government authority over all the most important sources of tax revenue, while leaving to the provinces only minor sources of taxation. In seeking to respond to social needs, policymakers in Ottawa were kept keenly aware of the need to avoid any appearance of intruding into provincial prerogatives. As

---

8. E. J. T. Brennan, *Education for Efficiency: The Contribution of Sydney and Beatrice Webb* (London: Athlone Press, 1975), p. 6.

9. Ibid., pp. 24–25.

Dennis Guest points out,[10] this resulted in an incongruity between legislative responsibility and financial capacity, thus indirectly contributing to Canada's delayed introduction of social security programs.

The same basic constraint existed in the United States. From 1789 up through the early 1930s the U.S. Constitution was interpreted by the Supreme Court as conferring upon state government the responsibility for social welfare, under the states' police power. The first general old age pensions in the United States were therefore state enactments. By 1933, twenty-one of the forty-eight American states had adopted such measures, and an additional seven had made pensions optional at the county level. Yet, as was true of Canada after 1927, these measures were widely viewed as not satisfactorily addressing the problem of old age hardship and dependency. While this problem was to become extremely acute in the context of the Great Depression, when several states became insolvent, it existed on a more limited scale even in the predepression years. Statistics documented that in the late 1920s at least 40 percent of elderly persons, and possibly as high as 67 percent, were unable to provide for themselves.[11]

The perceived constitutional barrier also explains why in the middle 1930s the Roosevelt White House became deeply concerned that the Supreme Court might soon invalidate the Social Security Act, on grounds of its exceeding the legitimate sphere of federal authority, and why as a consequence the act was drafted in a highly unusual manner, with the provisions relating to financing being sharply separated from those relating to benefits. A negative ruling by the Supreme Court on one section of the act based on states' rights considerations, so it was hoped, would not invalidate the act in its entirety.[12]

Urbanization and Population Aging

Aging of the population affected all the Western democracies to one degree or another, but its perceived importance varied cross-nationally, as did public recognition of its importance. A rough indicator of the point at which urbanization became a significant force in a given nation's public policy deliberations was when its population, as measured by the national census, shifted from predominantly rural to predominantly urban. In countries where this transition occurred fairly early, as was true in Britain, whose population became pre-

---

10. Dennis Guest, *The Emergence of Social Security in Canada* (Vancouver: University of British Columbia Press, 1980), pp. 6–7.

11. W. Andrew Achenbaum, *Old Age in the New Land: The American Experience since 1790* (Baltimore: Johns Hopkins University Press, 1978), p. 122.

12. Edwin E. Witte, *The Development of the Social Security Act* (Madison: University of Wisconsin Press, 1963).

dominantly urban as early as 1880, pressures were likely to build on government for a prompt, positive response, including the adoption of public pensions. But in the United States and Canada it came relatively late. In the former of these countries the official census revealed the nation as mainly urban only as of 1920, while in the latter the census-defined point of transition did not occur until 1931.

Population aging followed the same basic pattern, coming much sooner to most European countries, Britain included, than was true of North America. In Britain, the proportion of elderly persons (sixty-five and above) was 4.7 percent in 1900, a figure that would nearly double over the next thirty years to reach 7.4 percent in 1931—a rate of increase never again equaled in that country.[13] On the other hand, in Canada the sixty-five-plus population grew but slowly in the early part of the century, with elderly persons increasing as a proportion of the national total from 5.1 percent in census year 1901 to only 7.7 percent at mid-century (1951), and only later on beginning a more dramatic increase—such that by census year 1981 the nation was 9.6 percent elderly, representing, in absolute terms, a doubling in the number of elderly persons over the preceding thirty-year period.[14] In the United States, the proportion of elderly persons in the population likewise expanded but gradually over half the century 1900 to 1950—from 4.1 percent in 1900, to 5.4 percent in 1930, to 6.8 percent in 1940, and finally to 8.1 percent in 1950— and only then accelerated, to reach 11.3 percent in 1980. (Expressed in absolute terms, the latter increase was from 16.6 million in 1950 to 25.6 million in 1980.)[15] Even though the population pressures implicit in these figures did not directly produce the government response that later occurred in this field, their significance is not to be minimized.

Alternative Policy Arrangements in the United States

A final constraint applied to just one of the countries, namely the United States, and this, in combination with the others previously mentioned, largely explains why the U.S. government was the last of the three countries to launch a general old age pension system. A leading factor serving to frustrate national action on old age pension in the United States was the existence of the veterans' pension system established by Congress following the Civil

---

13. U. K. Central Statistical Office, *Annual Abstract of Statistics* (London: Her Majesty's Stationery Office, 1990).

14. Canada, Department of National Health and Welfare, *Old Age Security: Historical Statistics* (Ottawa: Queen's Printer, December 1986).

15. U.S. Bureau of the Census, *Statistical Abstract of the United States, 1990* (Washington, D.C.: Government Printing Office, 1990).

War.[16] While Congress had previously enacted service-related pensions—for veterans of the revolutionary war, the War of 1812, and the Mexican War—their scale in no way approximated those enacted during and following the Civil War. Following its initial launching (in 1862), and subsequent reformulation and liberalization (in 1879 and 1890), the U.S. Civil War pension system achieved remarkable scope, notwithstanding the exclusion of hundreds of thousands of war veterans (and their dependents) who had fought for the Confederacy, and also large numbers of nonsouthern elderly who for whatever reason had not served in the war. While pension eligibility under this program was initially restricted to Union army veterans who could prove injury in combat, that restriction later was lifted; old age itself was made a "disability" under the statute. Consequently, between 1890 and 1910 approximately one million American war veterans on the Union side were in receipt of pensions, and even as late as 1917 there were still some six hundred thousand pension beneficiaries. The scale of the program, both in numbers of clients and cost, was enormous. At its peak it encompassed some thirty percent of all men over age sixty-five, and fifty-six percent of all native-born white males in the entire population.[17] Not until the 1920s did the increasing death rates among Civil War veterans cause them no longer to be a significant fraction of the total U.S. aged population.

An additional constraint inhered in the abhorrence of public pensions on the part of leaders of the Progressive movement—a major force in American society from roughly 1890 to the close of World War I. Such abhorrence largely stemmed from the widespread corruption in the administration of veterans' pension benefits, and the resulting belief among these leaders that public pensions never could be administered honestly.[18]

As was predictable given the magnitude of the Civil War veterans' program, some major interest groups became very powerful. The decision by Congress to enlarge the program beyond its initial modest beginnings contributed to the rejuvenation of the leading Civil War veterans' organization, the Grand Army of the Republic. At the time of the GAR's formation in the immediate aftermath of the Union victory of 1865, and for more than a decade thereafter, its leaders remained indifferent to pensions established for the benefit of veterans with war-related injuries; these leaders refused to support

16. Ann Shola Orloff and Theda Skocpol, "Why Not Equal Protection? Explaining the Politics of Public Social Spending in Britain, 1900–1911, and the United States, 1880s-1920," *American Sociological Review* 49 (December 1984): 726–50.

17. Ibid., p. 728. See also John B. Williamson and Fred C. Pampel, *Old Age Security in Comparative Perspective* (New York: Oxford University Press, 1993).

18. Jill Quadragno, *The Transformation of Old Age Security: Class and Politics in the American Welfare State* (Chicago: University of Chicago Press, 1988), p. 40.

the policy recommendations of pension agents. During the 1870s the GAR struggled to survive, as membership fell alarmingly.

The adoption of the 1878 Arrears Pension Act was a critical element in changing this picture by helping to politicize veterans' benefits. The GAR promptly abandoned its previous standoffish attitude, and in the early 1880s, under the leadership of its newly elected national commander in chief, Paul Vandervoort, it shifted ground to make legislative activity on behalf of pension reform a central theme in a drive for increased membership. The tactic was successful. By 1884, in response to a rising clamor for pensions among rank-and-file members, the GAR had transformed itself into a pressure group. And a pronounced pension emphasis would remain central to the group's incentive system from that point forward, including the period after 1900 when membership had commenced its slow, inexorable decline and the political influence of organized Union veterans correspondingly waned.[19]

Only toward the end of the second decade of the twentieth century, as death began claiming Civil War veterans in ever-increasing numbers, and as the Progressive movement lost most of its former strength, were these constraints removed and fresh opportunities opened up.

It should be pointed out that neither Britain nor Canada had a war veterans' pension system on anything like the American scale. Since the British Empire, which included Canada, fought only small-scale wars between 1815 and the outbreak of World War I in 1914, and since subsequent to that war it would be many years before empire veterans in large numbers reached pensionable age, pensions for such individuals were dwarfed by their U.S. counterparts.

To summarize, the five factors mentioned—the existence of the Elizabethan poor law system, the strength of nineteenth-century classical liberalism and social Darwinism, the existence in the United States and Canada of a federal system, the existence in the same two countries of largely rural and still fairly youthful national populations, and alternative public programs that in part substituted for general pension schemes—all in varying degree helped to retard national action on public pensions in the three countries here under discussion. The fact that these barriers were more numerous and more potent in the United States than in the other two cases can serve as explanation for why it was among the last of the industrial democracies to establish public pensions for the elderly. Variance in the strength of the five factors appears useful, moreover, in accounting for the difference in timing of pension legislation among the three cases.

---

19. Ibid., p. 38; Mary R. Dearing, *Veterans in Politics: The Story of the G. A. R.* (Baton Rouge: Louisiana State University Press, 1952), pp. 213, 218, 270, 274, and 496.

CHAPTER 3

First Phase, Part Two: Foreign Models, Domestic Disseminators

The barriers to legislative action described in the preceding chapter were by no means absolute. Their capacity to thwart positive national action on social welfare concerns was dependent on the survival of public attitudes supportive of the limited government position, and over time that position would enjoy diminishing public and official support. This shift in outlook contributed to changes in constitutional interpretation. It contributed as well to the emergence of pension advocacy movements of an increasingly vocal character in all three of the countries. While organizationally fragile and resource starved, these movements in time would gain a political foothold. The present chapter is devoted to this campaign of social agitation and reform, with special emphasis being placed on the forces contributing to its coalescence, and to the interest groups that came to make up its core element. Before dealing with these matters directly, however, contributory factors of a social and demographic nature need to be considered.

Background Factors

The large-scale migration from rural to urban areas among the citizens of Canada, Britain, and the United States during the late nineteenth and early twentieth centuries, as described previously, served as background to the various reform crusades that were launched in support of public old age pensions. No population grouping was more strongly impacted by urbanization and the industrial revolution than the aged and aging. In rural society, elderly persons were typically fully employed, their health permitting—females as housewives and males as farmers or in trade. When not in good health, or when for some other reason unable to care for themselves, they could typically count on the informal support systems inherent in family, church, and neighborhood. In an urbanized world, however, employment opportunities for the able-bodied elderly were less abundant and, for those unable to care for themselves, support systems far less adequate. In addition, the first third of the twentieth century, as previously observed, saw substantial increases in the number of persons aged sixty-five and above, both absolutely and relative to total populations.

Urbanization, population aging, and increasing old age insecurity might help rationalize positive action by government, but by themselves they could not have compelled major age-related political initiatives. Required for that would be a relaxation of the formidable structural barriers, mentioned in chapter 2, that existed in both the United States and Canada, coupled with a political advocacy effort in all three countries capable of capitalizing on the shifting climate of public opinion and the new realities of electoral politics.

The relaxation of structural barriers occurred as politicians became adept at promoting fresh interpretations of basic constitutional principles. Thus, the Canadian prime minister, William Lyon Mackenzie King, took account of prevailing federal and provincial relations in 1925 when he avoided recommending to Parliament a national pension scheme based on the contributory insurance principle, despite his personal leanings in that direction. Instead, he embraced a noncontributory, flat-rate system, having judged that a contributory system, under which the dominion government would be given direct program responsibility, could well have resulted in a constitutional challenge, one from which Ottawa might well end up the loser.[1] On the basis of a careful calculation of the probable consequences, therefore, Canada's 1927 Old Age Pensions Act embodied a system of conditional grants under which the dominion government agreed to reimburse the provinces to the extent of one-half of provincially administered pension benefits. This scheme successfully met the constitutional test, even if at some sacrifice in terms of coverage and program adequacy.[2]

A roughly parallel set of political calculations surrounded the formulation and adoption of the 1935 U.S. Social Security Act. In drafting this legislation, the Roosevelt administration sharply separated the system of taxation, necessary to cover program costs, from the provision of benefits. The payoff from this strategy came in the form of a landmark 1936 U.S. Supreme Court decision turning back objections to the act of a constitutional nature (*Helvering v. Davis*, 301 U.S. 61). The court ruled that the payment of federal old age benefits did not violate the rights of the states defined by the Tenth Amendment of the Constitution and was also legitimate under the Constitution's general welfare clause.

Early Pensioner Advocacy

If relaxation of longstanding structural barriers was part of the picture, another was the emergence in each of the countries of influential pension advocacy organizations. The adoption by various foreign countries of public

---

1. Dennis Guest, *The Emergence of Social Security in Canada* (Vancouver: University of British Columbia Press, 1980), pp. 75–77.
   2. Ibid., pp. 78–79.

pension programs in the period leading up to and immediately following 1900 is pointed out in the previous chapter. As knowledge of these foreign models began to filter across international borders, reform-minded individuals in Canada, Britain, and the United States launched campaigns of propaganda, calling attention to those developments and seeking to educate both the general public and political elites regarding their appropriateness to the domestic social welfare need. In the United States, this process found early expression in an 1893 report published by the U.S. commissioner of labor, John Graham Brooks, who called attention to Germany's recent adoption of comprehensive social insurance covering old age and invalidism, in addition to sickness and industrial accidents. While Brooks's study found an audience, it produced little by way of immediate response, and it would be another two decades before the American social insurance movement was finally launched.

Lectures on social insurance delivered at the New York School of Philanthropy by Henry R. Seager and Isaac M. Rubinow, in 1910 and 1912 respectively, marked a turning point. Rubinow's lecture was particularly vehement—pointing out the successful European schemes and stressing the social necessity and practical feasibility, in an American setting, of all kinds of social insurance.[3] These views were later given fuller expression in his classic 1913 book, *Social Insurance, with Special Reference to American Conditions*,[4] which among other things calls attention to the recent foreign initiatives. The same process was also highly significant in Great Britain and Sweden, as pointed out by Hugh Heclo: "Very frequently, the contribution of reformers to adapting new policy responses consisted in perceiving and transmitting foreign experience . . . . [A]lmost all the characters involved in originating British and Swedish [old age] pensions followed international developments on the topic and drew inspiration from one or another foreign example."[5] Especially important in this effort at cross-border policy diffusion, which included Canada as well as Britain and Sweden, was the role played by the more moderate and reform-oriented (as opposed to the more doctrinaire) socialists, as the following discussion describes.

Britain

In Britain, the decline in social Darwinist thinking and its replacement by more progressive attitudes and assumptions during the last decade of the

3. Clarke Chambers, *Seedtime of Reform: American Social Service and Social Action, 1918–1933* (Minneapolis: University of Minnesota Press, 1963), p. 154.

4. Isaac M. Rubinow, *Social Insurance, with Special Reference to American Conditions* (New York: Henry Holt, 1913).

5. Hugh Heclo, *Modern Social Politics in Britain and Sweden* (New Haven: Yale University Press, 1974), p. 310.

nineteenth century contributed to a reevaluation of government's perceived responsibility toward the poor. The new thinking drew partially on Marxian socialism, as applied to the British setting by writers like Henry George and H. M. Hyndman, who challenged the foundations of individualist and ego-centric thinking, and also on non-Marxian Christian socialism, as originally articulated a quarter century previously by writers like Charles Kingsley and Frederick Denison Maurice. This is not to suggest that British socialism, and its close cousin collectivism, was from the beginning committed to the enact-ment of publicly funded programs of social welfare, old age pensions in-cluded. The collectivist outlook contained within it strands of profound dis-trust of positive government, and many of its adherents insisted that reform within a capitalist order can serve as, at best, a palliative and, at worst, a method to forestall the coming Socialist revolution. Thus, those in the move-ment who eventually became active in the campaign for old age pensions were identified with socialism's less doctrinaire, more reformist, school, and even they had to overcome profound initial misgivings. Yet, unlike their more doctrinaire counterparts, these moderate socialists in the end were prepared to join hands with like-minded figures in both the Liberal and Conservative parties in the pursuit of positive national solutions to social problems of all kinds.

An organized effort aimed at persuading Britain's Parliament to enact old age pension legislation commenced in the 1880s and continued to its culmina-tion two decades later in the Old Age Pensions Act of 1908. This campaign went through two distinct phases: an early phase dominated by middle-class reformers, many of them religiously oriented, and a later one where the leadership passed to a more working-class, union-affiliated, and secularized set of individuals. No sharp line of demarcation separates these, since throughout the 1880–1908 period there were activists in the movement of varying class origins and ideological and religious persuasions. Yet it is a useful distinction to bear in mind.

The more middle-class phase of the movement for government-sponsored old age pensions began in 1882 when Canon William L. Blackley, the rector of a poor Anglican parish and the administrator of a Friendly Society, formulated a plan under which the national government would com-pel working men within a certain age span to contribute to an annuity fund, the proceeds of which would be used to pay a very modest level of old age sickness and pension benefit. Blackley's Friendly Society involvement was significant, since those organizations, scattered throughout Britain, were the largest exclusively working-class groups of the period, having about 5.6 million members at a time when trade union movement had only 1.2 million.[6]

---

6. Pat Thane, "The Working Class and State 'Welfare' in Britain, 1880–1914," *Historical Journal* 27, no. 4 (1984): 878.

The Blackley plan was promoted vigorously by its author on the lecture circuit and through a newly launched pressure group, the National Providence League. His agitation contributed to the first serious public discussion of the problem of old age poverty in Britain, and of possible remedies.[7] Although Blackley's plan never achieved the status of a serious policy option—in part because the leaders of the Friendly Society movement were reluctant at this juncture to have the government enter this field—his campaign did prompt the Conservative government of the day into launching an investigation, the results of which were later published as a Royal Commission report.[8]

Further adding to the public's awareness of the plight of the aged poor was the publication of a series of official and privately sponsored studies aimed at determining the extent of poverty in Britain. These included the exhaustive statistical study of poverty in London undertaken by Charles Booth, whose findings were released in a series of seventeen volumes beginning in 1891. Booth lent his weight to the pension movement, and his 1899 book, *Old Age Pensions and the Aged Poor*, became one of its key source documents. A collaborator with Booth in his London surveys, and a major pension movement figure for other reasons also, was Beatrice Webb. On the basis of her involvement in one of the official investigations of this period, the Royal Commission on the Poor Laws, Webb would be asked later on, in 1907, to provide technical advice to government in connection with formulation of Britain's first old age pension statute.[9]

Perhaps the most concrete political expression of middle-class reform in this field was the founding in May 1899 of the National Committee of Organized Labor for the Promotion of Old Age Pensions for All (usually referred to by its shortened name, National Pensions Committee, or simply NPC). Despite the "organized labor" reference in its title and the inclusion of one or two union executives in its leadership, including George Barnes, a Socialist and the general secretary of the Amalgamated Society of Engineers, this group initially displayed more of a middle-class than a trade union character.[10] Spearheading its formation was the Rev. Francis H. Stead, a middle-class Congregationalist minister and the warden of Browning Hall, a settlement house. Its principal financial backers consisted of Charles Booth, the middle-class reformer mentioned earlier, and George and Elizabeth Cadbury (of the Cadbury chocolate firm). Another reform-oriented group, the Woman's Co-operative Guild (founded in 1884), likewise displayed middle-class leader-

7. Heclo, *Modern Social Politics in Britain and Sweden*, p. 159.

8. U.K. Parliamentary Papers, *Report of the Royal Commission on the Aged Poor* 14, Command 7684 (London: Her Majesty's Stationery Office, 1895).

9. P. M. Williams (Thane), "The Development of Old Age Pensions in the United Kingdom, 1878–1925" (Ph.D. dissertation, University of London, 1970), p. 196 (on file at the University of London Library)..

10. Heclo, *Modern Social Politics in Britain and Sweden*, pp. 169–70.

ship, exemplified by its first secretary, Margaret Llewellyn Davies, even though its rank-and-file membership was heavily working class. It was the largest female working-class organization of the period. Also of middle-class background—and also fairly conservative in his general outlook—was the only major politician of the late nineteenth century to lend his support to the pension cause, the Conservative party leader Joseph Chamberlain.

In contrast to this initially fairly middle-class cast, the NPC took on an increasingly working-class, Socialist, and trade union coloration in the years after 1900, with middle-class support now to some extent drifting away. In these years British organized labor came increasingly to embrace the public pension cause, a development related to the fact that the first countries to enact old age pensions did so under the sponsorship of Labour governments (as in New Zealand), or as a direct result of Socialist pressure (as in Denmark), or as a maneuver by Conservatives in power intended to outwit socialism (as in Germany). These developments were observed with keen interest among Socialists and trade unionists in Britain, whose leaders maintained close ties with their counterparts abroad.[11] From the 1890s onward, the need for public pensions was regularly debated at meetings of the Trades Union Congress (TUC), and resolutions supportive of that view began to win majority support. In addition to growing external pressure for old age pensions, resulting in part from Socialist influence, the TUC was responsive to pressures of an internal nature, especially from its general unions made up of workers employed in a common industry. Much more so than was true of the older craft unions, the general unions came to regard possible dependency in old age as a real and present danger for their members and members' dependents.[12]

Despite this growing labor movement consensus on the need to find solutions to the old age insecurity problem, there was no such early consensus regarding the notion that pensions should be provided through government, as opposed to directly by employers or the trade unions themselves. Equally controversial were proposals that such pensions be administered and financed by national government, as opposed to municipal government—as dictated by municipal socialism principles. These debates took time to resolve, considering the fractious and disparate character of the British labor movement in these years, which even as late as 1914 remained more an amalgam of factions than a unified force. Still, by the late 1890s labor support for the pensions movement had begun to emerge, and this carried with it an intensity of commitment that had not typified the middle-class pension supporters dominant in the movement's earlier phase. The fervor displayed by trade unions' representatives arose in part out of their increased awareness that

11. Ibid., p. 463.
12. Thane, "Working Class and State 'Welfare' in Britain," p. 884.

political demands for old age pensions enjoyed almost universal rank-and-file support, with unionists of many diverse and often conflicting tendencies finding common ground in this particular area. Support for public pensions thus came to be regarded as a useful consensus-building device within the labor movement.

The crystallization of working-class thinking in this field helped to bring about major shifts in the character and outlook of more than one of the political organizations of this period. One such shift occurred within NPC. Although granted a measure of working-class and trade union support even at its outset in 1898, such support now increased significantly. It had now become apparent to pension movement leaders that the Conservative party, which held power in Britain almost continuously for two decades beginning in 1886, had no intention of acquiescing to NPC demands, thereby rendering it highly unlikely that government would take action. This explains in part the tendency for the NPC's more middle-class elements to shift their attention elsewhere as the campaign went on beyond 1900. In cementing the trade union connection, it proved helpful that Frederick Rodgers, NPC's full-time secretary, was himself an active trade unionist and the first secretary of the Labor Representation in the House of Commons, and no less so that the chair of NPC's policy committee, W. C. Steadman, was an official in the barge builders' union.[13]

A second working-class organization to be affected by rising old age pension consciousness was the Grand United Order of Oddfellows, the peak association for Britain's Friendly Societies. As mentioned previously, the Friendly Societies were initially wary over proposed government involvement in this field. Indeed, some of the larger societies, including the very largest, the Manchester Unity of Oddfellows (with 713,000 members), originally had rejected the concept as one likely to result in competition with the various societies' own pension arrangements, and as inconsistent with their traditional self-help emphasis.[14] By the early 1890s, however, Friendly Societies, with their roots deeply planted in the British working class, had shifted ground. At their convention in 1904, the Oddfellows voted to endorse a proposal for public pensions as a humane and necessary measure, and this position was later conveyed to the 1906 annual conference by a large Friendly Society delegation. Friendly Society support for the NPC continued up through the final parliamentary victory two years later.[15] There is every reason to believe that pressure from interest groups representing various tendencies within the British working class became a crucial element in the enactment of the 1908

13. Ibid., p. 888.
14. Ibid., pp. 878–79.
15. Williams, "Development of Old Age Pensions in the United Kingdom," p. 180.

Old Age Pensions Act. Admittedly, labor strength had its limits: the measure as adopted was at most only a partial satisfaction of the demands put forward by NPC and its allies and was far more restrictive and narrowly focused than labor leaders had wished for or could readily accept. As Pat Thane remarks, "The act contained controls and limitations that were closer to the demands of politicians like [Joseph] Chamberlain and employers in the Chamber of Commerce than to those of the labor movement."[16]

Nevertheless, in the absence of pressure from NPC and its allies, it is highly unlikely that a public pension scheme would have been enacted at this time. Looking at the situation from the vantage point of 1906, one could scarcely have predicted that major pensions would pass in Parliament just two years later. The Liberal party, in its 1905 Election Manifesto, had refused to commit itself to any great initiatives in the field of social welfare. And following the Liberal victory in the general election of 1905, career officials in the Ministry of the Treasury began to exert powerful behind-the-scenes opposition to allowing pension measures to come before the House of Commons, just as these same officials had acted unswervingly, and successfully, to block similar proposals in both 1899 and 1902. Finally, Herbert Asquith, the chancellor of the exchequer and the informal deputy prime minister in the new government of Sir Henry Campbell-Bannerman, in 1906 rejected the pension scheme when it was first put before him and was markedly unresponsive to back-bench pressure both from within his own Liberal party and from NPC in support of positive action in this field.[17]

Obviously, then, powerful opposition forces were arrayed against the pension movement, and their existence presumably served to reinforce the laissez-faire orthodoxy in which all the ministers serving in the Liberal government had been schooled throughout their political careers. The normal tendency under such conditions would be for the government to do nothing in the way of enactment of a costly and radical social reform proposal. That this was not the course actually chosen points toward the apparent effectiveness of the most visible source of external pressure, namely the NPC.

Canada

The Canadian equivalent to Britain's enactment of 1908 was the Old Age Pensions Act, 1927, and as was true of Britain, it was preceded by a quarter century of prior pension agitation and advocacy. To what degree did this Canadian campaign resemble Britain's?

The Canadian federal government did not have a national old age pension

---

16. Thane, "Working Class and State 'Welfare' in Britain," p. 896.
17. Williams, "Development of Old Age Pensions in the United Kingdom," pp. 177 and 460.

scheme prior to 1927, but it did have in place a scheme of more-limited scope—the Government Annuities Act, enacted in 1908. Under this measure Canadian citizens could purchase, during their working years, annuities from the federal government, whose accrued value would become payable in monthly installments following retirement. The politician chiefly responsible for initiating this plan, and for steering it through the federal Parliament, one Sir Richard Cartwright, insisted that it was ideally suited to the Canadian situation. In parliamentary debate, Cartwright spoke out against the option of public pensions, which he looked upon as being perhaps a necessary evil in the old, densely populated countries of Europe, beset by "widespread poverty and destitution," but as inappropriate for Canada, an expanding and self-reliant nation.[18]

From its initial adoption in 1908 until its ultimate demise in 1967, the retirement annuities scheme led a kind of shadow existence. The program owed almost nothing to extraparliamentary public pressure, having been formulated by Cartwright from within the government. In the period preceding its enactment, no political party or interest group had endorsed the measure, and subsequent to its adoption the scheme failed to generate popular enthusiasm. It would be another two decades, fiscal year 1927–28, before the number of annuities sold in a given year would pass the one thousand mark; and even at the peak, shortly after World War II, annual sales of government annuities only slightly exceeded forty thousand. Kenneth Bryden remarks that the governmental annuities scheme might have evolved into a supplement to a larger system of government pensions, since it did serve the interests of a certain category of elderly persons. For this to occur, however, the federal government would have had to have adopted an expansionist outlook, not the restrictionist one that in fact became dominant in Ottawa.[19]

The annuities act was significant in one sense from the standpoint of later old age pension development: it served as a negative reference point for advocates of the pension cause, goading them toward increased effort in behalf of a broadly inclusive public pension program. Canadian labor leaders, for example, withheld their support of the annuities act when it was under discussion in Parliament in 1908. A decade later, in the wake of their abortive effort to win parliamentary acceptance of a national system of pensions, these same leaders became convinced that their defeat was in part attributable to the government annuities program, whose existence was used to rationalize legislative inaction.[20]

The Canadian pension movement, as it coalesced late in the second

---

18. Kenneth Bryden, *Old Age Pensions and Policy-making in Canada* (Montreal and London: McGill-Queens University Press, 1974), p. 49.

19. Ibid., p. 58.

20. H. A. Logan, *Trade Unions in Canada* (Toronto: Macmillan, 1948), pp. 503–4.

decade of the twentieth century, bore striking resemblance to its counterpart movement in Britain. As was true of the British case, one of its strands consisted of Christian clergy and laypeople, who in the Canadian case acted in the name of the Social Gospel movement. In 1907, Canada's Moral and Social Reform Council was organized, made up of representatives from the Anglican, Methodist, Presbyterian, and Baptist churches sharing a common Social Gospel orientation. Seven years later this same organization, by now renamed the Social Service Council of Canada, convened its first national congress on social problems, and the delegates voted to give special emphasis to needed social security initiatives. The conference appealed for social insurance to protect Canadians against the risks of work injury, unemployment, and old age insecurity, and among the several conference-adopted resolutions was one addressing the need for old age pensions. Pointed out in the resolution was the fact that the elites of Canadian society—nobility, statesmen, civil servants, military officers, and industrial magnates—all were protected by their own dedicated pension schemes, but that no such system applied to the common people. It was urgent, therefore, that legislation be enacted guaranteeing similar income security to elderly people generally.[21] Not among the leaders of the Moral and Social Reform Council, yet still among the most prominent Canadians associated with the Social Gospel movement, was the Rev. J. S. Woodsworth—a central figure in the development of Canadian public pensions, as the following discussion reveals. Church leaders thus helped spearhead the Canadian pension movement and were critical in helping to legitimate this otherwise radical concept of governmental activity.[22]

Another major contributor to the Canadian pension movement was organized labor. As was true in Britain, Canada's trade unions at this time were fractious and divided, both structurally and in terms of ideology. Still, in a land of vast distances, only poorly linked together by road, rail, and telecommunication, the Canadian labor movement was almost alone on the Canadian Left in its potential for knitting together widely dispersed local communities and for mounting a lobbying presence at both the national capital and among the several provinces.

In electing to become involved in this cause, the Canadian labor movement was markedly influenced by Socialist thought. Socialism here began to assume concrete form in the decade after 1900, with one of its wings consisting of doctrinaire Marxists, dismissive of the institutions of parliamentary democracy and intent upon revolution, and the other, more reform-oriented,

---

21. Guest, *Emergence of Social Security in Canada*, p. 32.
22. Guest, *Emergence of Social Security in Canada*; Bryden, *Old Age Pensions and Policy-making in Canada*.

made up of democratic Socialists committed to progress toward Socialist goals through legitimate parliamentary channels. Espousing the former of these views was the Socialist party, founded in 1902 as an outgrowth of the Socialist party of British Columbia, whereas the latter was championed by a Socialist party offshoot, the Social Democratic party, formed in 1909. While Canada's leading Socialist journal, the *Voice* (launched in 1894), sought to maintain a broad editorial policy, open to all tendencies, its general inclination was toward Social Democratic party-style social democracy. Socialists of both persuasions were responsive to contemporary social policy developments in Britain, and indeed the visit to Winnipeg in 1907 by Kier Hardy, the leader of the Independent Labour party in Britain, represented "one key to the growth of socialist thought in Canada."[23] The Socialist movement thus became one of the channels through which foreign models of public pensions were brought before the Canadian government and people, and of the many individuals involved, the name J. S. Woodsworth stands out as particularly important.

Woodsworth brought to the public pension cause a background in the Social Gospel movement and involvement in Canadian socialism. He was a product of the prairies, especially Manitoba, where he was born and lived most of his life. Yet, he traveled extensively and was responsive to wider world developments. As a young man, recently graduated from a university, he spent time in both Toronto and England, pursuing postgraduate studies and becoming aware that thousands, even millions, of his fellow human beings were forced to endure poverty and misery in big city slums. Although ordained to the Methodist ministry, Woodsworth was beset by religious doubt, and his inability to accept church doctrine caused him on more than one occasion to tender his resignation from the ministry. Always, however, his problems were brushed aside by more flexible supervisors. For some years, he was able to avoid an outright break by immersing himself in a series of nonpastoral social welfare roles, including that of national secretary of the Canadian Welfare League (1913–16). But World War I provoked a crisis. In 1918, finding that his pacifist views were increasingly alienating him from his fellow Methodists, he finally quit the clergy, and within a few months moved to Vancouver, where he accepted employment as a longshoreman.

During his time in Vancouver, Woodsworth immersed himself in the extraordinary 1918–19 discussions under way in British Columbia about socialism and social reform.[24] He concentrated on the educational work of the

23. Kenneth McNaught, *A Prophet in Politics: A Biography of J. S. Woodsworth* (Toronto: University of Toronto Press, 1959), p. 54.

24. Gerald Friesen, *The Canadian Prairies: A History* (Toronto: University of Toronto Press, 1984), pp. 378–79.

labor movement, becoming an activist and organizer in British Columbia's social democratic Federated Labour party. Woodsworth's biographer, Kenneth McNaught, places special emphasis on this Vancouver period as forming "the background against which [Woodsworth] developed his socialist ideas."[25]

In light of the great impact that his sojourn in Vancouver had on his mature political thought, it is highly probable that it was here—as one aspect of his involvement in the Federated Labour party—that he developed his passionate concern for the welfare of elderly people, and his conviction regarding the need for positive action on the part of government. Direct evidence is lacking, but it is highly plausible that Woodsworth was aware of the British Columbia labor movement's intense desire for old age pensions, and no less intense loathing for the existing government annuities scheme.[26]

Upon returning home to Winnipeg in 1919, Woodsworth became increasingly involved in efforts to translate his social reform views into political reality. Manitoba's Independent Labour party and the Canadian Labour party to which it was affiliated were both formed in 1921 in the context of the federal election called for late that year. The Independent Labour party chose Woodsworth as one of its candidates, and he soon proved himself an exceptionally strong campaigner, his lively campaign drawing heavily on his earlier Federated Labour party and Vancouver experiences. Woodsworth won his contest, as did another Independent Labor party–endorsed candidate from Manitoba, A. A. Heaps, and as did two other Canadian Labour party–affiliated candidates elsewhere in Canada.[27]

Woodsworth soon made himself the chief advocate in the cause of old age pensions in Ottawa. In taking on this role, he reflected not only his own personal experiences, but also the by now deeply held convictions of the

---

25. McNaught, *Prophet in Politics*, p. 90.

26. The *British Columbia Federationist* newspaper, voice of progressive unionism in the province, made frequent reference during 1910–19 to these concerns. On government annuities, a columnist wrote,

> If ever a damning indictment of the rottenness of the capitalist system was published, this appeal [a government poster promoting the sale of annuities] from the ruling class to its slaves, that they stint themselves still further and purchase annuities in order that when profit can no longer be squeezed out of their carcasses, they may not be a charge upon their masters, is such a one. The poster is frank, brutally frank, "Over the hill and to the workhouse." There is no covering up of conditions, no attempt to befool those with the eyes with which to see. It points out quite clearly that the lot of wealth producer when he is no longer able to produce sufficient profits for the master class is one of destitution and want. (May 9, 1913, p. 3, col. 4)

On state-funded old age pensions, the president of the British Columbia Federation of Labor, Christian Severtz, affirmed that "I have wholly and unreservedly been in favor of the principle [of old age pensions] . . . it is the duty of the State to provide a non-contributory pension to the aged as a matter of right" (*British Columbia Federationist*, April 25, 1913, p. 1, col. 1).

27. McNaught, *Prophet in Politics*, p. 150.

Canadian labor movement generally. Labor's campaign for old age pensions had begun in 1905, when the Trades and Labour Congress of Canada (TLC) passed a resolution on this topic at its annual convention. The TLC's voice was later joined by that of a second labor federation, the National Trades and Labour Congress (NTLC), whose 1907 convention had gone on record favoring old age and disability pensions for workers who were no longer able to support themselves.[28] Resolutions adopted by the two organizations at subsequent conventions had maintained this support, and at one point, 1911, such efforts appeared on the verge of gaining parliamentary approval. While that effort ultimately was thwarted, labor's commitment in this area was unwavering.

Woodsworth now took up this existing commitment, giving it voice and direction such as it had never enjoyed in the past. Upon entering the House of Commons, he and his colleague Heaps seized upon every opportunity afforded by parliamentary debate to advance the old age pension cause. These efforts initially met with little success, to the point that by 1925 the topic of pensions had dropped entirely off the legislative agenda of the governing Liberal party. The issue might have remained frozen in this manner had it not been that Liberals under Prime Minister King suffered a defeat in the autumn 1925 Canadian general elections, losing their former parliamentary majority and also falling behind the number of seats held by the opposition Conservatives. Yet, King was not disposed to resign as prime minister and saw in the situation a possibility to retain power by entering into a coalition with several minor parties, among them the Canadian Labour party and its affiliates. This gave the Canadian Labour party considerable political leverage, and Woodsworth and Heaps proceeded to exploit that advantage, making clear to the prime minister that their support for his remaining in power was contingent on his acceptance of two matters of deep concern to them and their party, one of them being old age pensions. In private negotiations between the three men, King reluctantly agreed to put pensions before the House without delay, and to seal that pledge with a written agreement that Woodsworth and Heaps would retain. King delivered on his promise, and the House of Commons granted its approval of the government's pension scheme, first in 1926, and then a second time a year later, following rejection of the initial enactment by the Canadian Senate. In the latter year the measure became law.

One should not assume that the prime minister necessarily acted against his will in these events. As early as 1916 an advisory committee of his own Liberal party had produced a detailed report on social security measures, and on King's recommendation this committee had included an item on old age pensions. Three years later, at the Liberal party's convention of 1919, a

---

28. Bryden, *Old Age Pensions and Policy-making in Canada*, p. 48.

resolution was adopted endorsing "an adequate system of . . . old age pensions," with King himself serving as chairman of the committee on labor and industrial relations through which it reached the floor.[29] One must assume, therefore, that the Liberals eventually would have initiated pension legislation on their own. Still, in the years following 1919 King displayed no sense of urgency in this area and might conceivably have put the matter off indefinitely, absent the pressure applied by Woodsworth and the larger pension movement of which he was a part.

United States

In none of the three countries treated here was the effort to achieve public pensions confronted by a more forbidding social and political environment than was true of the United States. The American social reform movement, as it crystallized around 1910, faced an uphill struggle, given the individualist assumptions that dominated public thinking about welfare issues, and for the various other reasons mentioned previously. Despite early indications of interest in the foreign models, hopes for positive action in this field were dealt a setback in 1917 with American entry into World War I. Suddenly it became pro-German to propose social insurance, and the Communist seizure of power in Russia the following year caused social insurance proposals to be branded also as "Bolshevist."[30] Moreover, within the American social welfare movement old age pensions were initially regarded as only secondarily important as compared to other pressing social needs.[31]

Despite these impediments, the pension movement (and the related social insurance movement) was launched around the end of World War I as an outgrowth of the postwar desire for reformulation and fresh thinking. Two events of significance now occurred within a twelve-month period. First, in December of 1918 a leading social reform organization, the American Association for Labor Legislation (AALL), upon the coming of peace following a war of unprecedented brutality and bloodshed, put forward a program of social reconstruction. Although from time to time since its beginnings a decade previous the AALL had paid lip service to the cause of pensions for the elderly, such statements had not been strongly emphasized. But its leadership now made social security needs its highest priority, including action relating to sickness, unemployment, and old age dependency. From this time forward to 1935, AALL continued to emphasize, in the pages of its *AALL*

---

29. Ibid., p. 66.

30. Chambers, *Seedtime of Reform*, p. 156.

31. Roy Lubove, *The Struggle for Social Security* (Cambridge: Harvard University Press, 1968).

Review and in other ways, the prevalence of old age dependency and the need for corrective action.[32]

Second, this period witnessed the appointment of a recent graduate of the University of Pittsburgh, Abraham Epstein, as research director of the Pennsylvania Old Age Pension Commission, thereby marking the beginning of what was to become a singular career in American pension advocacy. During his tenure on the Pennsylvania commission, Epstein became an expert on old age as a national problem. The insights arrived at while serving in this post were soon incorporated into his 1922 book, *Facing Old Age: A Study of Old Age Dependency and Old Age Pensions in the U.S.*[33], the first of several book-length studies that Epstein was to publish. Four years after joining the staff of the Pennsylvania commission, Epstein moved on to the staff of the Fraternal Order of Eagles, where he assisted in confronting the needs of the order's increasingly aged membership, and in forging an informal coalition between the Eagles and elements of the American labor movement, the United Mine Workers especially. The goal of this campaign was to achieve pension legislation at the state level.[34]

Finally, in 1927, having long been disillusioned with the Eagles and its basic political style, Epstein launched off on his own in forming the American Association for Old Age Security (AAOAS), a group later (1933) to be renamed the "American Association for Social Security" (AASS). (Epstein is credited with introducing the term *social security* into the lexicon of the English language.) The formation of AAOAS had special significance for the American pension movement since, unlike the other interest groups that lent their support, only it embraced old age issues as an overriding concern. By 1931, at the outset of the depression, Epstein's group had a budget of around $40,000 and a dues-paying membership of four thousand—a size sufficient for it to play a role in shaping public attitudes toward greater social security acceptance.[35]

The pension movement as a whole, however, was beset by serious problems. Relations between the AALL, under its director John B. Andrews, and the AAOAS, under Epstein, were never particularly close or cordial, and, indeed, endemic rivalries and occasional outright antagonisms took their toll, diminishing the movement's overall political effectiveness.[36] While one ought

---

32. Chambers, *Seedtime of Reform*, pp. 11–12, 160.

33. Abraham Epstein, *Facing Old Age: A Study of Old Age Dependency and Old Age Pensions in the U.S.* (New York: Knopf, 1922).

34. Jill Quadragno, *The Transformation of Old Age Security: Class and Politics in the American Welfare State* (Chicago: University of Chicago Press, 1988), pp. 66–72.

35. Chambers, *Seedtime of Reform*, p. 165.

36. Henry J. Pratt, *The Gray Lobby* (Chicago: University of Chicago Press, 1976), pp. 19–25.

not to discount entirely the level of pension movement success—a number of states, for example, enacted old age pensions under its prodding during the 1920s and early 1930s—programs were typically seriously underfunded and sharply limited in terms of the scope of coverage.[37] Furthermore, the movement was largely isolated from the American political mainstream, as brought home by the fact that the nation's two leading parties, Democratic and Republican, entirely ignored the topic of old age security in their predepression platforms of 1910–30, and also by the fact that in the depression year of 1932 the GOP remained silent on this topic, while the Democratic party, even though committing itself to the principle of federal involvement, limited itself to advocating *state* unemployment and old age insurance.

The pension movement's political marginality resulted in part from its inability to attract broad labor movement support. While individual labor leaders, mostly at the local and state levels, did occasionally lend their support to the efforts of the Eagles, AAOAS, and AALL, little of the sort was forthcoming from the larger national and international unions, the Mineworkers excepted, or from the American Federation of Labor (AFL). The AFL was generally hostile toward the public pension movement during the predepression period and even after the depression began was not a player in the developments preceding the adoption of Social Security in 1935. One could argue that labor was in no position to improve the prospects for old age pension legislation, given the antiunion, antisocial reform atmosphere that prevailed in the United States at this time. Still, the labor federation probably could have made a contribution had it been so inclined, and therefore the factors underlying its striking indifference merit discussion.

The AFL's refusal to act positively in favor of governmental financed old age insurance was attributable chiefly to the ideology of its founding leader and longtime president, Samuel Gompers, one also embraced by his successor, William Green, following Gompers's death in 1924. Gompers had a variety of reasons for opposing positive government involvement in labor-related matters. As he never tired of repeating, government intervention in the affairs of the worker would inevitably have negative consequences: it would subject workers to the shifting winds of political fortune, benefiting them today but punishing them tomorrow; it would cause workers to look to government rather than to union-negotiated contracts with owners for the protection of their vital interests, thereby weakening trade union resolve; political progress in securing legislation to improve working conditions through governmental action was necessarily slow, cumbersome, and uncertain; and new

---

37. Chambers, *Seedtime of Reform*, pp. 211–12.

legislation, even if enacted and signed into law, could well end up being declared unconstitutional by the courts.[38]

As early as 1902, at a point when Gompers's political philosophy had not yet become entirely dominant within the labor federation, his resolve in the area of social legislation was tested by a group of Democratic Socialists within the labor movement. At the AFL convention in that year, Victor Berger, a Socialist delegate from Milwaukee, introduced a resolution calling on the AFL to endorse the concept of general old age pensions, on the model of the law on the books in Germany for the past twenty years. Although debated on the floor, Berger's resolution was voted down, as was a similar motion put forward by him at the next AFL convention, held in 1904. By the latter date, Berger had become convinced that further efforts to enlist the AFL in support of pension and social insurance legislation would be futile.

And, indeed, it would not be until 1932, by which time the depression had shocked the labor federation into a reevaluation of certain long-held positions, that the federation would give its conditional endorsement to needed governmental action in this field. The shift in outlook had little apparent impact on New Deal social security thought and practice, however, given that the AFL, consistent with its traditional policy of neutrality in presidential politics, did not endorse Franklin D. Roosevelt in 1932 and was granted little by way of White House access after Roosevelt took office.

The pension movement was thus to a large extent cut off from what might be termed its most logical natural ally, the labor movement, and in its quest for coalition partners was obliged to pursue a course that departed significantly from that of its counterparts in both Britain and Canada. The leaders of the U.S. movement forged a coalition with the representatives of American organized religion. As World War I was nearing an end, the Federal Council of Churches of Christ (FCC) in America (representing Protestantism), the National Catholic War Council (representing America's Catholic bishops), and various Jewish organizations—especially the Rabbinical Council of America—all called attention in their social policy statements to the problem of old age dependency within the context of postwar reconstruction.

The first expression of FCC thinking came in a 1919 manifesto on social insurance issued by its Commission on the Church and Social Service. This statement includes a discussion of the risks associated with old age as one field appropriate for government-funded social insurance. While not making old age pensions a matter of top priority, the FCC continued throughout the next two decades to manifest concern in this area, calling attention to the need for

---

38. Philip S. Foner, *History of the Labor Movement in the United States*, vol. 3 (New York: International Publishers, 1964), p. 284.

appropriate corrective action.[39] Indicative of the church federation's commitment was the fact its president, Bishop Francis J. McConnell (Protestant Episcopal church), accepted an invitation to become the president of Abraham Epstein's AAOAS upon that group's formation in 1927.[40] The two organizations, it should be noted, had their headquarters within a few blocks of one another in New York.

An equally committed source of religious support for the old age pension movement arose from organized Jewry. Perhaps no individual of the pre-depression era more fully embodied the potential for fusion of Jewish communal activism and pension involvement than did Isaac M. Rubinow. Rubinow was the author of the first serious study of pensions and social insurance in North America, *Social Insurance, with Special Reference to American Conditions* (1913), and he would remain prominently identified with the pension movement through the 1920s. Yet he was no less prominent as a Jewish community leader, being selected in 1929 as secretary of B'nai B'rith, the nation's largest Jewish membership organization. Other Jews, some of them more prominent than Rubinow, also made this same fusion of religious involvement and pension advocacy. Among them were Solomon Lowenstein, director of the Federation of Jewish Philanthropy; Francis Taussig, president of the American Association of Social Workers; and Rabbi Stephen A. Wise, leader of New York's largest Reform synagogue and a founding board member of Epstein's AAOAS. Other names in this same vein also could be mentioned. Such involvement can be regarded as logical, combining as it did the principles underlying Jewish mutual aid societies—by now widespread in communities across the United States—and Jewish biblical teaching.[41] Reinforcing this linkage was the fact that New York City, where both the AALL and the AAOAS had their national offices, was heavily Jewish, and that the principal Jewish organizations in the United States for the most part had New York headquarters. Given such a setting, Abraham Epstein, himself a Jew, had no need to look far afield for supporters in his cause.

Roman Catholic support for the cause of old age pensions was implicit in the fact that John Lapp, the director of the Department of Social Action of the National Catholic Welfare Conference—successor organization to the National Catholic War Conference—included the problem of old age dependency in his many expressions of social concern during the 1920s, and in his

---

39. William Finley McKee, "The Attitude of the Federal Council of the Churches of Christ in America to the New Deal: A Study in Social Christianity" (M.A. thesis [history], University of Wisconsin, 1954), pp. 263–69 (available in the University of Wisconsin Memorial Library, Madison).

40. Louis Leotta, "Abraham Epstein and the Movement for Old Age Security," *Labor History* 16, no. 3 (1975): 374.

41. Chambers, *Seedtime of Reform*, pp. 213–14.

demand for social insurance, seen by him as essential to provide security, equity, and true Christian justice.[42]

Equal in importance to the support forthcoming from the nation's religious communities was that rendered to the pension cause by American socialism. As was true of their counterparts in both Britain and Canada, Socialists here looked upon old age pensions as consistent with their basic ideology. Two of the more prominent Socialist leaders of the early twentieth century, namely Eugene B. Debs and Victor Berger, were vocal in their support of public pensions for the elderly. The Socialist party was established at a meeting held in February 1900. One of its predecessors, the short-lived Social Democratic party of the United States, formed by Debs, Berger, and others in 1898, was quite likely the first national organization in the United States to pronounce in favor of national action in the pension field. In its platform, the Social Democratic party had affirmed the need for "insurance for working people, including insurance against . . . want in old age."[43] Thus, when the Socialist party was founded two years later, it took over virtually intact the platform of its predecessor, including the plank relating to old age pensions.

In the early 1900s Berger employed his skills as a publicist to keep up pressure for pension legislation. In one of his numerous broadsides, Berger in 1908 insisted that a nation whose government could afford a current annual expenditure of $140 million on Civil War pensions should be equally prepared to spend the same approximate amount (Berger put the figure at $144 million) for the protection of what he termed the "soldiers of the commonweal."[44] In 1911, now elected to the House of Representatives in Washington—the first Socialist to achieve this—Berger introduced the first bill into Congress that was an old age pension proposal. The bill had little congressional support and was killed in committee, but it nevertheless helped to give credibility to the public pension option.[45]

As described earlier, Berger's effort to being the American Federation of Labor around to his view on this topic was unsuccessful. Moreover, the Socialist party with which he was identified, despite a surge of national popularity in the 1912 presidential election, suffered severe setbacks later in the same decade, with American socialism fracturing into mutually contentious camps in the wake of the Russian Revolution of 1917–18. Thus, Socialist hopes that the party might one day become a major party in the United

42. Ibid., p. 159.

43. Daniel Bell, *Marxian Socialism in the United States* (Princeton: Princeton University Press, 1967), p. 53.

44. Victor L. Berger, *Broadsides* (Milwaukee: Social Democratic Publishing Company, 1913).

45. Lubove, *Struggle for Social Security*, p. 135.

States, on the model of the Labour party in Britain, did not survive the second decade of the twentieth century.

Nevertheless, while Socialists had little or no direct impact on the chain of events leading up to the 1935 Social Security Act, they did play an important behind-the-scenes role through their close connections with pension movement leaders. Around the time that Victor Berger was presenting his pension bill in the House of Representatives, Isaac M. Rubinow, a Russian immigrant to the United States, was delivering his previously mentioned lectures at the New School of Philosophy in New York, while also completing work on his 1913 book on social insurance. Rubinow was prominent in Socialist circles in New York and a member of the Marx Institute of America. There seems to have been no one whom Abraham Epstein held in higher esteem or felt closer to personally. Rubinow was a fellow Russian-Jewish émigré, and sufficiently older (by seventeen years) to serve for Epstein as a role model and father figure.[46] The latter's affection for the older man can be inferred from the wording of Epstein's dedication to the 1938 revised edition of his magnum opus, *Insecurity, A Challenge to America: A Study of Social Insurance in the United States and Abroad*: "to the memory of Dr. I. M. Rubinow, cherished friend and profound teacher."[47]

Socialist support for the social insurance and old age pension movement, while pervasive, went largely unacknowledged, especially in the aftermath of the 1918 Bolshevik revolution and the resulting "Red Scare" in the United States. Thus, for example, Abraham Epstein remained intimately connected with several Socialist party members, and "often received his most vocal support from local leaders of the Socialist Party and League for Industrial Democracy."[48] The AAOAS files contained letters from local Socialist leaders affirming the importance of their role at old age conferences and deriding the caution of professional social workers. Yet for tactical reasons the AAOAS, like other national pension organizations, generally avoided mention of such support in its publicity and propaganda messages.

The various age-advocacy organizations mentioned here played a significant, if secondary, role in shaping the 1935 Social Security Act. The enactment of legislation was chiefly attributable to other forces, including, at the elite level, President Franklin D. Roosevelt and various class interests as brought to a focus through key members of Congress,[49] and, at a mass level, a

---

46. Leotta, "Abraham Epstein and the Movement for Old Age Security."
47. Abraham Epstein, *Insecurity, A Challenge to America: A Study of Social Insurance in the United States and Abroad*, 2d rev. ed. (New York: Random House, 1938).
48. Chambers, *Seedtime of Reform*, p. 165.
49. Quadragno, *Transformation of Old Age Security*, p. 100.

broad base of public support that cut across class lines to include rich and poor, white and blue-collar workers, and care givers for elderly persons.[50] Nevertheless, interest groups were not an inconsiderable factor. Their propaganda contributed toward shifting the national opinion climate toward acceptance of the principles underlying the proposed 1935 legislation.

And Franklin D. Roosevelt clearly was aware of Abraham Epstein and his post-1927 pension movement. He had first been sensitized to this group's demands during his period as governor of New York, 1929–33. (As governor, Roosevelt had earned a reputation among his fellow governors for leadership in the old age pension field, and AAOAS representatives had met with him more than once during that period.) And in 1934, in making their selection for the post of executive director of the Committee on Economic Security, Roosevelt and his labor secretary, Frances Perkins, opted in favor of Edwin Witte, a professor on the faculty of the University of Wisconsin whose qualifications included longstanding ties to both the AALL and the AAOAS and AASS.[51] Moreover, Epstein and his allies took the lead in organizing a protest over Roosevelt's statement, made in a speech before the November 1934 National Conference on Old Age Security, to the effect that "I do not know whether this is the time for any federal legislation on old age security." (In apparent response, the White House soon changed its line, submitting its draft legislation without further delay.)[52] Finally, while Roosevelt mostly refused to accept the particulars of AALL and AAOAS/AASS, policy proposals, he did go along with Epstein's idea of federal subsidization as the only feasible approach in caring for those too old to participate in a social insurance system.[53]

Conclusion

While the political arena associated with phase one is made up of a diverse set of actors, none stands out as more important in the three countries here under discussion than do the models of public old age pensions provided by other countries. Not only were such models important to the timing and content of pension legislation, but they also served as a stimulus in the formation of pension-advocacy lobby groups and in the redefinitions of political goals on

---

50. Michael B. Katz, *In the Shadow of the Poorhouse: A Social History of Welfare in America* (New York: Basic Books, 1986).

51. Theron F. Schlabach, *Edwin E. Witte: Cautious Reformer* (Madison: Wisconsin State Historical Society, 1969), pp. 91–92.

52. W. Andrew Achenbaum, *Social Security: Visions and Revisions* (New York: Cambridge University Press, 1986), p. 20.

53. Leotta, "Abraham Epstein and the Movement for Old Age Security," p. 377.

the part of existing voluntary organizations. The domestic advocates for public pensions in Britain, Canada, and the United States were without exception familiar with the foreign models. Committed Socialists were especially knowledgeable of foreign developments, in part from their participation in Socialist international congresses and meetings.

This first phase was characterized by an instability of interest group involvement, an ebb and flow of political commitment. Church assemblies, middle-class reformers, trade unions, and social welfare activists were responsive in varying degree to the logic of initiating government-financed and government-administered pensions for the elderly and were prepared to make positive contributions.

Yet such enthusiasm was in competition with their other social reform concerns, and elderly persons were not always the concern of highest priority. Phase one, evidently, was a setting that lacked a firm pension reform anchor, one that might have prevented, or diminished greatly, the downstream drift that so frustrated pension movement leaders. This tendency toward "goals drift" can be seen in all types of organizations active in the cause, but it was more evident in some types than others. It was especially visible among the secularized middle-class and religious group reformers. Various explanations for this are possible, but it presumably owed something to the fact that in their case the basis of concern over old age insecurity, while informed by the desire for social uplift, was lacking in any genuine element of direct benefit or perceived personal stake. On the other hand, among the trade unions and socialist cadres, where the personal stake was more tangible and more clearly perceived, such drift appears to have been far less marked.

The role of socialism in this process is one of special interest. Socialists became direct participants in the events occurring in Canada and Britain but were shoved to the sidelines in the United States, where their influence, even though tangible, was exerted only indirectly. There is no little irony in the fact that American Socialists, and their left-leaning allies in the Christian denominations and in the Jewish community, managed to play a role in the early pension movement, while finding it impossible to wield influence over the course of events in Washington leading up to the Social Security Act. In all three of the countries the measures adopted involved little by way of national income redistribution (regarded by Socialists and others on the Left as essential) and made major concessions to capitalist class interests. The reforms as finally enacted were not of Socialists' choosing and received only their grudging acceptance at most. The larger principle illustrated by this is that interest group influence, when mediated through other institutions—labor unions, political parties, and other interest groups—is prone to unpredictability in terms of its public policy outcomes.

The British, Canadian, and American labor movements all figured in early pension and social security advocacy. Whereas in Britain and Canada organized labor became early and heavily involved, this did not apply to the United States where labor leaders in many, not all, cases forswore political commitment in this area. Such absence of support in the U.S. case was not without consequence, given that organized labor occasionally did win legislative victories in the United States, both at the state level and in Washington.

Given the then-prevailing public attitudes, substantial barriers confronted any effort to transform the existing highly restricted state schemes on aging—veterans' pensions and civil service pensions—into a more universalized concern for old age welfare. The pension movement was often frustrated by its inability to arouse firm backing among the general public and by an absence of consistent support among financial backers. This explains, in part, the movement's strong emphasis on foreign models, whose existence could serve to enhance both the perceived feasibility and the legitimacy of the proposals being advanced domestically.

It was also a barrier that the elderly themselves could not be appealed to directly in substantial numbers. It is not difficult to see why seniors' organizations did not emerge at this time: in the absence of universal age-benefit programs, under which the more politically aware, participatory, and articulate elderly were made pension eligible along with others, there was little glue to mold such persons into a cohesive force. As the following chapters reveal, such elderly consciousness would eventually emerge, making possible the formation of interest groups both broadly based and professionally led. But at this initial stage such consciousness had yet to arrive.

CHAPTER 4

Second Phase: Organizational Disincentives and the Dismal Years

Legislation enacted in Britain, Canada, and the United States—in 1908, 1927, and 1935—represented public policy breakthroughs, involving acceptance of the principle, however limited in its application, that national government bears a responsibility for elderly peoples' welfare and income security. Even though far from adequate given the scope of the existing need, these enactments embraced significant social welfare principles and established foundations upon which later enlargements could be erected. And in addition to their substantive content, the measures authorized the establishment of new governmental bureaus and agencies—units having the potential for serving as rallying points around which efforts to achieve benefit increases and program enhancements might later crystallize. This latter possibility was enhanced by the fact that the legislative enactments were cast in broad language, with many questions left open for later administrative resolution. Executives serving in the newly authorized bureaus and departments might therefore assist in shaping the course of future pension policy while also helping to shape the wider pension policy arena.

The present chapter, therefore, explores the extent to which these possibilities were in fact realized. The discussion centers upon the following questions: Did interest groups continue to play as influential a role now as had been the case in phase one? If so, were these the same groups, essentially, that had been active earlier on, or instead ones for the most part newly formed? To what extent, if at all, did the newly authorized age-benefit programs serve as a source of incentives toward the formation of viable new interest groups on aging? What would be the relative levels of political strength between within-government program advocates—civil servants and governmental officials especially—and nongovernmental advocates—interest groups especially?

Program Content as a Definer of "Space"

In cross-national comparison it becomes apparent that the old age pension measures of 1908, 1927, and 1935 were similar in certain respects, yet in others sharply contrasting. In the section to follow both the resemblances and the contrasts are identified, as each of the three countries is taken up in turn.

United States

In the United States, the Social Security Act of 1935 established a program of dual dimension, with means-tested benefits, grounded on relief principles, mandated under Title I, and universal benefits, determined on the basis of one's employment record, authorized under Title II. The legislative sponsors had anticipated that Title I benefits would be transitional. Such benefits were expected to provide a needed source of relief during the depression emergency, and then to be phased out as the national economy revived and the reserve accounts provided for under Title II had reached sufficient size to cover the anticipated cost of benefit payout.

Contrary to these expectations, however, Old Age Assistance (OAA) soon took on a life of its own, continuing to expand while displaying no tendency to disappear naturally.[1] Initially, such continuance of OAA strength was explainable in terms of the Great Depression's persistence into the late 1930s and the felt need to maintain federal relief programs of all kinds, OAA included. Yet there was no such ready explanation for the trend of policy development in the post–World War II period, with its booming prosperity and dramatic upsurge in job availability. Thus, whereas it was not regarded as particularly surprising that as of 1937 Title I (OAA) payouts were $244 million whereas those under Title II (Old Age Insurance, or OAI) were a scant $1 million, or even that three years later the disparity between the two programs remained very wide—$450 million for OAA and $35 million for OAI (now retitled as Old Age and Survivors Insurance [OASI], it was not so easy to explain the wide gulf between the two titles that persisted into the middle and late 1940s. As of 1946, for example, the average OAA payment remained 29 percent higher than the comparable figure for OASI.[2] And as late as June 1950—fully fifteen years after the enactment of the original Social Security statute—more elderly persons were getting OAA than OASI: 2.8 to 2.1 million. Moreover, "the OAA rolls were growing steadily and at a pace fast enough to stay ahead of insurance."[3]

It was not long before a well-placed group of appointive federal officials

---

    1. The following discussion is based on Jerry R. Cates, *Insuring Inequality: Administrative Leadership in Social Security, 1935–1954* (Ann Arbor: University of Michigan Press, 1983), chap. 1.

    2. Ibid., p. 108.

    3. Martha Derthick, *Policymaking for Social Security* (Washington, D.C.: Brookings Institution, 1979), p. 273.

coalesced into a concerted effort to reinvigorate the insurance title under Social Security (OASI), and to resist OAA's continuance as a major program. Chief among these was Arthur Altmeyer, the man appointed by Franklin D. Roosevelt in 1936 to the post of chairperson of the Social Security Board (SSB), and who later on, in 1946, assumed the same post in its successor agency, the Social Security Administration (SSA). Altmeyer's administrative behavior is fully documented in books published since his departure from public life in 1954. The leading sources include Altmeyer's own memoirs, which appeared in 1966, and the more recent scholarship of two social scientists—Martha Derthick and Jerry R. Cates.[4] From these sources, it is apparent that Altmeyer, acting in collaboration with his fellow board members and senior civil servants in the SSB and SSA, launched a campaign in the late 1930s, which continued into the 1940s, aimed at winning congressional approval of amendments designed to ensure the supremacy of the Title II Social Security "insurance" benefits, as opposed to Title I "relief and assistance."

Making use of its agency's publications and press releases, in addition to other more informal avenues, Altmeyer and the SSB/SSA mobilized their resources on behalf of this cause. Among other things, they helped draft legislative proposals and took steps designed to punish, through the threatened withholding of federal funds, any states that saw fit to offer an enhancement or supplement to the federally provided OAA benefits, thereby to maintain the public support base of Title I benefits.

In the end, Altmeyer's position prevailed, even though this success was not as prompt or as totally decisive as he personally would have preferred. After lengthy deliberation, Congress in 1950 adopted corrective amendments to the Social Security Act designed to ensure the success of the Title II alternative. In the early 1950s, with the new legislation now taking effect, the United States entered a new period in its social welfare history. OASI and the Social Security Trust Fund became increasingly central to the overall federal effort in the field of old age security, whereas Title I benefits now faded in relative importance.

Still, up to the close of the 1940s the prevailing political arena for the Social Security system continued to depart markedly from the conservative social insurance model that Altmeyer so strongly favored. Until at least the end of 1950, Social Security retained its strongly means-tested, poverty-targeted character. In addition, the great bulk of persons aged sixty-five and above remained unprotected by old age insurance: as late as 1950, only 133 out of every 1,000 individuals in this age group were drawing any OASI

---

4. Arthur Altmeyer, *The Formative Years of Social Security* (Madison: University of Wisconsin Press, 1966); Derthick, *Policymaking for Social Security*; Cates, *Insuring Inequality*.

benefit.[5] Elderly persons in large numbers had not yet become a meaningful part of the U.S. old age insurance system.

Canada and Britain

The description for the United States also applies broadly to Britain and Canada at the comparable phase two. In both of these countries, policymakers elected to adopt means-tested systems, financed out of general tax revenues, despite urgings that they establish instead a state pension system of the universal type, financed on the basis of shared contributions from workers, businesses, and the state. The plans adopted involved benefits targeted toward elderly persons who could demonstrate acute need, with no provision made, necessarily, for elderly persons slightly higher up the income scale who might face financial insecurity and risk of hardship. When confronted by objections to the means test—arising from its tendency to deprive applicants of dignity, while discouraging many eligible, yet proud, individuals from ever applying for benefits—policymakers remained unmoved. Critics' objections notwithstanding, means-tested, nonuniversal old age benefits were mandated.

A variety of considerations entered into the choice of this course of action. One related to immediacy of payout: means-tested programs had the capacity to deliver substantial, immediate relief to those in the most visible distress, based upon an administrative determination of need. Also involved was a pronounced cost element: a restricted program would be relatively cheap and would minimize the necessity to make painful choices, as between competing government programs. Thus, with cost considerations in mind, British policymakers framed that country's 1908 Old Age Pensions Act so as to restrict eligibility to men aged seventy and above whose annual incomes from other sources did not exceed a very modest 21£. (Also authorized were pensions at reduced rates for those earning more than this amount but not in excess of 31£.)[6] Restrictions also related to the clients' perceived character. In order to be declared as pension eligible, clients must not have received poor law relief after 1908, must not have been imprisoned for any offense including drunkenness during the ten years preceding the claim, could not be an alien, and must be able to satisfy the authorities that they had not been guilty of habitual failure to work according to their ability.[7] The British system was, as

---

5. U.S. Congress, House, Committee on Ways and Means, *Social Security Act Amendments of 1949* (Hearings on H.R. 2893), 81st Cong., 1st sess., pt. 2, 1949, p. 1171.

6. Bentley B. Gilbert, *British Social Policy, 1914–1939* (Ithaca: Cornell University Press, 1970), p. 236.

7. A. I. Ogus, "Great Britain," in Peter A. Kohler and Hans Zacher, eds., *The Evolution of Social Insurance, 1881–1981* (London: Frances Pinter, 1982), p. 178.

one historian has aptly described it, one "for the very old, the very poor and the very respectable."[8]

Fiscal considerations were no less salient in the decision-making process in Canada. It is true that the politicians and civil servants who helped formulate the 1927 act had more than one thing on their minds. For example, they were concerned over the complexity involved in any contributory social insurance scheme and worried that such an approach could well overwhelm the capacity of Canada's still-immature federal bureaucracy. Still, in Canada as in Britain the crux of the matter was cost. Canadian leaders feared that a universal system might disastrously impact the government's tax base and fiscal resources. As Kenneth Bryden observes in reference to the key parliamentary body involved in this matter, "[The 1924 committee] was breaking new ground in Canada and it proceeded with caution. It was careful to keep the estimated costs within limits. . . . That automatically ruled out a universal plan financed out of general revenues."[9] Poverty among Canada's elderly in the 1920s was acute, widespread, and chronic, and political leaders involved in drafting the 1927 legislation could maintain with some plausibility that this program, even though low in benefit payout and modest in scope, represented a significant step forward. With little in the way of research or empirical evidence, therefore, the 1924 committee proposed, and Parliament later accepted, the premise that an old person needed just $1 per day to live on, notwithstanding that this level of benefit represented an "empirically unverified assumption prevalent in government circles."[10] From this, the committee calculated the benefit needed to support a person at age seventy or above to be $365 per year, thereby excluding all single persons having incomes exceeding that level, as well as all married couples having incomes

---

8. Pat Thane, "Non-Contributory versus Insurance Pensions, 1878–1908," in Pat Thane, ed., *The Origins of British Social Policy* (London: Croom Helm, 1978), p. 103. The degree of restrictiveness of the 1908 program is apparent from the following figures. In England and Wales there were some 987,000 persons over age seventy at this time, representing 2.7 percent of the total population for those regions. Of that number, some 442,000 (or 44.7 percent) were old age pension recipients. The main exclusionary factor, aside from the obvious exclusion of all individuals under seventy years, was the disqualification of any person who had received poor law relief since January 1, 1908. In Scotland, the proportion of persons seventy and above declared as pension eligible was slightly higher, namely 53.8 percent. Since policymakers were unable to find any obvious explanation for Scotland's perceived excess, a special parliamentary enquiry was ordered. Noel A. Humphreys, "Old Age Pensions in the United Kingdom," *Journal of the Royal Statistical Society* 74 (December 1910): 71–73.

9. Kenneth Bryden, *Old Age Pensions and Policy-making in Canada* (Montreal and London: McGill-Queens University Press, 1974), p. 77.

10. Ibid.

above $730 per year (365 × 2).[11] Canada's Old Age Pensions Act, 1927, embraced this set of assumptions and related benefit levels.

One should not pass by this period of Canadian policy development without taking note of an obvious paradox: the expansion of scale (i.e., in terms of numbers of persons now declared as benefit eligible) and the narrowing of scope (i.e., as compared to the size of benefits that were potentially available under the existing government annuities program.) Thus, while progressive and forward looking in certain ways, the 1927 act involved such a large concession to perceived fiscal realities as to render ambiguous its claim as a social welfare measure.

Narrowing of Scope of Political Involvement

One consequence of the fairly circumscribed character of these early national schemes—one not consciously intended by their respective framers but real nevertheless—was a marked narrowing in the scope of organized age advocacy. In part, this probably reflected a decline in the numbers of relatively affluent individuals who were prepared to contribute, financially and otherwise, to this type of political organization. With old age pension legislation now on the statute books, it is highly probable that the cause of government-sponsored pensions lost much of its earlier appeal for reform-minded citizens—persons who had featured prominently during the previous era of policy development. It is useful to remind oneself of the heavily middle-class character of the early pension-advocacy movement, as brought out in the previous chapter. Middle-class support for public pension schemes whose beneficiaries consisted largely, and in some cases entirely, of low-income individuals was problematic even under the best of circumstances. What is perhaps most surprising is that persons of middle-class background were prepared to support such a reform effort in the first place, from which they would derive no personal, tangible benefit, and not that such support was prone to later displacement in favor of other, competing priorities.

Losses from that particular source conceivably could have been offset by a corresponding increase in support from elsewhere—for example, from individuals recently declared as state pension eligible, and who therefore had an objective interest in the continuance of their state benefit, and even its possible enlargement. Yet no such compensating gain in pension movement support was forthcoming. The apparent reason for this is not difficult to identify. As demonstrated in the social science literature, political participation, including voting and other forms of political action, varies significantly by social class. This applies to involvement in politically active voluntary organi-

11. Ibid., pp. 76 and 62.

zations, where the likelihood of one's joining up and making a voluntary contribution declines the lower one's position on the social ladder, and with especially low rates tending to occur among those on the bottom rung.[12] A logical corollary to this is that age-benefit programs that are poverty focused and narrowly restrictive probably will have little stimulative effect in terms of collective senior citizen action, even assuming that the benefits represent a substantial, or even total, share of most recipients' incomes. Such persons are not for the most part easily recruited into mass campaigns of political agitation and protest.

To what extent, then, do the preceding rather general observations square with the pattern of interest group dynamics apparent during phase two of policy development? In responding, one can usefully begin by examining those interest groups initially formed in phase one, now seeking to maintain themselves, and then move on to consider any newly formed groups, peculiar to phase two.

Previously Active Organizations

In the United States, the two organizations that together had formed the core of the old age pension movement of the 1920s and early 1930s, namely the American Association for Social Security (AASS) and the American Association for Labor Legislation (AALL), initially seemed capable of maintaining themselves into the era that opened up in the wake of the 1935 Social Security Act. Immediately following 1935, these two groups continued their accustomed range of activities: publication of newsletters and occasional writings, sponsorship of meetings and conferences, arrangement of appearances by their leaders and representatives at congressional hearings, and so on. Yet such outward signs of health were misleading. All was not well with them, and neither one would endure for more than a few more years. At one level, each group's demise can be accounted for in terms of the untimely death of its longtime leader—Abraham Epstein in the case of AASS, who died at age fifty in 1942, and John B. Andrews of AALL, who died the following year at age sixty-three. The untimely death of its principal leader and spokesperson can represent a crisis for any voluntary organization, and these cases evidently were no exceptions. Yet other factors, reflective of a deeper malaise, also were present. Even while Epstein and Andrews were alive and in apparent good health, their organizations had begun to deteriorate. Both groups had drawn their support from fairly narrow middle-class elites, and with the Social Security Act on the statute books former supporters now began to drift away,

---

12. Raymond A. Wolfinger and Stephen Rosenstone, *Who Votes?* (New Haven: Yale University Press, 1980), chap. 2.

evidently unwilling any longer to make the required sacrifices in time, money, and energy.[13] In addition, the two groups for different reasons refused to endorse the model of conservative social insurance that Arthur Altmeyer and the SSB were now so fervently embracing, and thus their leaders were denied privileged access to Altmeyer himself and the SSB as a whole. Direct evidence is lacking, but such lack of access most likely diminished these groups' perceived legitimacy in the eyes of supporters and friends.

The third U.S. age-advocacy organization emergent before 1935, the Old Age and Revolving Pensions—better known by its informal title, the "Townsend Movement"—also survived into the period following adoption of Social Security. As with the other two groups mentioned, however, it did not long remain a significant political force; within three years it had begun to fade, first into political quiescence, and later on into organizational oblivion. The Townsend movement took its name and much of its unique flavor from its founder and national president, Dr. Francis E. Townsend, a Long Beach, California, physician who was in his late sixties when his organization was formed in 1934. The organization enjoyed mushroom growth at its outset, reaching an all-time high membership of six hundred thousand in 1935, the bulk of it in California, but with pockets of strength elsewhere, especially in the American West.

This group was in many respects more of a depression era protest against the dislocations and insecurities of the time than a genuine senior citizens' organization—an advantage from the standpoint of that particular era, but a disadvantage from the standpoint of its long-term survival. The Townsend plan, which the leadership promoted vigorously, aimed to restore the U.S. economy and at the same time provide immediate relief for elderly persons. (Under it, beneficiaries would be given $200 per month—an extremely generous amount by then-prevailing standards—on the condition that the money be spent within a predefined, short period.) Although, conceivably, the Townsend movement might have enlarged its range of goals and direct member benefits, thereby broadening its popular appeal and improving its chances for long-term survival, any such possibility was undercut by a series of early mistakes and questionable practices. There were scandals involving certain national leaders that ended up in embarrassing court battles. And there was Townsend's ill-advised participation in the 1936 presidential campaign under a third-party banner, the Union party, along with two other depression era messiahs: the far-right Gerald L. K. Smith and the Detroit radio evangelist, Father Charles Coughlin. Thus, the Townsend movement was unable to capitalize on its brief moments in the political spotlight, especially the 1938

---

13. Henry J. Pratt, *The Gray Lobby* (Chicago: University of Chicago Press, 1976), chap. 3.

hearings before a committee of the U.S. House of Representatives where Townsend-backed bills served as the focus of discussion.[14]

It is useful to reflect upon the larger significance of the Townsend movement's brief span of popularity and political importance. This organization's spurt of popularity was reflective in part of the special significance of middle-class individuals in the context of senior citizen mass movements. The Great Depression rendered elderly persons of widely divergent social backgrounds financially insecure, including many who before the depression had been relatively advantaged and accustomed to having their voices heard among politicians and elective officeholders. It is significant that the Townsend movement was California-centered, since this was a state to which elderly persons by the tens of thousands had only recently migrated,[15] elderly who were cut off from, and unable easily to replace, their previous linkages to family, neighbors, and friends. Thus, in addition to tapping an obvious dimension of acute financial need, the Townsend movement appealed to members on the basis of solidarity, as fostered through its affiliated local clubs where loneliness and isolation could be combated and a sense of belongingness promoted. (The Townsend movement also found support in the other western states with similarly large immigrant populations from the more-settled East.) In addition, the enactment in 1935 of the Social Security Act almost certainly contributed to the Townsend movement's early demise as a national political force. The promise of substantial age-based relief—inherent in the 1935 act—tended to undercut the movement's repeated charges of governmental indifference toward elderly people. Such impact was presumably augmented by President Franklin D. Roosevelt's known abhorrence of the Townsend plan, and related distancing from Townsend personally.[16]

The common demise of AALL, AASS, and the Townsend movement—all within the decade of the adoption of the Social Security Act—was therefore at least partially the result of organizational disincentives implicit in the act itself, as reflected in the behavior of appointive officials and elective

---

14. Abraham Holtzman, *The Townsend Movement* (New York: Bookman Associates, 1963); Alan Brinkley, *Voices of Protest: Huey Long, Father Coughlin, and the Great Depression* (New York: Vintage Books, 1983), pp. 222–26; Jackson K. Putnam, *Old-Age Politics in California: From Richardson to Reagan* (Stanford: Stanford University, 1970).

15. Between 1920 and 1930 the California population, aged sixty-five and above, increased 83 percent, from 200,000 to 366,000. How much of this large increase arose from in-migration and how much from population aging is unknown. Still, it is worthwhile mentioning that this sixty-five-plus increase significantly exceeded that for the California population generally, which increased only 67 percent over this same time span. It is reasonable to infer that a large fraction of the state's older population was made up of recent migrants. This is based on U.S. Bureau of the Census, *Historical Statistics of the United States*, series A, pp. 195–209.

16. Holtzman, *Townsend Movement*.

politicians. The three voluntary organizations were critically dependent on achieving and maintaining access to government, and once it became clear that such access would not be forthcoming, their leaders' standing in the eyes of members and supporters clearly suffered.

The pattern for the United States is broadly applicable to the other two countries. In the case of Canada, no nongovernmental group had more to do with the adoption of the Canadian 1927 pension act than the Moral and Social Reform Council (MSRC), whose base of support included elites identified with certain important elements in Canadian society: the Social Gospel movement, liberal Protestantism and Anglicanism, and the social work community. Yet in the late 1920s, the MSRC, now reorganized as the Social Service Council, parted company with its social work constituency and, in the wake of a redefinition of goals, no longer gave high priority to pension reform and age-related issues.[17] With respect to Britain, one sees a similar pattern of organizational exit from the political stage. The leaders of the National Committee of Organized Labor made no serious effort to extend their pension-advocacy efforts into the post-1908 period, and within a year's time the group had formally disbanded.

Efforts at New Group Formation

In principle, the disbanding (or in one case the redirecting of energies) of preexisting organizations active in behalf of old age pensions should logically have opened up attractive vistas to enterprising individuals interested in launching new age-advocacy voluntary organizations. Yet no such wave of new group formation occurred. Only in Britain did a serious pension reform organization emerge at this time, and even it did not represent a marked departure from the pattern displayed in the other two cases.

In both Canada and the United States, no serious attempt was made to establish a lobby group at the federal level of government, notwithstanding the new policy space opened up by the 1927 Old Age Pensions Act and the 1935 Social Security Act. There was, admittedly, some degree of pension group development among the Canadian provinces and in the American states. One such, the Old Age Pensioners' Organization of British Columbia, the first general membership group of senior citizens in North America, was established in 1932. (This group has remained active to the present time.) A decade later, 1942, a viable membership organization was formed in Saskatchewan, and around this same time similar groups began to emerge in

---

17. Dennis Guest, *The Emergence of Social Security in Canada* (Vancouver: University of British Columbia Press, 1980), p. 126.

California, Colorado, and one or two other American states.[18] Yet of greater interest for present purposes was the absence in either country of any serious effort to forge seniors into a collective voice, capable of lobbying effectively in national government.

In a previous writing,[19] I suggest that the absence of such a group capable of involvement in U.S. government in Washington, D.C., was a factor in rendering the 1940s, from an age-policy standpoint, "the dismal years." It now appears that the same characterization may apply to the Canadian federal government. Admittedly, an organization styling itself the Canadian Old Age Pensions Federation (later renamed the National Pensioners and Senior Citizens Federation [NP&SCF]) was formed in 1945, toward the close of phase two of Canada's policy development that lasted until 1951. Yet this group had little legitimacy at this time as a representative of seniors throughout the country. Its early headquarters, actually the home of its national president, Nathan Medd, was situated in Saskatoon, Saskatchewan, fifteen hundred miles distant from the national capital, and it had not at this time been chartered by the federal government, which is considered a minimum requirement for legitimacy in the Canadian system.

In the case of Britain, phase two of policy development did witness the formation of a new national pensioners' organization. This group's history, even though fairly short, offers some intriguing insights into the organizational constraints that existed at this time. The group in question, the National Conference on Old Age Pensions (NCOAP), was voted into existence at a July 1916 meeting in London made up of delegates from several existing voluntary organizations. It set for itself the goal of becoming a membership organization of pensioners and senior citizens, and with that in mind its leaders directed appeals toward several sectors of British society: trade unions, Friendly Societies, the cooperative movement, and the "free churches." The group's leading figure, Sir Thomas Oliver, quickly gained recognition as an effective fund-raiser and a competent, if not brilliant, strategist and administrator.

The NCOAP enjoyed some early successes. It managed to generate revenues sufficient to permit its hiring a full-time secretary, and within a few months it had formulated a set of demands to lay before Parliament. Within a year of its inception over one hundred members of Parliament had indicated their support for its work, and in 1919 an NCOAP-led all-parties deputation

---

18. Bryden, *Old Age Pensions and Policy-making in Canada*, p. 194; Senior Citizens' Provincial Council, *A Short History of Senior Citizens Organizations in Saskatchewan* (Regina, Canada: Senior Citizens' Provincial Council, 1981).

19. Pratt, *Gray Lobby*, chap. 3.

was a factor in compelling Austen Chamberlain, the chancellor of the exchequer and half brother of Neville Chamberlain, to convene a parliamentary committee on pensions, whose report was subsequently presented to the cabinet. Upon its release, however, this official report was condemned by NCOAP as wholly inadequate. Its leaders launched a propaganda offensive designed to impress upon members of Parliament the view that the proposed reforms did not adequately address the inequities in the means limits, whose rigorous enforcement was leaving many old age pensioners in pitiable condition. The committee went on to emphasize that state spending on pensioners compared unfavorably to that spent on paupers and prison inmates. Parliamentary response to this pressure was prompt: a revised proposal was soon drafted and brought up for vote on the floor. The NCOAP had the satisfaction of seeing this reform measure enacted into law in January 1920.[20]

Despite this promising start, the NCOAP early on began to display evidence of instability and poor judgment at the top. At one point its national executive adopted a set of proposals that essentially compromised its own professed concern for the welfare of poorer elements among Britain's elderly. And the organization's insistence on the need for a universal, nonmeans-tested pension, and refusal to consider the alternative state contributory insurance approach, cost it dearly in terms of member support. Its doctrinaire stand in favor of the universal pension restricted its governmental access, especially after 1921, when a newly installed Labour government, breaking with its earlier support for universal pensions, embraced instead the contributory principle. Although the NCOAP proclaimed itself as the voice of over ten million organized people, there was no substance to this boast, and indeed it never succeeded in realizing a mass membership base.

These deficiencies eventually resulted in disintegration. From 1921 onward the original supporters began drifting away. And at what proved to be its final national convention, in 1925, the organization voted to condemn the newly enacted Widows', Orphans', and Old Age Contributory Pensions Act for its inclusion of only 70 percent of the population and perceived failure to eliminate the "Means, Residency and Nationality tests." Such rhetoric had not the slightest effect on government policy, and the following year the NCOAP passed quietly out of existence.[21]

Summing up, the available evidence points toward a connection between public policy outputs and age-organizational activity during stage two. Except

---

20. Andrew Blaikie, "The Emerging Political Power of the Elderly in Britain, 1908–1948," *Ageing and Society* 10 (1990): 17–39.

21. Ibid., pp. 25–27. See also Pat M. Williams (Thane), "The Development of Old Age Pensions Policy in Great Britain, 1878–1925" (Ph.D. dissertation, University of London, 1970) (on file at the University of London Library).

in Britain, the level of pension benefits provided was apparently insufficient to produce major organizational incentives, and even in Britain the level of incentives seems to have been only rather modest. A case can be made that the primary impact of policy change was depressive from an organizational standpoint, considering the disappearance from the stage of existing age-advocacy organizations, and the drifting away of former supporters and members. It would appear, in other words, that the critical decisions associated with phase two proved to be more productive of disincentives than of incentives when regarded from the standpoint of age-group mobilization and political activism.

Fragmentation of Administrative Mechanisms

There was at least one additional factor involved in the fragility of age-advocacy organizations at this time, one having more to do with the manner of pension administration than with program content and scope. As revealed in the existing literature, the successful launching of new political interest groups, and the perpetuation of ones already in existence, depends in part on their having a clear governmental focus toward which to direct their political energies.[22] Absent such a target, it may be difficult to achieve organizational focus and to achieve positive results. This situation seems to have confronted pension advocacy organizations in the period under discussion.

The administrative arrangements initially adopted for old age pensions had the following common features in all three of the countries: the placing of certain functions under national jurisdiction and others under that of regional government, and an overall absence of clear administrative responsibility. In two of the countries, namely Canada and the United States, civil servants at the provincial or state level were made responsible for the distribution of important old age benefits, but funding was centralized. The Canadian provinces were made entirely responsible for benefit payout under the 1927 enactment, while in the United States state governments assumed responsibility for Old Age Assistance (OAA), which as previously noted was the more substantial facit of the Social Security system in stage two. Yet in both cases central bureaucracies, in Ottawa and Washington, respectively, were granted a major role in program administration.

In Britain, the absence of clear focus was more reflective of expediency and convenience than of a constitutionally determined division of powers between levels of government as is inherent in a federal system. As far back

---

22. For a discussion of the possible connection between governmental structure and the character of voluntary political organizations, see James Q. Wilson, *Political Organizations* (New York: Basic Books, 1973), chap. 5.

as medieval times, British local government functioned under authority of the Crown, and was overseen by crown servants headquartered at the national capital. Consistent with this traditional pattern, the 1908 Old Age Pensions Act placed responsibility for pension administration in the hands of a central ministry in London. Still, the administrative arrangement chosen pursuant to this act informally mixed program responsibilities as between London and the localities in a manner not entirely rational. Administrative practice under Britain's 1908 Old Age Pensions Act gave overall authority to appointive officials in London, while informally leaving much to local discretion. And locally, the administrative pattern was fairly confused, as Maurice Bruce points out:

> Old Age pensions were the first national social service and no offices existed to administer them . . . . The administrative problem was overcome by the establishment, through the Local Authorities, of local committees, which were assisted in their investigations by the only government department which possessed the network of local offices and experienced investigators which were needed, the Board of Customs and Excise. . . . The actual payment of pensions was committed to the only government department with the local facilities for making payments, the Post Office.[23]

All of this appears to have adversely affected the chances for success on the part of interest groups concerned with pensioners and senior citizens. Given the multiplicity of levels—national, regional, and local—where significant administrative discretion now was being exercised, and the resulting absence of any clear target, their leaders must have found it difficult and frustrating to determine where to apply their limited political resources. Assuming this was so, it must have represented an additional strain on their organizations.

The Government Actors

The political weakness and instability that typified pension-advocacy groups at this time probably contributed to the ascendency of other political actors, better adapted to that particular environment and less constrained by the phase two atmosphere. Two types of actors were especially significant in this regard, namely civil servants and elective politicians.

---

23. Maurice Bruce, *The Coming of the Welfare State* (London: B. T. Batsford, 1961), p. 156.

Civil Servants

Appointive officials in government came to play highly significant roles with respect to state pensions in the years following the 1908, 1927, and 1935 enactments. In each of the countries, civil servants came to be relied on for their mastery of technical detail, grasp of the viable options, and informed opinions regarding the best course of action. Even though neutral with respect to partisan politics, such officials were seldom neutral in program terms, having strong policy preferences that they were prepared to voice and, on occasion, actively to promote.

With respect to Canada, it is apparent that within a decade of the nation's 1927 pension legislation officials such as these had become important in the course of policy deliberations. During the years immediately preceding Canada's 1951 universal pension, civil servants were closely in touch with all the ministers having authority in this area: the prime minister (first, William Lyon Mackenzie King and then, beginning in 1948, Louis St. Laurent), the minister of justice, the minister of munitions and supply (retitled after World War II as minister of reconstruction), and the minister of finance. If one was to single out a single civil servant for special mention in the pension area, it would probably be George Davidson, the deputy minister of welfare and a man described by Kenneth Bryden as "a continuous influence for the universal pension plan [that was eventually adopted]."[24]

The prominence of civil servants evidently marked the British case no less than the Canadian. In 1919, with World War I only just ended, the government of Prime Minister David Lloyd George saw grounds for serious concern that a returning army of war veterans and an increasingly restless British working class might combine to force immediate enactment of pension legislation of an overly radical and fiscally burdensome character. Seeking to forestall such an unwanted outcome, while holding open the possibility for more moderate pension reform, the Lloyd George government convened a departmental investigating committee—heavily larded with senior civil servants—to review the options, listen to deputations and experts, and produce a set of policy recommendations. The committee's final report did not win immediate approval, and in fact was subject to searching, occasionally harsh, cabinet-level criticism. Still, it became the foundation for the moderately reformist Old Age Pension Act of 1919—a measure that left intact the essentials of the existing 1908 program, while raising benefit levels and introducing some minor administrative reforms.[25]

---

24. Bryden, *Old Age Pensions and Policy-making in Canada*, pp. 113–14 and 123.
25. Gilbert, *British Social Policy*, pp. 236–38.

A roughly similar pattern of participation was evident a few years later, 1923, when Britain's government had before it a far more sweeping proposal involving overhaul of the existing state pension system. As had been true earlier, civil servants were called upon for advice, and their views were to prove quite influential. They were among the major inputs into the Widows', Orphans', and Old Age Contributory Pensions Act (1925), whose enactment ushered in stage three in Britain.[26]

Turning to the United States, the abundant available materials enable one to explore the role of civil servants at some depth. As earlier mentioned, the individual who stands out above all others for the forcefulness of his views and the extent of his policy impact at this stage was Dr. Arthur Altmeyer. In combination with his lieutenants, Altmeyer succeeded in enforcing a substantial degree of conformity to his particular interpretation of congressional intent on Social Security. The commissioner came to occupy a position of vast importance, as evident by his ability to influence several sets of decision makers: his superiors in the Federal Security Agency (FSA), the members of the House Ways and Means and other congressional committees, and (prior to his death in April 1945) President Franklin D. Roosevelt. The full extent of Altmeyer's clout becomes evident when it is observed that he successfully overcame substantial opposition, including that of vocal critics in both the House and Senate and restive subordinates within his own agency. The commissioner's preference for conservative, as opposed to liberal, or redistributive, social insurance was the position that eventually prevailed on Capitol Hill. Going well beyond the fairly passive role often ascribed to civil servants, Altmeyer became essentially a program politician—waging duels with his detractors while simultaneously shoring up and reassuring his political allies and supporters.[27]

Participation by Cabinet Members and Government Heads

In addition to civil servants, stage two also saw elective officials and cabinet members becoming actively identified with the public pension cause. Their proactiveness involved a shift from that of their counterparts at the previous phase of pension policy, when, it will be recalled, politicians mostly displayed considerable reticence and reluctance to commit themselves until almost the last moment. (The exceptions to this had been few—most notably Joseph Chamberlain in England.) With pension legislation now on the statute books and with the rolls of pension beneficiaries expanding—initially into the hun-

---

26. Ibid., p. 242.
27. Cates, *Insuring Inequality*, chaps. 3 and 4.

dreds of thousands and then into the millions—elective officials began to see much political advantage, and little offsetting risk, in seizing the initiative in this area. There were, obviously, limits to such willingness; it stopped well short of the point where program expansion might threaten to place an unreasonable burden on available fiscal resources or on competing domestic programs. Yet, the shift in behavior was still substantial.

In all three cases, this new outlook was apparent a few years into the phase two era. The British case illustrates the general pattern nicely. Late in the second and early in the third decade of the twentieth century Britain's government came generally to accept the proposition that overhaul of the 1908 pension scheme was required. World War I had delayed any early coming to grips with the old age pension issues, and the initial postwar response, as embodied in the legislation of 1919, was looked upon as essentially a stopgap. Serious discussion within government directed toward possible fundamental changes thus began in the early 1920s. In 1924 the newly installed minister of health, Neville Chamberlain—son of Joseph Chamberlain, now recently deceased—moved for the appointment of a study commission, while also making clear his own support for needed legislation. (Chamberlain's motives appear to have reflected in part his family origins, since he regarded himself as following in his father's footsteps as advocate for Britain's needy elderly, although having the advantage, denied to his father, of being a political insider, not a maverick.) The minister put forward a proposal for a new, contributory pension to be offered to individuals between age sixty-five and seventy, with the existing, noncontributory, scheme to be left in place for eligible persons seventy and above. The measure further provided that persons who earlier had qualified for the contributory pension at sixty-five, and were still in receipt of a pension from that source, would pass automatically into the noncontributory pension at age seventy without having to undergo a means test.

For the proposal to move ahead, Chamberlain required the support of his fellow cabinet members, and in the end such support was forthcoming. Most significant was that provided by the two officials having the greatest veto power, namely the chancellor of the exchequer, Winston Churchill, and the prime minister, Stanley Baldwin. (Baldwin had replaced David Lloyd George as prime minister following the Conservative victory in the 1922 national elections.) No significant opposition having been voiced, the cabinet voted its assent to Chamberlain's proposal. With cabinet support thus secured, and with the opposition Liberal and Labour parties disinclined to contest the issue, eventual approval by the House of Commons and House of Lords now became a foregone conclusion.[28] It was a far different political atmosphere than

---

28. Gilbert, *British Social Policy*, pp. 235–51.

the timidity that had characterized Herbert Asquith in 1906–8 under comparable circumstances.

The behavior of leading politicians in both Canada and the United States resembled that of their British counterparts when comparable pension reforms were under discussion. There was this difference, however: whereas in Britain the debate was fairly restricted in scope—essentially confined to the cabinet and senior civil servants—in the other two countries the topic of pension reform became a matter of high public visibility and interest. In Canada, the Liberal party was dominant in Ottawa throughout these years, and Liberal leaders early on came to appreciate the possible electoral advantages of becoming positively identified with the pension reform cause. As early as 1943 Prime Minister William Lyon Mackenzie King declared that "a comprehensive national scheme of social insurance should be worked out at once."[29] Five years later, by which time he had stepped down, King's successor, Louis St. Laurent, voiced similarly firm commitment. Indeed, support for reform of Canada's pension system was voiced at this point by all the key members of the cabinet, including Brooke Claxton and Paul Martin—the first and second individuals, respectively, to occupy the post of minister of national health and welfare.[30]

The 1951 overhaul of Canada's pension system consisted of two companion pieces of legislation, the Old Age Assistance Act and the Old Age Security Act. The former of these was the less controversial, since it involved little in the way of programmatic change. Authorized under this statute was an increase in the size of the existing federal subsidy to the 1927 means-tested benefit, thereby enabling the ten provinces to raise existing pension benefit levels, and a lowering of the age of pension eligibility under OAA from the previous seventy years to sixty-five. The latter measure proposed more fundamental change. The Old Age Security Act established a universal pension for every Canadian at age seventy subject only to a residency requirement. At a single stroke, Canada's federal pension scheme was now enlarged from one involving benefits payable only to the demonstrably indigent and needy into one covering every Canadian citizen above a defined age regardless of need or circumstance. Although a topic of lively debate, neither of these measures proved especially controversial, and in the end the opposition Progressive Conservatives joined with the ruling Liberals in endorsing the two reforms when they came before the federal Parliament.[31]

The U.S. case also illustrates the powerful attraction of pension reform legislation for elective leaders and politicians. The critically important 1950

---

29. Quoted in Bryden, *Old Age Pensions and Policy-making in Canada*, p. 113.
30. Ibid., p. 117.
31. Bryden, *Old Age Pensions and Policy-making in Canada*.

amendments to the Social Security Act embraced principles that the Democratic party, then in power in the White House and also in both houses of Congress, had espoused for a number of years. In their 1940 platform, the Democrats had pledged to extend the Social Security system to "millions of workers not now protected under its terms" and to establish "more adequate and uniform benefits." The platform also rebuked the Republicans for their alleged lack of support for Social Security. Congressional action on this pledge was impeded by the U.S. entry into World War II, but in the run up to the 1948 election, the Democratic standard-bearer, President Harry Truman—now seeking election to office in his own right, having initially assumed the presidency on the death of his predecessor—powerfully rekindled the campaign. Truman appealed for a vast expansion in worker coverage under Social Security and for an improvement in benefit levels, while also making clear his preference for social insurance (OASI) as opposed to public assistance (OAA). With the election less than a year ahead, the president used his January 1948 State of the Union Address to speak up in favor of this legislation, emphasizing his belief that the existing system "has gaps and inconsistencies and is only half finished."[32] Later, with the November election close at hand and polls showing him trailing, Truman refocused his campaign, giving special emphasis to the concerns of the core Democratic, New Deal coalition—labor, liberals, and Afro-Americans—and in this context gave his Social Security proposals a heightened emphasis. He stressed the need to increase OASI benefits by at least 50 percent and to extend OASI coverage to an additional twenty million uncovered workers. (Both these proposals had appeared in the 1948 Democratic platform, adopted the previous summer, but without the emphasis now given them by the presidential candidate.) Subsequently, with his upset 1948 election victory behind him, Truman submitted Social Security proposals embodying his administration's views, and shortly thereafter, in slightly revised form, these were enacted by Congress as the 1950 Social Security amendments.[33]

A common thread of assertiveness ties together the behavior of the British, Canadian, and U.S. politicians. Obviously, the element of risk—so much part of the calculations of their counterparts at the earlier stage of policy development—was now essentially removed. One was dealing now with established programs, not untested and arguably risky proposals as had been the case previously. Moreover, *partisan controversy*, so prominent a feature of policy debates during the stage immediately preceding, now receded in importance, to be replaced in large part by an increasing degree of *partisan consensus*.

---

32. Pratt, *Gray Lobby*, p. 32.
33. Ibid.

Such decline in the element of controversy probably was felt in all three countries, but nowhere was it quite so obvious, perhaps, as in the United States. In the 1936 U.S. presidential election, held in the immediate aftermath of the adoption of the Social Security Act, the Republicans had made a campaign issue out of this vast extension in the role of the federal government. Alfred E. Landon, the GOP standard-bearer, attacked the 1935 act as a leading example of everything that was wrong with the Roosevelt New Deal.[34] Yet the GOP under Landon suffered a crushing defeat in 1936, and with the Supreme Court's decision at around this same time to uphold the Social Security Act as constitutionally valid, the political atmosphere surrounding Social Security underwent a shift. In the 1940 presidential election, the Republican leadership reversed its previous stance, and in its platform was in favor of extending old age and unemployment insurance to all employees not already covered. Moreover, in 1944 and again in 1948 the GOP reaffirmed this position, and in increasingly unqualified terms. Thus, an astute politician like Harry Truman could seize on Social Security reform as a major campaign theme in 1948, knowing that there was no possibility of his being outflanked by the GOP or even by those within his own party to the right of him politically.

Regional Patterns: The Case of Canada

As mentioned, phase two of pension policy, even though not in general very supportive of seniors' collective action, did witness significant organizational development in the provinces of western Canada. Any effort to account for this unique regional pattern must consider the possible significance of policy outputs emanating from the region's provincial governments. Indeed, the governments in question were all in advance of the rest of Canada with regard to the full adoption of implementing legislation under the 1927 Old Age Pensions Act. Whereas all four of the western provincial governments had adopted such legislation by 1929, such early adoption applied to only one of the governments further to the east, namely Ontario, where the implementing legislation took effect in 1929. In the other four eastern provinces such legislation did not come into effect until 1933 or later. Furthermore, the five eastern provinces established and enforced fairly strict eligibility standards, thereby making pension benefits available to but a limited sector of the elderly population, consisting chiefly of the more aged and severely disadvantaged. In the West, on the other hand, eligibility standards were more flexible: in a typical year, 1949, between 70 and 80 percent of pensioners in the four

---

34. W. Andrew Achenbaum, *Social Security: Visions and Revisions* (New York: Cambridge University Press, 1986), p. 29.

western provinces were receiving the full pension benefit—far above what applied elsewhere in the country. Given this setting, it is not surprising that the first Canadian province to see the formation of a provincial seniors' federation, namely British Columbia (1932), was also the first to adopt provincial enabling legislation (1927), or that the second such federation, the Alberta Pensioners' Federation (1937), emerged in a province whose government was likewise among the early adopters (1929).[35]

Conclusion

Several themes characterizing phase two have become apparent in the preceding discussion. One is the important role, in all three countries, of both elective politicians and senior civil servants. Such officials participated in the deliberations leading up to the introduction of new pension reform proposals, and also in the efforts made to enhance public understanding and support. Some degree of variation existed, cross-nationally, in how such support was manifested. In the United States and Canada, the pension enactments of 1950 and 1951 involved open collaboration between the appointive and elective public officials and the various nongovernmental actors. In Britain, on the other hand, the process was more behind closed doors and more dependent on a single individual, Neville Chamberlain. (Chamberlain's ultimate success in this campaign would later be viewed as his most singular domestic policy accomplishment.) Civil servants took part in these events on the basis of their reputations for technical expertise and feel for the viable options; their actual role transcended their usual public image as neutral and faceless.

Such comparisons cross-nationally at this common stage are worthwhile making, yet they are perhaps less instructive than is a comparison across time between phase two and phase one. The new stage involved some diminution in the capacity of age-advocacy interest groups to intervene effectively in pension policy debates. In place of government leaders being *acted upon* with respect to such matters, such leaders now became far more autonomous and self-directing. Upon reflection, it is not especially surprising that elective officeholders and civil servants should have acted with such autonomy and initiative. Such individuals were required to shift their focus only slightly in

---

35. (For the pattern of legislation) Bryden, *Old Age Pensions and Policy-making in Canada*, pp. 81 and 101 and chap. 5. (For the dates of the provincial federations) Gifford, *Canada's Fighting Seniors*, pp. 260–61. Other factors than simply the content of public policy obviously were involved in this regional contrast. In the Canadian West, for example, both the cooperative movement and the labor movement were stronger than in the East, and they in turn contributed to the rise of progressive politics in that region, and the resulting strong pressure for more generous pension benefits during the late 1920s, 1930s, and 1940s. I am indebted to C. G. Gifford (personal correspondence) for enlightening me on these matters.

order to produce the desired political outcome, and their risks in so doing were but minimal.

With respect to age-active interest groups, the level of incentives newly created was evidently insufficient to overcome the apparent sense of quiescense that the new environment evidently engendered. Government programs providing small benefits, restricted in scope, appear to have constituted a net interest group disincentive, given their tendency to convey an illusion of progress while offering little in the way of genuine clientele improvement.

As mentioned, the Canadian West was atypical, given the fairly pronounced pattern there of vigorous group activity. Yet this exception does not basically alter the overall picture. The general pattern of organizational quiescence and related public policy disincentives have certain interesting theoretical implications, and these are perhaps best postponed until the concluding chapter.

CHAPTER 5

Third Phase: Universal Benefits, Universal Organizations

There is a sound basis for characterizing the previously mentioned measures of 1925, 1950, and 1951—in Britain, the United States, and Canada, respectively—as marking the transition from phase two to phase three of pension policy development. Previous analysts, although not using this same formulation, have shared the view that these enactments were genuine public policy departures, not mere elaborations on existing themes. Thus, Martha Derthick, in assessing the 1950 amendments to the U.S. Social Security Act, remarks that this represented no less than "the program's third and final statutory 'founding.'"[1] (The earlier "foundings" were the original act of 1935 and the amendments of 1939.) Another leading U.S. observer, Robert M. Ball, shares Derthick's opinion of this legislation's importance. The Social Security system, given its inadequacy of benefits and narrowness of scope, was "imperiled" as of 1949, Ball writes, and the 1950 amendments "may well have preserved the system."[2] Likewise, a leading student of Canadian social welfare policy, Dennis Guest, in commenting upon that country's 1951 legislation, points out that "the Old Age Security Act, a universal demogrant, removed once and for all the sense of personal failure that accompanied the acceptance of an old age pension under the original act."[3] Finally, a leading British social historian, Pat Thane, observes that the individualistic, self-help values that informed Britain's 1925 Contributory Pensions Act represented a radical departure from the more collectivistic thinking that had underlaid the legislation of 1908, and that the former of these for the first time created "a vested right in a contributory pension [and thereby] absolved the state from

---

1. Martha Derthick, *Policymaking for Social Security* (Washington, D.C.: Brookings Institution, 1979), p. 273.

2. Robert M. Ball, "The Original Understanding on Social Security: Implications for Later Developments," in Theodore R. Marmor and Jerry L. Mashaw, eds., *Social Security: Beyond the Rhetoric of Crisis* (Princeton: Princeton University Press, 1988), p. 31.

3. Dennis Guest, *The Emergence of Social Security in Canada* (Vancouver: University of British Columbia Press, 1980), p. 145.

the odium incurred since 1908 by the necessity to accept or reject pensioners by often arbitrary criteria."[4]

Common to all these reformulations of policy was a major expansion in the scope of coverage. As discussed at greater depth in this chapter, decision makers in each country now opted to shift the emphasis of pension policy away from the former, near-exclusive stress on the oldest, most acutely needy individuals, and instead to place it upon the income security needs of retirees generally, including their dependents if any. There existed, of course, considerable country-to-country variation in the precise terms of these measures. Britain offered an earnings-related pension tied to that country's existing national insurance program, the United States reformulated its Social Security system so as to reinvigorate social insurance (Old Age and Survivors Insurance [OASI]), which had languished somewhat in comparison to Old Age Assistance (OAA), and Canadian policymakers embraced a "demogrant"—a scheme of fairly modest, flat-rate benefits universal in their coverage for persons aged seventy and above. (In 1965 the eligibility age was lowered to sixty-five.) Although these and other variations in program content are of interest, they are perhaps less interesting in a larger sense than is the fundamental point of similarity, namely the common abandonment by these three countries of their previously very restrictive state pension systems in favor of programs embracing broad-scale, in one case even universal, entitlement at some predefined age.

While the newly formulated programs thus departed from the principles of previous years, none of the countries had yet arrived at, nor even closely approximated, a genuinely mature system of state-funded pensions for the elderly. The new schemes were not especially generous in terms of individual benefits, and policymakers manifested little inclination to launch a direct, frontal attack on the existence of old age poverty. The concept of pension adequacy was not embraced as a fundamental principle, or even vigorously advanced as a feasible public policy alternative. Taking these realities into account, the following discussion examines the degree to which, if at all, the new enactments affected the basic character of interest group activity in aging. The working hypothesis is that even though the expanded coverage provided for in the new legislation augmented the incentives available to seniors' groups, its organizational impact was far from unlimited, and the fledgling groups of the time faced daunting odds against their own viability and survival. This hypothesis is tested in each of the countries, beginning with Canada.

---

4. P. M. Williams (Thane), "The Development of Old Age Pensions in the United Kingdom, 1878–1925" (Ph.D. dissertation, University of London, 1970), p. 466 (on file at the University of London Library).

Canada in the Phase Three Setting

Canada's legislation of 1951 vastly increased the scope of persons covered under the nation's state pension program. In place of a means-tested system, as mandated under the existing Old Age Pensions Act of 1927, the nation's old age pension now was made universal at age seventy, and in addition, eligibility for a means-tested pension now was lowered to sixty-five (from seventy). These changes had the effect of augmenting the number of pension beneficiaries by hundreds of thousands. At the point that benefits under the former Old Age Pensions Act ended in December 1951, 309,000 Canadians were in receipt of a state pension; when the new program went into effect the following year their number more than doubled to 643,000. And within the space of fifteen years, with the new system gaining increasing acceptance among the provinces, this number would double again, so that by 1966, at the end of Canada's third phase, there were 1.3 million recipients.

The same 1951 legislation increased the size of the individual pension benefit to an initial $40 monthly—a major increase over the $25 figure of just eight years previous. There can be little doubt, then, that one is dealing here with a major redirection of pension policy.

Yet the new act was less expansive in terms of the size of individual benefits. With respect to that aspect, some enduring policy constraints made themselves felt, as policymakers continued to embrace the principle of minimal adequacy and basic need as opposed to income adequacy. From an original maximum monthly rate of $40 per month, the Old Age Security (OAS) pension increased but slowly, so that by late 1961, a decade after the program took effect, the maximum had risen only modestly to $55 and, moreover, by the close of phase three in the late 1960s the figure was still only a modest $75—less than double the original figure for January 1952, and below the rate of inflation for the period as a whole.[5] And overall expenditures reflected the same basic assumption. When OAS first became operational in fiscal year 1952–53 expenditures amounted to $323 million, and it would not be until 1966–67 that this figure would pass $1 billion (to $1.03 billion)—despite a substantial enlargement in the number of beneficiaries over this same fifteen-year period. Likewise, it would be twenty years after the program went into

---

5. (For Old Age Pensions Act) Canada Department of National Health and Welfare, *Reports of the Administration of Old Age and Blind Persons in Canada, Fiscal Years Ended March 31, 1948 to 1952* (Ottawa: Queens Printer, 1952), p. 39 (table 21), and (for Old Age Security Act) *Old Age Security: Historical Statistics* (Ottawa: Queens Printer, December 1986), p. 1 (table 1) and p. 6 (table 6-A).

effect before the basic pension for individuals would double in size, namely from $40 (1952) to $80 (1972).[6]

This was not a policy setting that proved especially congenial to formation of nationally active seniors' organizations. Canada's third phase of policy development lasted from 1951—the year of enactment of the OAS pension—until 1966, the year of adoption of the Guaranteed Income Supplement (GIS), introduced to assist the most poverty-stricken seniors. At both the national and provincial levels, seniors' organizations for the most part did not find this an atmosphere in which they could flourish. It can be said of Canadian interest groups generally that as a condition of such groups' achieving sustained political influence they must establish a foundation of support in the several provinces. This principle applies to senior citizens' groups no less than to those operating in other spheres, and thus, in the words of one leading analyst, C. G. Gifford, "From the beginning, the backbone of Canada's seniors' movement has been formed by the provincial federations of senior citizens clubs."[7] In light of this, it is striking that phase three of Canadian pension politics saw but one new provincial federation, namely the United Senior Citizens of Ontario, whose formation in the late 1950s, when added to the provincial federations that already existed in Alberta, British Columbia, and Saskatchewan, increased to four the number of provinces with seniors' federations then in existence. With respect to the six unorganized provinces, it is not known, save for one case, whether efforts were undertaken to form provincial federations, only to meet with failure, or instead potential organizers did not even make the effort. The one case where evidence on this point exists points toward the former of these possibilities. A group styling itself the "Manitoba Federation of Pensioners and Senior Citizens" was formed sometime in the late 1950s or early 1960s only to die out after about a decade.[8]

This should not be taken as suggesting that the atmosphere was entirely uncongenial to the establishment of seniors' organizations. Successful organizing efforts did occur at a scattering of places at the local, grass roots level, including areas where provincial federations had yet to emerge.[9] Also, the NP&SCF now for the first time succeeded in gaining a marked degree of visibility and governmental access.

6. Canada Department of National Health and Welfare, *Old Age Security*, pp. 1 (table 1) and 18 (table 7-H).

7. C. G. Gifford, *Canada's Fighting Seniors* (Toronto: James Lorimer, 1990), p. 41.

8. Ibid., pp. 262–63.

9. Ibid., pp. 262–63.

NP&SCF

As mentioned in the preceding chapter, the group that originally styled itself the "Canadian Old Age Pensions Federation" was formed in 1945, toward the close of Canada's second phase—its political interventions much constrained by a fairly narrow geographic base and general reputation in Ottawa as a regional, and not a national, presence. (The question of why the Canadian seniors' movement should have coalesced originally in the West, and only much later—after the third phase had ended—in the East, is an interesting one to contemplate.)[10]

As Canadians in large numbers now began to experience the full impact of the 1951 OAS pension, however, this picture began to change, with the Canadian Old Age Pensions Federation coming to realize increased access to the Canadian government in Ottawa. In 1954, ten years after its founding, the group was granted its federal charter—a significant, if modest, recognition by Ottawa of its political legitimacy. And in 1959, it formally renamed itself the National Pensioners and Senior Citizens Federation (NP&SCF)—the name still employed at the present time. Moreover, in the middle and late 1950s this group's original western support base was enlarged so as to include the emer-

---

10. It was more than forty years after the enactment of the 1927 Old Age Pensions Act, and more than thirty years after the last of Canada's provinces had opted to participate in the 1927 program, before viable provincewide seniors' federations emerged in the five Canadian provinces to the east of Ontario. While no single explanation is adequate to account for this long delay, one key element probably relates to the marked difference between western Canada and the East in their extent of provincial in-migration. In the East, where the number of immigrants from other provinces and from foreign countries relative to total population was small, it is highly plausible that elderly typically maintained themselves in their long-accustomed family and community roles. In the West, on the other hand, immigrants were a major fraction of the total population, and here it is highly plausible that seniors were less well integrated into their families and communities, given the distance—often very great—from their places of origin. Such a lack of community and family integration would logically lead to seniors in large numbers lending support to senior citizen associations and clubs, seen by them as venues for social solidarity and support. It is also plausible that they would tend to support the proposed creation of provincial federations of seniors' clubs.

While these propositions cannot be directly tested, there is supportive evidence of an indirect nature. Analyses of 1951 census data and provincial federation histories reveal a high correlation between the proportions of persons of "foreign" birth (i.e., not native to the province) in 1951 and dates of formation of provincial seniors' federations. When the rank order of provinces arranged according to date of founding is compared to the rank order according to the proportion of the non–native-born population (i.e., foreign), the positive correlation (Spearman's rho) is found to be a quite high .94. This is consistent with the thought that the mobilization of seniors is easier to accomplish in locations having relatively large numbers of less-settled individuals. Source: Ninth Census of Canada, 1951, *Population,* vol. 1 (Ottawa: Queens Printer, 1951), table 45.

gent seniors' movements further to the east, especially in Manitoba and Ontario.

The Ontario group, United Senior Citizens of Ontario (USCO), was formed in 1956, its policy orientation strongly progressive—an ideology reflective of the leaders' industrial-union backgrounds and Left political leanings. By the early 1960s USCO was regularly sending representatives fifteen hundred miles westward to Saskatoon, for purposes of participating in the annual meetings of NP&SCF. Their presence soon began to transform the national organization, especially after 1962 when Jack C. Lerette, USCO activist and retired United Rubber Workers organizer, was elected the national group's vice-president. Lerette's prominence within the pensioners' movement was augmented the year following, when he was elected president of USCO, and further so over the subsequent six years, 1964–69, when USCO under his direction succeeded in building its membership base from just thirteen affiliated chapters at the outset to over four hundred.[11]

Lerette originally sought to avoid a direct challenge to Nathan Medd's fairly leisurely, politically conservative style of leadership. Yet he objected strenuously to Medd's practice of holding all NP&SCF national meetings in Saskatchewan, the president's home base and also that of the parent organization, the Saskatchewan Federation of Pensioners and Senior Citizens. Lerette also objected to the practice of including as members only provincial federations of seniors, and thereby excluding local seniors' clubs and individuals. His repeated criticisms ultimately had their effect: toward the close of Medd's presidential tenure the organization voted to diversify itself by holding its annual meetings elsewhere, and the base of membership was changed in line with Lerette's demands. Given his position at the head of USCO, Canada's largest senior citizen group in terms of numbers, Lerette was favorably positioned to challenge Medd's position at the helm of the national organization. In the end Lerette did win the delegate support necessary to oust Medd as president—in a bruising floor fight at the NP&SCF annual meeting in 1969. Lerette's victory at Medd's expense represented more than just leadership turnover at the top—the first since the organization's founding a quarter century earlier. It also represented a cultural shift: progressivism replaced moderation as the organization's dominant ideological mode.

These organizational developments were associated with a reinvigoration of NP&SCF's lobbying activity at the national capital. From an earlier position of obscurity, the group emerged in the middle 1960s as a major actor on public pension issues. A leading analyst, Kenneth Bryden, refers to these years as ones of increased pensioner activism in Ottawa, and while more than one interest group was involved, he stresses NP&SCF's special significance:

11. Gifford, *Canada's Fighting Seniors*, pp. 27–28.

[NP&SCF] undertook extensive lobbying at Ottawa and elicited vocal support in the House of Commons. The national health and welfare minister of the time has attested to the vigor of the campaign. *Undoubtedly it was a factor in the substantial changes made in the universal plan, not originally contemplated by the government, culminating in the guaranteed income supplement in 1966.*[12]

It should be pointed out that this lobbying was entirely a volunteer, shoestring effort. NP&SCF at this time employed no full-time staff and was lacking an office in Ottawa proper, or anywhere in the national capital vicinity. And there was no nationwide mobilization of seniors to back up its political demands. The group's success resulted, therefore, not from any large base of tangible resources, or from the skills of a cadre of professional lobbyists, or from a nationwide campaign of agitation and protest—all or some of which frequently attend interest group victories in other fields in the face of substantial opposition. Rather, it resulted from the exceptional intensity of conviction and motivation that existed among a fairly small group of NP&SCF activists, as well as from the aforementioned absence of serious rivals to this group in speaking for the retiree and old age pensioner population.

The New Social Security Climate in the United States

The 1950 amendments to the U.S. Social Security Act introduced substantial changes in the programmatic character and clientele base of this vastly important social program. At the time this legislation was adopted, the American work force comprised some 59 million persons, of whom only about 60 percent were in occupations covered by OASI. And after fifteen years, Social Security still was not very important, with a mere 16 percent of persons sixty-five and above then in receipt of Social Security benefits.[13] The new legislation altered this picture fundamentally. An additional 20 million workers were now brought into the system, representing an increase of 35 percent in the number of covered workers. Moreover, the expansion in coverage shifted OASI's clientele base in a pronounced middle-class direction. Brought under the Social Security and OASI umbrella now would be such previously uncovered groups as self-employed business and professional people (their number estimated initially at 5.1 million), state and local government employees (estimated at 3.3 million), civilian and uniformed armed services personnel

---

12. Kenneth Bryden, *Old Age Pensions and Policy-making in Canada* (Montreal and London: McGill-Queens University Press, 1974), p. 196. Emphasis added.
13. Ball, "Original Understanding on Social Security," p. 27.

(estimate of 2 million), self-employed farmers (estimate of 3.8 million), among other categories of workers.[14]

This change in the Social Security clientele base takes on added significance in light of national survey data that demonstrate that political participation of all kinds, including voting, varies by social class, with more highly educated, white-collar workers more inclined than persons of lesser education and lower social status to become politically active.[15] This characteristic of the American electorate has been essentially unchanged over time; the definitive study covering this point employs data from the late 1960s and early 1970s,[16] but its findings are consistent with those dating from the 1940s and 1950s. One study from the late 1950s that focused on political behavior in old age found that older persons, sixty-five and above, with white-collar, middle-class backgrounds were more organizationally involved than was true of their age peers from blue-collar backgrounds.[17] It would appear, then, the 1950 amendments enlarged significantly the ranks of the more easily mobilizable elderly, thereby indirectly enhancing the potential for successful organizing efforts within this sector of the U.S. population.

As the clientele base for Social Security took on an increasingly middle-class aspect, a new attitudinal dimension was introduced. Direct evidence is lacking, but it is highly plausible that political age advocacy now became imbued by a more optimistic attitude among persons eligible for membership in seniors' organizations regarding the possible payoffs of age-based collective action. As noted by one analyst, Carol Pateman, although without special reference to the elderly, attitudes of fatalism are substantially more prevalent among working-class than among middle-class individuals. Persons in the former of these classes, she remarks, are considerably more likely "to believe that participation 'may not be worth it,' whereas middle class citizens have good reasons to be full members of the civic culture."[18] It would appear, therefore, that the 1950 expansion of Social Security coverage—and the augmentations in OASI benefit levels that were enacted by Congress over the succeeding decade and a half—had major implications for American politics, including interest group activity. While it would be an exaggeration to suggest

---

14. U.S. Congress, House, Committee on Ways and Means, *Social Security Act Amendments of 1949* (Hearings on H.R. 2893), 81st Cong., 2d sess., pt. 2, 1949, pp. 1161 and 1169; Ball, "Original Understanding on Social Security," p. 31.

15. Raymond A. Wolfinger and Stephen Rosenstone, *Who Votes?* (New Haven: Yale University Press, 1980), chaps. 2 and 3.

16. Ibid.

17. Frank A. Pinner, Paul Jacobs, and Philip Selznick, *Old Age and Political Behavior: A Case Study* (Berkeley: University of California Press, 1959), p. 285 (table 4).

18. Carol Pateman, "The Civic Culture, A Philosophical Critique," in Gabriel Almond and Sidney Verba, eds., *The Civic Culture Revisited* (Boston: Little, Brown, 1980), pp. 84–85.

that individuals already OASI eligible as of 1950 were entirely without collective awareness or voice, it is still the case that a sensitive observer might well have predicted, following the 1950 amendments, that significant changes were in the offing in regard to the size and degree of political awareness of that client population.

And there was at least one other way in which the 1950 Social Security amendments helped to reshape America's age-political arena. From the outset of Social Security in the 1930s the age of eligibility for retirement benefits was set at sixty-five years. Although this age criterion had the force of law only with respect to those covered under federal programs—particularly the civil service retirement system, railroad retirement system, and OASI—it indirectly influenced private sector pension schemes that then were being established in large number across the United States. Prior to 1935, and for some years thereafter, such private pension plans had given only tentative and spotty acceptance to age sixty-five as the "normal" retirement age, with many plans withholding until some later age full eligibility for private pension benefits. Yet in the wake of the 1950 amendments such acceptance now became well-nigh universal (at least for white-collar workers). As of 1950, roughly half (46 percent) of male workers aged sixty-five and over were still regularly employed, representing only a modest decline, from 62 percent, for the same age group in the pre–Social Security year of 1930. That percentage now shrank dramatically, such that by 1970, with the 1950 amendments now in effect for twenty years, male work force participation for this age-group rate stood at a mere 28 percent.[19]

It would be an error to attribute this change in work force participation entirely to the effect of federal policy changes, including the 1950 legislation. A variety of influences obviously were at work. Still, leading analysts point toward federal policy shifts as perhaps the most significant determinant. As brought out in a 1969 book by William G. Bowen and T. Aldrich Finegan, the declines in work force participation rates among older men during the 1950s and 1960s were a result chiefly of two things: the *increased ability to afford leisure*, resulting in part from expanded payout by both the Social Security system and private pension plans, and the *decreased ability to qualify for work*, resulting from the increasing prevalence of compulsory retirement policies, ones rationalized by corporate officials partly on grounds of the recently enacted expansion in Social Security coverage.[20]

This new environment provided strong encouragement for political

19. Quoted in W. Andrew Achenbaum, *Social Security: Visions and Revisions* (New York: Cambridge University Press, 1986), p. 103.

20. William G. Bowen and T. Aldrich Finegan, *The Economics of Labor Force Participation* (Princeton: Princeton University Press, 1969), pp. 279 and 303.

entrepreneurs—ones sensitive to the needs and aspirations of older Americans and prepared to incur the necessary sacrifices of time, money, and energy required in the formation of new voluntary organizations. And indeed, within a few years of the amendments' going into effect there were efforts made to launch such new voluntary organizations. Two of these were senior citizen and retiree "membership" organizations: the American Association of Retired Persons (AARP), founded in 1958, and the National Council of Senior Citizens (NCSC), founded 1961. The third group, the National Council on the Aging (NCOA), composed chiefly of professional workers employed in the field of aging, was chartered in 1960 and carried forward, on an expanded basis, the work of the former National Committee on the Aging of the National Social Welfare Assembly, formed in 1950. Among these, the NCSC was of special interest for reasons made clear shortly.

In previously published writings, I discuss the genesis and early organizational development of these age-advocacy organizations.[21] Two points from those commentaries are worthy of repetition here. First, common to all these groups in their early, formative years was an absence of governmental patronage and a related organizational fragility. Even though at a later stage of policy development all of these groups would benefit financially in their role as "middlemen"[22] between the federal government and various elderly clientele populations, there was essentially nothing of the sort available at their point of gestation and infancy.

Admittedly, a limited amount of patronage was bestowed on these fledgling groups by nongovernmental institutions. Thus, AARP was subsidized at its outset by its parent group, the National Retired Teachers Association (NRTA), and also by a private entrepreneur, Leonard Davis, a Poughkeepsie, New York, insurance agent. (AARP's founder and first president, Ethel Percy Andrus, had founded NRTA in 1947.) Likewise, the NCSC was critically dependent on funding forthcoming from several large industrial unions, especially the United Steel Workers and United Automobile Workers. And finally, NCOA was in a position within a short time of its creation to successfully compete for grants from various philanthropic foundations, and in addition it was partially subsidized by its parent organization, the National Social Welfare Assembly.

---

21. Henry J. Pratt, *The Gray Lobby* (Chicago: University of Chicago Press, 1976), chap. 4, and "National Interest Groups among the Elderly: Consolidation and Constraint," in William P. Browne and Laura K. Olson, eds., *Aging and Public Policy: The Politics of Growing Old in America* (Westport, Conn.: Greenwood Press, 1983), pp. 145–79.

22. On "middleman" [sic] programs, see Robert Binstock, "Aging and the Future of American Politics," in Frederick Eisele, ed., special issue devoted to "The Political Consequences of Aging," *Annals of the American Academy of Political and Social Science* 415 (September 1974): 208.

Yet none of this early private sector patronage amounted to a great deal absolutely, and what there was of it was insufficient to permit each of these fledgling organizations to achieve more than a slim margin of organizational security. The risks of organizational insolvency were greatest, perhaps, for the two general membership groups, AARP and NCSC. Their particular objectives included the rendering of direct services to dues-paying members, then growing rapidly in number, but with revenues that were inadequate to provide for such services above a very modest level. "When I came down here," the early NCSC executive director William Hutton remarked to an interviewer in 1965, "the office was a dilapidated flat, the one secretary worked at the kitchen table and kept the press releases in the bathtub, and there was precious little in the way of funds."[23] Given such an atmosphere, there could be no very solid basis for confidence over the chances for the group's long-term survival; it was more of a calculated risk than anything approaching a certainty.

Second, indicative of the unstable senior group environment that was characteristic of this period, the fledgling organizations frequently fell victim to forces beyond their control, disappearing from the stage almost as quickly as they had emerged. The 1950s and 1960s were witness to a series of bankruptcies among American age-active voluntary organizations. Little is known about these several failed attempts, other than the names of organizations and the approximate dates. Still, judging from the listings provided under the rubrics "senior citizen" and "retirement" in the annually published *Encyclopedia of Associations*, such failure was not an isolated phenomenon. Its ranks included Senior Advocates International, the Senior Citizens League, Senior Citizens of America, and the National Association for the Advancement of Older People.

In short, the national groups that did manage to endure were the survivors in a sea that swallowed up many of their contemporaries. The newly reshaped political context of aging presented new possibilities for interest group formation, but ones not extending beyond a fairly limited, circumscribed scope.

From a lobbying standpoint it is worthwhile singling out one of the surviving groups for special attention. Among the successful seniors' organizations formed at stage three, only the NCSC embraced as a primary, explicitly stated goal that of political advocacy on behalf of retirees and senior citizens. The other two leading age-advocacy organizations in Washington, namely AARP and NCOA, would occasionally put in appearances on Capitol Hill or in the executive branch. Yet they did not do this systematically, and in

---

23. Quoted in Richard Harris, *A Sacred Trust* (New York: New American Library, 1966), pp. 137–38.

fact both defined themselves as nonpolitical. This did not apply, however, to the NCSC, where public policy goals were considered as crucially important from the outset. This group's early leaders were drawn heavily from the ranks of the more politically conscious and militant sectors of the American labor movement, and NCSC's immediate precursor, Senior Citizens for Kennedy, had been a wing of John F. Kennedy's successful 1960 bid for the U.S. presidency. Further testifying to the NCSC's public policy cast in its early, formative years was its name: "National Council of Senior Citizens for Health Care through Social Security." (The last six words in the name were later dropped in the wake of Congress's enactment of Medicare in 1965.)

Indeed, one of NCSC's great advantages at this point was its essential near monopoly of political advocacy on behalf of senior citizens. This is not to suggest, obviously, that this group's Left-leaning message was universally embraced, either among all politically aware seniors or among nonseniors concerned over the same set of issues. What it does suggest is that lawmakers and elected officials, in seeking to evaluate policy options in light of clientele group demands, had few, if any, alternative sources of broad-based organizational advice other than that provided by NCSC. By the standards of what would later develop during the fourth phase of pension politics, it was a decidedly simple world, as is documented in greater detail in the chapter to follow. This unrivaled status, combined with other advantages, resulted in NCSC's gaining considerable reputation on Capitol Hill for influence over Social Security policy.[24]

Britain in the Third Phase

In the preceding chapter the events leading up to the adoption of Britain's Widows', Orphans', and Old Age Contributory Pensions Act of 1925 are outlined and characterized as marking a point of transition in Britain's age-policy development. (While this characterization is somewhat controversial, it is a defensible one based on the available evidence.)[25] What has yet to be fully

---

24. Pratt, *Gray Lobby*, chap. 11.

25. The more usual view is that the nation's transition from an immature to a relatively mature system of old age pensions occurred with the enactment of the National Insurance Act of 1946, a move closely associated with Sir William Beveridge and the "Beveridge Report." As is considered in more depth in chapter 6, the 1946 enactment admittedly contained some important elderly related aspects: it helped institutionalize the nation's retirement age, ended the last vestiges of the centuries-old poor law system, and helped to shape the growth of occupational pension systems. Yet, as I also show in chapter 6, the act had scarcely gone into effect before it was subjected to withering attack, especially by the Left, for its perceived failure to protect millions of elderly persons against the risk of poverty and destitution. Indeed, by the middle 1960s the Beveridge revolution had essentially run its course, to be replaced by new approaches.

clarified is this act's substantive content and apparent long-term significance. The new legislation integrated the old age pension scheme into the British social insurance program, initially adopted in 1911. Under the new law, equal contributions were made into the system by all insured workers, regardless of differences in wages. When the enactment took effect in January 1926, it boosted from over 300,000 to *10.5 million* the number of male workers made eligible at retirement for pension benefits. The act brought middle-class people in large numbers under the old age pension umbrella and also declared as pension eligible most full-time employed women. Whereas under the old system females generally were not covered by health or old-age pension protection, such coverage now was extended to a vast multitude of working women, 4,645,000, aged sixteen to seventy.

These figures take on added significance when a comparison is made with the total of the population in this same age range. At the time of the British census of 1931—the one closest to 1926—there was a total of 15,214,700 men in the age range fifteen to seventy years.[26] The minimum age of entry into the National Health Insurance and Contributory Pensions system was set at sixteen, but unfortunately census data at this time were aggregated only in five-year cohorts (i.e., fifteen to nineteen, twenty to twenty-four, etc.). Thus, the following comparisons should be regarded as representing close approximations only. (The same data are unavailable for employed women. What can be said of them is that their numbers covered under social insurance increased as a result of the new legislation, but that relative to men they still lagged far behind as a share of the total clientele population.) In the wake of the 1925 enactment, fully two-thirds of the British male work force was now brought into the state pension system—a massive departure from the previous residual scheme designed for only the poorest. The new scheme gave pension eligibility to millions of individuals who were politically significant in any of several ways: as voters, as workers and trade unionists, and as employees of business firms large and small.

Yet, while the legislation enlarged substantially the scope of state pension coverage, individual pension benefits remained modest. Whereas per capita income levels during phase three rose substantially for the British population as a whole, the real value of pension benefits failed to keep up. Thus, as of 1950 Britain's national assistance rate stood at £1.00 weekly (single person) and £1.75 (married couple), and the basic old age pension was set at £1.30 (single person) and £2.10 shillings (married couple). Even though

---

On the other hand, the 1925 legislation, while more far-reaching in its impact, passed quickly into the realm of political consensus.

26. Source: B. R. Mitchell and P. Deane, *Abstract of British Historical Statistics* (Cambridge: Cambridge University Press, 1962), p. 12.

these benefit levels were later boosted over the next quarter century—in the course of various "upratings," which, for example, saw the single-person pension boosted to £2.50 in 1961 and £4.50 in 1967[27]—there remained a pronounced individualistic aspect to the total pension system, with strong emphasis placed on family self-reliance and what was termed "voluntary action."[28]

Organizational Fragility

This new policy setting did not, apparently, serve to incline elderly people in large numbers to regard national government as a principal source of remedies for their income security and other social welfare needs. Such persons were now made conscious of their stake in the pension system but were given little reason to anticipate that the government would be highly responsive to their individual circumstances.

Newly emergent pensioner organizations at this time could opt for either one of two routes. On the one hand, they could choose to emphasize the welfare needs of elderly persons, defined in philanthropic and charitable terms. On the other, they could adopt a political approach, involving attempts to pressure government in behalf of expanding the existing old age pension system and of ironing out the anomalies and imperfections of the existing program. The former of these approaches was favored by several newly formed organizations of this period. It seems best to postpone until chapter 6 the discussion of this point, considering that these groups' latent political inclinations did not become fully manifest until the fourth phase.

The latter approach was taken up by other organizations, notwithstanding the risks involved in a group's becoming overly identified with its political agenda to the detriment of other group objectives. Several nationally based age-advocacy organizations were formed during Britain's third phase, 1925–75, and it is notable that most of them soon faded, leaving little trace of their existence. Among the groups fitting this mold were the Old Age Non-Pensioners Association (formed in 1961 and then disbanded in the early 1970s), the National Old Age Pensioners Association (formed at an unknown date prior to 1965; no longer active by 1967), the British Association of Retired Persons (formed in 1970; no longer active by the early 1980s), and the Scottish Pensioners Association (formed in the early 1940s; disbanded some-

---

27. Ken Judge, "State Pensions and the Growth of Social Welfare Expenditure," *Journal of Social Policy* 10, no. 4 (1981): 516.

28. Alan Walker, "Pensions and the Production of Poverty in Old Age," in Chris Phillipson and Alan Walker, eds., *Aging and Social Policy: A Critical Assessment* (Aldershot, England: Gower Publishing, 1986), p. 200.

time prior to 1965).[29] The common British pattern of organizational fragility thus paralleled that in the United States.

Remarkable, therefore, for its organizational viability and survival capacity is the one enduring nationally active pension group formed in this period, the National Federation of Old Age Pensions Associations (NFOAPA)—the name it employed at this time, although not the one employed at the present time. It should therefore prove informative to investigate how this group functioned at this time, and with what, if any, political results.

NFOAPA: Origins and Early Development

The interwar period in Britain, 1919–39, was one of protracted economic hardship for vast numbers in the population, the elderly included. Hopelessness and despair were widespread among the lower and working classes. Although one might suppose that such conditions would serve to stimulate the political mobilization of senior citizens, their actual effect was quite the opposite, blunting and delaying the full impact of whatever organizational incentives were inherent in the 1925 legislation. Thus, instead of emerging a decade or more earlier, the NFOAPA was a product of the late 1930s, the point at which Britain was experiencing a modest economic upturn after years of fairly hard times.

Several persons, some from the south of England, others from the north, collaborated in forming this first true mass membership organization of British pensioners.[30] Prominent within the southern contingent was the Reverend W. W. Paton, a Presbyterian clergyman from London's East End, whereas among those from the north was J. C. Birtles, a Manchester justice of the peace and active Anglican layman whose father had been a trade union organizer. At a meeting held at the Tottenham Court Road, London, offices of the YMCA in March 1939 delegates from both the southern and northern regions convened to officially constitute the NFOAPA, with Birtles chosen as presi-

---

29. *Directory of British Associations* (Beckenham, England: CBD Research, selected years, 1965–86). The unusually named Old Age Non-Pensioners Association had as its purpose "to obtain pensions and concessions for the people who were excluded by the National Insurance Act of 1946." A few years before passing out of existence this group changed its name— obviously in response to recent changes in pension law—to Old Age *Part-Pensioners* Association.

30. The following account of the origins and early development of the NFOAPA is primarily based on J. C. Birtles, *The Ties That Bind: Being the Story of the Pensions Movement in Britain* (Blackburn, England: NFOAPA, n.d.), chaps. 4–6. Copies of this booklet are on file at the federation's national headquarters. A secondary source is the federation's files of the *Pensioner* and the *Old Age Pensioner*. I am also indebted to the federation's longtime general secretary, George Dunn, who generously consented to interviews and was responsive to my written enquiries.

dent and Paton the honorary secretary. The delegates agreed that an immediate doubling of the existing £.50 (ten shillings) pension to £1.00 (twenty) was a matter of great urgency, and the fledgling organization committed itself to achieving this policy objective, in addition to certain others. Plans were laid for a national petition drive to bring the proposed pension boost forcefully to the attention of Parliament.

During its formative decade, 1939–48, the organization's political approach was characterized by militancy and abrasiveness, with heavy emphasis placed on mass rallies and national petition drives. The group's political style did not differ substantially from that later identified with the U.S.-based NCSC, which has also made heavy use of mass rallies and protests. Yet, as compared to the NCSC, the British group's appeal was (and remains) less strongly class based and trade union oriented. Where the NCSC enjoyed labor movement patronage and enthusiastic backing from its outset, NFOAPA's relations with the labor movement were traditionally fairly unstable—a point developed at greater depth in chapter 7.

The NFOAPA's efforts to stabilize its internal affairs were severely strained by World War II, especially the German bombing blitz of 1940–41, which caused widespread death, injury, and destruction. The organization's southern, or London, wing was especially hard hit. Paton, for example, was killed. The chaos in London helps to explain why the organization found it necessary within eighteen months to reorganize and subsequently to hold all its wartime annual conventions in the North, where the German bombing was less intense and socially disruptive.

From his base in Manchester, Birtles spearheaded the organization's early development in his role as president. Tireless in his devotion, he traveled seven thousand miles in a typical year under difficult wartime conditions to help organize chapters and build support for the cause. Almost equally important was Birtles's close associate, Ernest Melling, who edited the federation's house organ—originally the *Pensioner* and later retitled as the *Old Age Pensioner*. Melling resided in the northern industrial city of Blackburn, and from 1940 onward he made available his home for the organization's national headquarters. (Blackburn remains the organization's headquarters to the present day, but no longer in the late Melling's former residence.)

Melling, H. W. Tyrrell, and the other early NFOAPA leaders always insisted that their agitation for old age pension improvements led directly to positive steps along that line taken by government. It is impossible to verify such claims of political effectiveness, given the long lapse in time and the absence of independent verification.[31] Whatever the degree of influence, if

---

31. Andrew Blaikie, "The Emerging Political Power of the Elderly in Britain, 1908–1948," *Ageing and Society* 10 (1990): 17–39.

any, it could not have been very great, given that the British government took only modest steps on pension policy at this time—considerably less than what the group was demanding. Not subject to debate, however, is the organization's wartime survival and membership growth under difficult circumstances, and emergence in the postwar era favorably positioned to campaign for further old age pension reforms and enhancements.

Building on wartime and immediate postwar organizing efforts, the national federation set itself the task of gaining favorable access to national government. In seeking this, it was favorably situated to capitalize upon a domestic politics setting that was to prove highly congenial and manipulable in line with NFOAPA interests and policy demands.

The year 1950 appears to have marked the beginnings of a reinvigorated NFOAPA effort aimed at increasing its level of access in national government. At the NFOAPA's annual conference that year, delegate attendance, numbering eighteen hundred, exceeded by a wide margin the figure for any previous conference and was more than triple the highest attendance figure for the conferences held in any of the years just previous, 1947–49. Furthermore, the NFOAPA now for the first time comprised over 1,000 branches, roughly double the 538 branches of 1947. (Throughout the subsequent quarter century the federation's annual conferences never drew less than a thousand delegates, and more typically around three thousand, and the count of its local branches reached an impressive 1,300—figures that placed this federation among the numerically larger British pressure groups of this period.)

The federation at this time also benefited from its essential monopoly of organized pension reform advocacy in Britain. Obviously, it was not the sole interest group concerned with seeking improvement in old age pension benefits. One ought not to overlook, for example, the political potential of the nation's leading trade unions, and especially that of the Trades Union Congress (TUC), several of which were intensely active on this front. Yet, for many years the federation was unique as a politically active, *general membership* organization of pensioners—a uniqueness that was challenged only toward the close of Britain's third phase, when two large-membership charity organizations, Age Concern England and Help the Aged, began to shift their energies in a more politically active direction.

In addition, the federation drew strength from its blending of the twin roles of lobbying force for the elderly and locus of old folks' social support and camaraderie. The group's leaders never tired of emphasizing the former of these roles, as is illustrated by the following passage drawn from a brochure produced in the 1970s:

The Federation is, and always has been, a pressure group. Every increase in the pension, every betterment in conditions for the elderly, has been won only by prolonged pressure on Government—through Branches, individually and at Conference, through Press and Television, and most of all through face-to-face confrontation by Federation Officers in deputation. On these occasions Federation Officers sit around the table and no punches are pulled.[32]

Nevertheless, the federation would have found it difficult, and possibly impossible, to survive solely on the basis of such a political appeal, no matter how widespread the backing among potential supporters for the group's public policy goals. The NFOAPA was no exception to the rule, expounded by the political economist Mancur Olson,[33] that rationally motivated old age individuals would refuse in any numbers to support a pressure group whose sole purpose was to promote their political objectives in government. NFOAPA leaders, evidently aware of the dangers inherent in placing any undue emphasis on purely political concerns, elected early on to give high priority to fostering a branch structure and "branch ideal." In urban neighborhoods, in rural villages, and in other communities throughout the nation, pensioners were encouraged to join their local NFOAPA branch. Here, they were encouraged to achieve solidarity with others of like age and life circumstances, based upon mutual interests and shared social activity. Solidarity forged in this manner thus served as a method for the initial recruitment of members, and for binding members more closely into the organization's ongoing program and structure.

The federation also derived benefit from a favorable setting for social welfare politics generally—one fairly fluid in character and potentially amenable to age-group demands. This atmosphere arose in part from a shared perception among politicians that, despite rising levels of personal incomes among the British people generally, the material circumstances of needy individuals were falling behind. Among those not keeping pace with rising living standards were old age pensioners, among whom extreme personal hardship was not uncommon. Even though the national insurance scheme of 1946 had raised the basic state pension to well above that of earlier years, poverty and near poverty among the elderly remained a problem into the 1950s and even beyond.

NFOAPA was therefore in a position to fashion a lobbying effort that avoided becoming enmeshed in statutory detail and could base itself upon simple moral imperatives backed up by case histories and personal testi-

---

32. *What Do We Get Out of It?* (Blackburn, England: NFOAPA, circa 1975), pamphlet.

33. On the difficulties inherent in seeking to establish an interest group on the basis of purely political incentives, see Mancur Olson, *The Logic of Collective Action* (Cambridge: Harvard University Press, 1965).

monies provided to its leaders by rank-and-file members and supporters. Moreover, as Ken Judge notes, it was well within the fiscal capacity of government, assuming a desire on its part to move in that direction, to increase substantially the level of pension benefit. The post-1950 growth in Britain's economy and the related improvements in per capita incomes opened up possibilities for increased pension benefits, both nominally and in real terms, without necessarily raising taxes or imposing draconian cuts in other government programs.[34]

Further adding to NFOAPA's advantaged position was the unique party balance in Parliament at this time, and the resulting high degree of sensitivity to issues deemed important to swing votes in the British electorate. As Samuel Beer notes, the decade of the 1950s witnessed a close balance of strength between the Labour and Conservative parties, with, for example, a 1955 Gallup Poll showing the Conservatives ahead of Labour by only 1 percentage point. In such a context, obvious incentives existed for politicians to fashion electoral appeals aimed at attracting support, at the margins, from various swing groups. Thus, Beer characterizes the era of the 1950s as one of "bidding for the pensioners' votes," although in applying this label he warns against any crude and oversimplified image of what bidding might appear to entail. He continues:

> . . . the elderly were a large and growing proportion of the population, some 4.6 million men and women being in receipt of retirement benefits under National Insurance. It would be callous to claim that the pensions were generous; in addition their earning power was being continuously eroded by inflation. In short, among these millions, there was a large group to whom an increase would be a significant benefit.[35]

In discussing this period, Beer makes passing reference to the role of NFOAPA representatives in influencing the pension deliberations of the Labour party.[36] Yet it would appear that this group's interventions extended well beyond a limited Labour party context. Accounts appearing in the NFOAPA house organ make it clear that its representatives appeared on an annual basis before the ministries and departments responsible for advising on, and administering, pensions and other old age benefits, while also making regular appearances at political party conferences, not just of the Labourites, but also of the Conservatives.

---

34. Judge, "State Pensions and the Growth of Social Welfare Expenditure," p. 317.

35. Samuel Beer, *Modern British Politics: A Study in Politics and Pressure Groups* (London: Faber and Faber, 1965), p. 341.

36. Ibid., p. 342.

Efforts were made to ensure that such appearances were perceived positively by the target audiences. Deputations of national federation representatives, in their regular pilgrimages to Parliament, typically were selected in a way intended to convey the group's broad support base. Included would be the federation's national president and vice-president, two or more of its regional vice-presidents, and the general secretary—all drawn from various regions of the country. In support of their recurrent demands to increase the basic old age pension, and likewise the benefits available to the elderly under national assistance, these deputations typically presented the results of one of the organization's so-called surveys. These surveys were not infrequently challenged by ministers and civil servants on grounds of their unscientific character, but such challenges may not have entirely negated their impact.

Illustrative of the extent of government access enjoyed by the federation was a series of meetings occurring over a three-day period in March 1954, as reported in detail in its official house organ. After an initial daylong meeting in London to plan strategy, the deputation made prearranged visits to various offices: the social services committees of all three of Britain's national parties (Labour, Liberal, and Conservative), the offices of the National Assistance Board, and the offices of the Ministry of Pensions and National Insurance. The day ended with an arranged visit to the House of Lords, for a meeting with Sir William Beveridge, the father of Britain's welfare state and a figure of eminence in matters in any way related to social policy. The deputations came away from these several visitations convinced that in all cases they had received a fair and attentive hearing; the discussion with officials and lawmakers had been for the most part rather lengthy. At the two ministry offices, officials expressed reservations concerning the government's ability to afford the high price tag attached to the demands being put before them. The minister of pensions, for example, voiced alarm that the pension increase as demanded by the delegation would cost some additional £400 million the very first year, and a boost of more than £1,000 million several years down the road. Nevertheless, such concern did not prevent the minister from closing the meeting by assuring the deputation that its policy proposals would be carefully weighed, a remark that the NFOAPA people perceived as more than mere ritual politeness. The deputation also came away pleased by the outcome of its House of Lords visitation, especially Beveridge's remark that he agreed in principle with what the deputation had to say, and that "some new method may have to be adopted to finance a decent pension at retirement age."

It was not always the case that the deputations were this warmly received. In 1956, an account of a meeting with the minister of pensions and national insurance noted that the session had ended with "no satisfaction . . . given to us by the Minister."[37] Likewise, on another occasion the NFOAPA

---

37. *Our Fight for Your Pension* (Blackburn, England: NFOAPA, n.d., circa 1958), p. 11.

believed that the Conservative government had reneged on a promise to hold a full parliamentary debate on its proposal (put forward in the House of Commons by Labour members) to provide an immediate increase in old age pension and national assistance benefit.[38] Yet such occasional rebuffs never resulted in NFOAPA representatives being denied access to the key ministries of government, since the group's house organ makes it clear that its representatives met at least annually at those offices throughout this period.

In pursuance of its pension reform objectives, the federation made use of a variety of tactics. The tools of public relations and propaganda were extensively employed. These included appearances by its spokespersons on radio and television, mass letter-writing campaigns, petition drives, and so on. A favorite tactic was the pledge drive, in which members of Parliament at national election time were asked to commit themselves on issues of pensioner concern. Such drives often were backed up by the federation's releasing a listing of members of Parliament who had carried their last elections by narrow margins, and who therefore might be more inclined than most to make a firm pledge.

Not every NFOAPA publication of this period was explicitly aimed at winning support for proposed pension benefit increases, but it seems unlikely that anything released by the national office was entirely innocent of political intent. For example, beginning in 1952 the federation released an objectively worded, factually based brochure, *Your Pension*, offered by headquarters for sale to members and nonmembers alike. Sales of the booklets were brisk—ten thousand copies the first year, rising to sixty thousand in a revised edition of four years later. While making no mention of proposed pension legislation (the brochure stressed the NFOAPA's importance), readers might reasonably have concluded that the federation was both objective and fair-minded—a perception valuable for any lobby group seeking to enhance its political standing. Moreover, the monthly circulation figure for its house organ, the *Old Age Pensioner*—mostly informational and nonpolitical—reached sixty thousand by the late 1950s and rose even slightly above that in the decade that followed.

It is obvious, therefore, that during the period under discussion NFOAPA succeeded in gaining considerable attention for its views, both among government elites and among interested publics. It would appear as well that in this period the organization became a significant influence upon the course of pension policy development. This view, it should be pointed out, is one rejected by an earlier analyst who has addressed this topic.[39] At the very least,

---

38. Ibid., p. 13.

39. Hugh Heclo, *Modern Social Politics in Britain and Sweden* (New Haven: Yale University Press, 1974), p. 260. Heclo writes: "By all accounts but its own, [NFOAPA] has played little substantial part in postwar policy developments." This author concedes that the evolution of

there was a relationship in time between the demands repeatedly advanced by the federation and the general trend of government decision making on pensions. Over the quarter century 1950–75, this group gave high priority to a needed expansion of old age pension benefits, and its demands in this vein corresponded fairly closely to the actions taken subsequently by government. By the early 1970s, following enactment of numerous pension upratings and boosts in national assistance benefits, Britain's policy in this field was scarcely recognizable in its original 1925 foundations. By now, the nation had begun the transition into its fourth phase, which dates from the State Earnings-related Pension Scheme (SERPS) of 1975. It is highly plausible that the NFOAPA provided impetus to this transition in policy, whether or not its leaders consciously intended that outcome.

In a wider cross-national perspective, there is evidence to suggest that the level of third-phase political influence enjoyed by NFOAPA in the British context was roughly equal to that wielded by the NCSC in the American context and also the NP&SCF in the Canadian. All three organizations were in a position to claim partial credit for securing the enactment of pension reform measures, notwithstanding strong opposition.

There can be little question, therefore, that during stage three the NFOAPA gained significant advantage from its status as Britain's only nationally based and politically active membership organization of pensioners and senior citizens. Given the absence of rivals for its large potential and actual membership base, politicians could not easily play off NFOAPA against other interest groups or significantly restrict its governmental access. If the interest group universe had been more competitive, NFOAPA might well have found its lobbying efforts more constrained, and indeed, at a later stage of policy development just such competition began to make itself felt, and with the predictable adverse effects.

Conclusion

The third phase of pension politics was characterized in all three countries by a major expansion in the scope of state pension coverage, coupled with an unwillingness, or inability perhaps, among policymakers to raise benefit levels above fairly modest levels. In contrast to the earlier period, policymakers were no longer always the dominant actors. There is evidence to

---

British pension policy in the twentieth century was attributable in no small part to interest group pressure, particularly on the part of trade unions. Without denying the power potential of trade unions, I would point out that union influence varied widely over time, waxing in times of Labour party rule and waning in times of Conservative governance. And the Conservatives held office in Britain for all but a few years during the quarter century that began in 1950. A nonpartisan organization, such as NFOAPA, would be less subject to such variability in political access.

suggest that senior citizens in large numbers now became aware of the national government's role as potential guarantor of elderly people's income security and personal well-being, and that the formation of a limited number of seniors' organizations was among its more important indirect consequences. Still, age-group consciousness was not for the most part very deeply or intensely felt at this time, and this probably contributed to the fairly large number of organizational bankruptcies occurring at this time.

Seniors' group development in the three countries followed a common pattern: the formation of a number of fledgling voluntary organizations, most of them soon to pass out of existence; the formation of a smaller number of successful organizations on aging, most of them geared toward seniors-oriented business enterprise, charity work, and/or other essentially apolitical enterprises; and the formation of a single nationally based general membership organization of strongly held political and pension reform views. Groups of the latter type, while quite limited in terms of resources, nevertheless succeeded in gaining a measure of governmental access. This can be attributed in part to their monopoly, or near monopoly, of the age-advocacy role, and to the desire on the part of government officials and lawmakers more fully to inform themselves regarding senior citizens' needs and expectations.

CHAPTER 6

Scope for Governmental Choice
at a Point of Transition

It seems appropriate at this point to draw back from the presentation of data having to do with seniors' organization and advocacy, and to recast the discussion along two lines. The first line consists of a recapitulation, phase by phase, of the changing sphere of pension policy, beginning with the early events described in chapter 2 and extending up through phase three. The second involves an exploration of the range of choice and the degree of freedom open to decision makers at the point of transition from phase three to phase four—a uniquely important transition as is apparent in chapters 7, 8, and 9. My aim here is not that of accounting for pension policy outcomes; such discussion can appropriately await later chapters. Instead, it is identifying the social, demographic, economic, and partisan political forces that together formed the wider context within which public decision making was to occur. In short, the chapter's purpose is partly retrospective, a look back, and partly prospective, a look forward.

Retrospective

Phase One

The pension legislation adopted in various foreign countries in the late nineteenth century, and in the first few years of the twentieth, served as a stimulus toward the subsequent enactment of similar measures in the three countries here under investigation. The impact of the foreign models was considerable, especially as a stimulus to action on the part of humanitarians and policy intellectuals concerned with social welfare. Having initially become aware of the compelling domestic need in the area of old age security, many such individuals now committed themselves to securing a place for the foreign models on their own nations' political agendas. These policy disseminators spearheaded the formation of lobby groups devoted to the public pension cause and committed themselves to securing the adoption of pension legislation.

Having little by way of financial autonomy, the pension-advocacy groups of this period were highly vulnerable to the occasional shifts in priorities of their patrons. Thus, in Canada the increasing professionalism of the social work profession during the 1920s, coinciding with a reordering of social concerns among the nation's Protestant churches, served to weaken the fledgling movement for old age pensions.[1] Likewise, the National Pensions Committee (NPC) in Britain faced something of a crisis in the late 1890s, at the point that many middle-class reformers turned their financial support and attention elsewhere. While managing to survive and achieve considerable credibility, it never became organizationally robust.

Yet, while weak in terms of autonomy and vulnerable to supporters' occasional reorderings of priorities, these early interest groups did succeed in exerting an appreciable measure of political influence. That such small and seemingly fragile groups should realize such influence is not entirely a surprise, considering that the groups involved, unlike their counterparts at later phases of pension development, were not obliged to demonstrate any great technical expertise or policy-analytic capacity, or to confront significant program or legislative complexities. The issues at this time were framed in fairly simple, straightforward terms that did not overwhelm these groups' limited resources and capacity. With fair likelihood of success, they could pitch their appeals at the level of moral imperatives and employ slogans like "simple justice," "soldiers for the commonweal," "an end to the poorhouse," and "an old age with dignity, not with penury." Moreover, they enjoyed a pronounced degree of organizational focus and singleness of purpose. Unlike their counterparts of later periods, obliged to deal with aging as a complex, multifaceted phenomenon and to cover a wide domestic policy landscape, these interest groups could concentrate their attention on either/or choices of enacting, or failing to enact, state pension legislation.

It is highly significant that in all three countries the leading pension crusaders were involved—sometimes overtly, other times less publicly—in either organized religion or the Socialist movement and, occasionally (as in the cases of both J. S. Woodsworth and Isaac M. Rubinow), in both at one time or another during their careers. An emphasis on morality, and the moral imperative that must underlie any just society, would come naturally to persons in the Judeo-Christian tradition or in a secular religion such as socialism. Moral passion has never been entirely irrelevant in the long history of pension politics, but this was never quite so true, perhaps, as at this earliest point in pension policy development.

While phase one witnessed a number of common responses to age-related social problems among the three countries here under discussion, such

---

1. Dennis Guest, *The Emergence of Social Security in Canada* (Vancouver: University of British Columbia Press, 1980), p. 70.

commonalities ought not to obscure one or two interesting points of cross-national contrast. The three countries differed in the timing of their initial involvement in the state pension field, with more than a quarter century separating the action taken by Britain, the first of the three to act, and the United States, the last to do so. And while organized labor played an extremely important role in both Britain and Canada, this was not the case in the United States, where the American Federation of Labor (AFL) and most of its constituent unions held back from the crusade that culminated in the 1935 Social Security Act. In both Canada and the United States governmental structure served as a source of constraint in the timing and content of government decision making, but this did not apply to Britain, whose unitary form of government posed no such structural impediments to the adoption of legislation for the entire country. In the United States, the earlier large-scale system of war veterans' pensions became the functional equivalent of old age pensions for millions of the country's older male citizens and their dependents, but this did not apply to Britain or Canada, whose veterans' pension schemes encompassed far fewer beneficiaries and were of less overall significance. Clearly, then, differing history, demography, and constitutional structure combined to produce three somewhat contrasting patterns.

Phase Two

The phrase "dismal years" can be applied to the second phase, given that the effect of government policy at this time ended up being more depressive than stimulative of age-advocacy organizations. The interest groups active in this early period were in all cases fragile and vulnerable and faced with formidable competition from other political actors. In the United States, the period was notable more for the demise of several preexisting advocacy groups than for the success of fledgling organizations only recently established. Indeed, no national age-advocacy organization formed at this time would remain viable beyond the 1940s. In regard to Canada, the only seniors' organization to extend its base beyond a single province, namely the Canadian Old Age Pensions Federation, lacked support outside the four western provinces. This group's mode of operations remained one-man-dominated and amateur, and even though managing to survive up to the present writing, one could easily exaggerate its political importance at its fledgling stage. Britain saw the formation of a national group on aging, the National Conference on Old Age Pensions (NCOAP), but it would pass out of existence within a decade, leaving in its wake little in the way of tangible result or accomplishment.

Given this fragility of pension group organization, the agenda-setting function normally fulfilled by interest groups was largely assumed by other political actors, career civil servants and elective officeholders especially.

Civil servants were unique at this time by virtue of their near monopoly of specialized state pension knowledge, and the capacity to focus on this field in single-minded fashion. They came to play a critical role in the formulation of regulations relating to the implementation of pension programs, and in terms of advice giving relating to proposed new enactments and reforms. And elective politicians easily moved to center stage, given the authority vested in their offices, and the absence at this time of any great risk, fiscal or political, attendant upon their identification with reform of public pensions.

Phase Three

The beginning point for the third phase consisted in the adoption in each country of revisions in their existing old age security programs. Benefits now for the first time were made available on a universal, or near-universal, basis. The least universal case was the United States, which even after the Social Security amendments of 1950 left certain categories of workers uncovered by old age insurance (Old Age, Survivors, and Disability Insurance [OASDI]). Yet even here it would not be long after 1950 before Congress would enact further public pension expansions, such that by the 1970s well over 90 percent of the U.S. work force had been brought within the system.

This new breadth of coverage did not, however, involve any genuine commitment to the provision of pension benefits commensurate with need; in all countries, poverty in old age would remain fairly widespread and endemic. Given existing pension benefit limitations, therefore, elderly persons remained mostly dependent on various nongovernment sources: personal savings, family, the country poorhouse, and occasional charity.

This enlargement in program content had significant consequences for the political arena on aging. On the one hand, it contributed to a new climate for senior citizen organizing. With tens of millions of persons now newly in receipt of national pension benefits, and with many for the first time becoming aware of government's potential for ensuring their well-being and income security, the atmosphere was conducive to new senior group organizing efforts, and with fair likelihood of success. The creation of viable, politically active, age-membership organizations evidenced the new climate: in Britain, the National Federation of Old Age Pensions Associations (NFOAPA, informally referred to as Pensioners' Voice); in Canada, the National Pensioners and Senior Citizens Federation (NP&SCF, outgrowth of the Canadian Old Age Pensions Federation); and in the United States, the National Council of Senior Citizens (NCSC). (The American Association of Retired Persons [AARP], despite its large size, is not included in this listing, given its low involvement in government at this time.)

This same period was important also in terms of the emergence of nationally based advocacy organizations, whose aim was that of promoting elderly persons' well-being through nongovernmental, private channels. Such an approach did not entirely rule out occasional interventions with selected government ministries, but it did mostly preclude the groups' developing much by way of explicit political mandates or legislative strategies. Even though of little apparent political importance at this time, such welfare-oriented voluntary organizations possessed long-term potential as political actors, as made clear in later chapters.

On the other hand, the climate also entailed a large degree of constraint, with sharp limits placed on both the scope for new group formation and the potential for existing group survival. None of the three countries had more than a single general purpose seniors' advocacy organization, except perhaps toward the very end of the third phase when certain of the social welfare organizations began moving toward involvement in the governmental process. Moreover, the available, somewhat fragmentary, evidence suggests that this period witnessed more than a normal share of abortive organizing attempts. In the case of the United States, where evidence on the point is fairly conclusive, the number of interest groups formed initially, only later on to become defunct, far exceeded the number of successful organizing ventures. The same also probably applied in Britain. And finally, despite their growing memberships and apparent good health, there is reason to doubt the adequacy of the resource base enjoyed by even the few cases of apparent organizational success. Although successful occasionally in their lobbying attempts in government, these groups were in large part resource starved—lacking such usual accoutrements of professionalism as trained full-time staff, targeted lists of members and supporters, and state-of-the-art methods of internal and external communication.

Offsetting, to some degree, these elements of phase three constraint was the fact that the organizations in question enjoyed what amounted to a monopoly of organized senior group representation. This accounts, in part, for their ability to achieve a significant measure of governmental access and influence despite slender resources.

Phase Four

Chapters 7–9 identify the developments in public policy that collectively, in each of the countries, closed out phase three and ushered in the one to follow. Equally worthy of attention is the degree to which those developments were associated with subsequent changes in the number, size, and political behavior of seniors' organizations.

Policy Scope at the Point of Transition

The Wider Context of Policy

As mentioned, the second line of thought pursued in this chapter is a discussion of the wider context of pension policy in the three countries at the point of transition from the third to the fourth phase. For reasons to be made clear, this transition was one of exceptional significance, more compelling in certain respects than any of those previously occurring. In light of this, it seems worthwhile to give attention in the remainder of this chapter to the following question: Did policymakers now find themselves confronted with but a limited set of options, tightly constrained by contextual factors, or instead was their range of choice fairly wide, and more determined by their own sense of what the situation called for than by any compelling external considerations? In responding to this query, the discussion can usefully focus on the following topics: (1) the state of the world economy, given that economic conditions inevitably affect domestic policy making, (2) the ideological climate, as manifested in the attitudes and behavior of political elites, and (3) the prevailing public and elite-group perceptions respecting both elderly people in general, and more particularly their capacity for collective action.

The State of the Economy

The Arab oil embargo of 1973 was a major event in world economics, producing dislocations that soon rippled through the non-Communist, industrialized world. This event, and the related Iranian oil crisis that followed it beginning in 1979, were of such magnitude as to compel policymakers' attention, especially after becoming recognized as contributory factors in the hyperinflation marking the middle and late 1970s.

The most obvious effect of the oil-related world economic shocks consisted in their bringing to a close the era of seemingly uninterrupted prosperity that had marked the 1950s, 1960s, and early 1970s. The earlier period had seen substantial growth in all three of the countries here under discussion. In Britain, according to figures compiled by the Organization for Economic Cooperation and Development (OECD), the period 1955–70 had seen the gross national product rise in real (inflation-adjusted) terms by approximately 50 percent, or from £21.9 billion to £32.9 billion (in British usage a billion is equal to a million million, not a thousand million). In Canada, the rate of real growth had been even more marked, with a more than doubling of the gross national product from the 1955 figure of $31.8 billion to that of $63.9 billion in 1970. And roughly the Canadian pattern had applied as well to the United

States, where real gross national product had risen from \$438 billion to \$742 billion over the same, 1955–70, time span. Furthermore, in each of the countries the rate of growth had been not only large for the period as a whole but remarkably constant, year to year. For example, over the same span of years, Canada had increased its gross national product in every year save one, 1958, and the United States had likewise boosted its rate in all years save two, 1958 and 1970. Finally, in all three countries inflation levels had been consistently low and unemployment only an occasional inconvenience, confined to relatively brief periods or else to defined geographic regions of the country.[2] Not surprisingly, therefore, the Canadian-born economist and longtime Harvard University faculty member, John Kenneth Galbraith, could publish at the end of the 1950s *The Affluent Society*[3]—a book chiefly devoted to North America—while an economist in Britain, Vernon Bogdanor, a decade later could produce *The Age of Affluence, 1951–1964*[4]—a work dealing with the British economy.

In contrast to all that, the world economic tone of the 1970s and 1980s took on a cloudier, more turbulent cast. Several sharp economic breaks and an overall slackening in real growth served to dim somewhat the earlier fairly rosy picture. In both Britain and the United States the sixteen-year period 1971–86 saw four years of real gross national product decline. And while Canada managed the period with but a single year of declining real income, it too faced economic difficulties: hyperinflation, double-digit unemployment, trade imbalances, and substantial increases in the national debt. Between 1971 and 1982, Canada's federal deficit soared fifteenfold from roughly \$1 billion in the former year to \$15 billion in the latter. The nation experienced a near depression in 1981 and 1982 and remained in the economic doldrums as late as 1984.[5] Writing in 1986, a Canadian economist offered this assessment of her nation's economic health: "Most countries, including Canada, aim to achieve full employment, a high economic growth rate, and equitable income distribution, and a viable balance of payments . . . . Canada has not realized these goals."[6] This world economic climate posed an obvious threat to the national income base out of which governments, through taxation and other revenue sources, must finance their large social programs, not least importantly social security and state pensions.

Yet, despite the vicissitudes and uncertainties of the fifteen-year period

---

2. OECD.

3. John Kenneth Galbraith, *The Affluent Society* (Boston: Houghton Mifflin, 1958).

4. Vernon Bogdanor, *The Age of Affluence, 1951–1964* (London: Macmillan, 1970).

5. David Bercuson, J. L. Granatstein, and Walter R. Young, *Sacred Trust? Brian Mulroney and the Conservative Party in Power* (Toronto: Doubleday, 1986), pp. 94–95.

6. Ingrid A. Bryan, *Economic Policies in Canada*, 2d ed. (Toronto: Butterworths, 1986), p. 13.

1965–80, decision makers in government continued to enjoy a fairly wide margin of policy choice and discretion. The real gross domestic product in all three countries continued to rise. And, moreover, the clientele population for public pensions, while increasing, did so at a modest pace, and one that did not preclude, by the sheer weight of numbers, possible further enhancements in benefit levels.

New Ideological Climate

The 1970s and 1980s also were distinguished by a particular ideological climate, one right of center in its tone and strikingly different from the era of liberal politics that had characterized the 1950s and 1960s. In the United States, the new era can be dated from Richard Nixon's election to a second term in 1972, and an accompanying shift in his style of governance toward a more conservative posture than the one characterizing his first term in office beginning in 1969.[7] This conservative cast continued, now strongly augmented, under his Republican successors in the presidency, Gerald Ford (1974–77) and Ronald Reagan (1981–89), and it included as well, though to lesser degree, the Democratic presidency of Jimmy Carter, 1977–81. (Carter was arguably the most conservative Democratic president of the twentieth century.)

It is useful in this context to make special note of the Reagan administration's policy views in the Social Security field, since Reagan, among all the U.S. presidents since Franklin D. Roosevelt, was the one who succeeded most fully in dominating the political landscape, at least during his first term in office. There were legitimate grounds for the pre-1980 concerns often expressed that a Reagan presidency would see a revolution in U.S. old age security policy. From as far back as the 1950s Reagan had expressed skepticism regarding the essential tenets of the Social Security system, and during his years as governor of California his public statements and speeches had shown him as seriously doubting the wisdom of continuing on the current course. As governor, he had expressed thoughts of making Social Security an essentially voluntary arrangement, with exception made only for those elderly living at the poverty level for whom a government-funded retirement guarantee was justifiable. And in his 1980 presidential race Reagan campaigned not only against big government, big taxes, and big expenditures "but more or less specifically, against the innovations in social policy that had characterized

---

7. Richard P. Nathan, *The Plot That Failed: Nixon and the Administrative Presidency* (New York: John Wiley, 1975), p. 16.

the preceding two decades."[8] Finally, on the basis of the early months of his presidency, 1981–82, Mr. Reagan's behavior led some observers to conclude that the Social Security anxieties previously expressed in some quarters were now in the course of achieving reality. Thus, for example, a book on this early segment of the Reagan era devotes a chapter to the president's alleged "war on Social Security."[9]

Yet, with respect to federal programs on aging, Social Security included, the Reagan presidency was not in fact as harsh as the president's conservative rhetoric and the concerns expressed in some quarters might have led one to predict. In addressing social policy issues during the 1980 campaign, Reagan made exception for the aged, whose Social Security benefits would be maintained, unlike those of others heavily dependent on public programs such as the poor, the housing-deprived, and the welfare-dependent. It is perhaps immaterial whether this stance reflected political expediency and the calculus of elections or instead was grounded in conservative ideology, which the candidate (and later the president) so fervently embraced.[10] The point is that Reagan avoided drastic cuts in Social Security expenditures, and even acquiesced to a continuing rise in program outlays, as mandated under various indexation formulas. Both in his presidential campaign and later as president, Reagan treated Social Security as sacrosanct.[11]

Canada and Britain also underwent ideological swings to the Right at about the time that Reagan entered the White House. And as was true in the United States, concern was expressed in both countries over the possibility that age-benefit programs might be jeopardized by conservatively inclined public officials. In Canada, some observers voiced concern that the election of Brian Mulroney under the banner of the Progressive Conservative party in 1984 foretold reductions in social program expenditures. Fears were voiced that the alleged dominance of the Progressive Conservative party by right-wing ideologies—antagonistic toward social welfare and sharing in the basic

---

8. Nathan Glazer, "The Social Policy of the Reagan Administration," in D. Lee Bawden, ed., *The Social Contract Revisited: Aims and Outcomes of President Reagan's Social Welfare Policy* (Washington, D.C.: Urban Institute Press, 1984), p. 223.

9. Ronnie Dugger, *On Reagan: The Man and His Presidency* (New York: McGraw-Hill, 1983), chap. 3.

10. It is possible to find, in the writings of some conservatively inclined theoreticians, an apparent willingness to accept Social Security pensions as congenial to a free market, antiwelfare state ideology. The concession is not accorded any degree of prominence, however, and could be easily overlooked. See George Gilder, *Wealth and Poverty* (New York: Basic Books, 1981), pp. 111–12; Charles Murray, *Losing Ground: American Social Welfare Policy, 1950–1980* (New York: Basic Books, 1984), p. 17.

11. Dugger, *On Reagan*, p. 225.

views of Ronald Reagan—would now express itself in a frontal assault on social programs, of which none offered a larger and more inviting target than did Old Age Security (OAS).[12] In Britain, a similar shift toward the Right, already apparent in the early 1970s, found concrete expression in the person of Margaret Thatcher, elected as prime minister for the first time in May 1979. (Thatcher's mandate was subsequently renewed in 1983 and 1987, making her the longest-serving British prime minister of this century.) Again, as in Canada, concerns were voiced that Thatcherite ideology foretold drastic changes in all areas of social insurance expenditure, state pensions included.[13]

Even though the preceding inferences derived logically from the basic principles of the conservative, free market ideology, now in the ascendancy, it was also the case that conservatively inclined Canadian and British politicians were not entirely the captives of their own conservative rhetoric. On the basis of pragmatic considerations, reflective of electoral politics, they might well express a preference for maintaining existing spending levels in the public pension and age-benefit program areas, and even permit further expansions in line with established indexation formulas. In other words, a plausible case could be made that ideology, while influential up to a point, would not become a determining factor in decision making. The margin of choice open to conservatively oriented officeholders was, in other words, considerably wider than their own political rhetoric might have suggested.

Partisan Political Climate

In addition to the prevailing economic climate and newly ascendent ideology, an additional problematic element was present in the wider setting that prevailed during the 1970s and 1980s. It consisted of popular and elite-level attitudes toward elderly people and their expressed needs. While in past years a favorable set of attitudes had contributed toward the enactment of the wide array of age-benefit programs existing in the three countries, uncertainty now developed over whether or not such favorable responses would continue, given the recent substantial improvements in well-being and income security among elderly persons in general. Was it possible, some observers wondered, that policymakers would now find their range of choice in the pension area substantially narrowed, given growing public awareness of old people's increased income security and declining rates of poverty? Were we not witnessing a public backlash against the heavy outlays from the public treasury

---

12. Bercuson, Granatstein, and Young, *Sacred Trust?* p. 94.

13. Joel Krieger, *Reagan, Thatcher, and the Politics of Decline* (Cambridge, England: Polity Press, 1986); Raymond Plant, "The Resurgence of Ideology," in Henry Drucker, ed., *Developments in British Politics* (London: Macmillan, 1985), pp. 7–26.

required to fund such programs? Such questions could not be entirely brushed aside, especially given that the widespread poverty and hardship among the elderly, which in the past had helped to arouse public concern over their situation, now no longer applied in any broad sense to the elderly as a category of the population. The so-called compassionate stereotype continued to be employed by many senior citizen activists, but it bore less and less relationship to the objective condition of senior citizens generally.[14]

In seeking to address these questions, a variety of approaches could be taken. National survey data could be scrutinized, as it has been by other authors.[15] Another possibility would be to examine the content of testimony delivered at legislative public hearings dealing with social welfare concerns. The speeches and other public statements of elective officeholders represent another fruitful possibility. Yet for reasons of space and convenience the following discussion employs none of these approaches, but instead makes use of political party platforms and election manifestos. Such partisan rhetoric proves informative in seeking to comprehend the attitudinal climate existing at this time in regard to public pensions and other age-benefit programs. The rhetoric's value for this purpose is not diminished by party leaders' well-known tendency to avoid strict conformity to such party platforms, once nominated and subsequently installed in office. The platforms' usefulness inheres, not in the extent of programmatic carry through on the pledges made, but rather in their embodiment of the prevailing party consensus and in the potential for identifying changes in the consensus.

Before documenting what these platform statements may suggest with respect to the degree of emphasis devoted to age-related issues, it should be mentioned that Canada presents something of a problem for this analysis. Neither of Canada's two leading parties—the Progressive Conservative nor the Liberal— has traditionally drafted and disseminated party platform statements in the context of national elections. While Progressive Conservative and Liberal party leaders do make known their views on leading issues of the day, in speeches and at party rallies, they do not typically express these views in a form that is easily accessible for analysis. Still, published expressions of partisan thinking in Canada are not entirely lacking, since there are platform statements available, covering an extended period, for Canada's perennial third party—now the New Democratic party, previously the Cooperative Commonwealth Federation. These statements can be consulted for clues into attitudes among the Canadian political elite generally, considering that this party has consistently participated in Canadian electoral politics and on sev-

---

14. Robert Binstock, "The Aged as Scapegoat," *Gerontologist* 23 (1983): 136–43.

15. See, for example, Christine L. Day, *What Older Americans Think: Interest Groups and Aging Policy* (Princeton: Princeton University Press, 1990).

eral occasions in recent history has seen its statements on social welfare matters taken up and embraced by one of Canada's major political parties.

Platform statements referring in some way to the elderly and to age-benefit governmental programs fall into two categories: (1) "assurances," arising out of purported accomplishments and successes, and (2) "viewing with alarm," calling attention to the wide scope of unmet social need. The former type tends to characterize the "in" parties—those currently holding office—whereas the latter is more typical of the "outs," whose aim it is to dislodge the "ins." Before directly examining the content of party platforms during the transition from phase three to four, it may prove helpful to take account of how party platforms and manifestos traditionally dealt with state pension and other issues of senior citizen concern.

During the first half of the twentieth century, party platforms and election manifestos only rarely gave space to either "reassurance" or "viewing with alarm" in regard to public pensions, but instead displayed little apparent concern over this particular area.[16] Thus, the Conservative party of Britain, in its election-time "Prime Minister's Election Address"—its preferred manner of addressing the British electorate up through the 1950s—and later on in its published election manifestos, made only a single, passing reference to old age pensions during the entire period 1900 to 1945. (The exception was 1924 when the prime minister in his address alluded rather offhandedly to the need to correct certain "defects in the present old age pension scheme.") Likewise, the Republican party in the United States avoided any specific mention of an age-related issue until its platform of 1940, when it declared itself in favor of reform of the American system of Social Security. Not greatly different was the level of interest in this area that was displayed by the parties of the center and the center-left. Thus, Britain's Liberal party, the party that more than any other was responsible, perhaps, for the erection of that nation's early welfare state, made no reference to pensions or old age in its election manifestos over the time span mentioned. A similar lack of concern for the problems of the elderly, save for the support given to civil service and war veterans' pensions,

---

16. The following discussion is based on (for Britain) F. W. S. Craig, *British Election Manifestos, 1900–1974* (London: Macmillan, 1974); Labour and Conservative manifestos for late 1970s and 1980s: Conservative Party Central Office, Labour Party Headquarters; (for Canada) M. S. Cross, *The Decline and Fall of a Good Idea* (Toronto: New Hogtown Press, 1974) (book deals with the Cooperative Commonwealth Federation); New Democratic Party, *Policy Resolutions Passed by Plenary Session, 1961–1986* and *1987 Policy Resolutions Supplement*, mimeos (both on file at National Library of Canada, Ottawa); (for the United States) Bruce Johnson, ed., *National Party Platforms*, 2d ed. (Urbana: University of Illinois Press, 1978); Democratic and Republican party statements for elections of 1980, 1984, and 1988: *Congressional Quarterly Weekly Reports*.

was expressed by the Democratic and Republican parties in the United States in the years before the Roosevelt New Deal.[17]

Partial exceptions to the general reluctance of platform writers to adopt planks supportive of proposed public pension schemes in this period were parties of the Left, ones Socialist-inclined and labor-oriented. Even here, admittedly, expressions of support in this area were not consistently voiced in all three of the countries. The most consistent case was Britain, where Labour party support for public pensions was consistent and unwavering. Even before taking on its present name and organizational form, this party, at its outset in 1900, voiced a demand for pension protection for Britain's elderly, and especially for those in poverty. The manifesto of the Labour Representation Committee listed first in order among its several platform pledges the demand for "adequate maintenance from national funds for the aged poor." Restatements of this theme were to occur in subsequent election campaigns, such that the party's manifesto of 1922 could justifiably remark, after first setting forth the need for "more generous provision for the old age pensioners," that this "has been one of Labour's consistent demands."[18]

No such consistency of public pension support can be found in the published campaign statements of the Cooperative Commonwealth Federation—Canada's approximate counterpart to the Labour party in Britain. The Cooperative Commonwealth Federation's Regina manifesto, adopted at its founding convention in that city in 1933, made no reference to the elderly or old age pensions. And in the manifestos emerging from the party's two subsequent conventions, held in 1944 and 1956, Canada's emergent system of state pensions was mentioned, but only briefly, and with no special emphasis.

What the statements of this era most notably did *not* contain was any sense of the elderly as a constituency in their own right, with their own unique set of political aspirations and power potential at the ballot box. There was, it is true, a firming up at this point in platform support for old age security programs, with regular election-time alarm expressed by the "outs" over the government's alleged inaction in this field, and affirmations by the "ins" of what government was managing to accomplish. Nevertheless, the manifestos neither sought to arouse the elderly negatively—demanding punishment for those politicians deemed as insufficiently committed to addressing their needs and aspirations—nor to do so positively—pointing out to voters where previous platform pledges had been fulfilled and progress allegedly realized. Among parties of the Left, Right, and center the statements reveal a common

17. Dale Vinyard, "Political Rhetoric and the Elderly," Occasional Paper, Department of Political Science, Wayne State University, 1981.

18. Craig, *British Election Manifestos*.

tendency to advance schemes embodying government *assistance* to the elderly, yet with the intended beneficiaries regarded as essentially *passive* recipients of public largesse. Thus, the Labour party of Britain pledged in its 1924 manifesto "complete and non-arguable provision for the sick, the infirm and the aged, and the children . . . apart from the workhouse and pauperism." Likewise, the Cooperative Commonwealth Federation in Canada, in its 1944 manifesto, pledged "adequate old age pensions for all at age 60." In other words, the elderly were not seen as possessing collective consciousness or group identity; they were viewed in the platforms, not as actual or potential actors, but instead as a collectivity that is (or should be) acted upon in their own best interest.

This information adds weight to the important shift in platform content occurring toward the close of the third phase of policy development in each of the countries. In Britain, as the preceding chapter documents in some detail, the 1950s was marked by an unprecedented bidding for pensioners' votes. With the country's two major parties, Labour and Conservative, holding approximately equal levels of public support at this time, party leaders evidently came to regard older voters as a potential swing vote whose interests it was highly prudent to take account of. Thus, the manifestos of Britain's two leading parties now for the first time became highly explicit in setting forth what the parties were prepared to do for this electoral constituency. The election year statements of this period came to employ ringing age-related slogans as subheads: "ending poverty in old age" (Labour, 1959), for example, and "to provide care for those most in need" (Conservative, 1966). And it became the rule, no longer the exception, for British party manifestos to point out various age-related concerns and to promise corrective action.

Even more-interesting shifts in platform content were to occur just a few years later. In the early 1970s party platforms for the first time began making regular reference to old people as a political constituency, one having its own unique circumstances and aspirations. The precise terms for such references varied slightly among the three countries, and among each country's several parties. Yet, a common emphasis is apparent in the use of collective terms for the elderly in partisan rhetoric at this time. Elderly persons were no longer regarded simply as clients of government programs, with government being viewed as protector and benefactor, but as active voters, important in the larger election context.

The most striking thing about the platform statements produced toward the end of phase three and at the onset of phase four is their common affirmation that an elderly vote exists and that it is one worthy of being appealed to and, if possible, won over. One can give a fairly precise date in all three cases for this shift in election manifesto rhetoric. For Britain, it occurred in the context of the general election of 1974, when for the first time both of the nation's leading parties used their manifestos to spell out needed state benefits for "the pensioners." From this point forward, British election year manifestos have almost invariably identified the elderly as a distinct sector of the electorate, with use made of some group-specific label and mention made of its particular circumstances and unmet needs.

With respect to Canada, the New Democratic party began regularly referring to the elderly in group terms at almost exactly the same time. When in 1961 the old Cooperative Commonwealth Federation was succeeded by the New Democratic party, its party declaration pledged "a new and realistic retirement plan for *Canada's older citizens*" and went on to affirm that "all *elderly people* will have an income equal to at least half of their working income" (emphasis added). New Democratic party manifestos issued in the context of the 1963 and 1967 federal elections omitted any similar age-group references, even though the manifestos for these years did advocate a strong Canadian "family policy and need for a stronger system of old age pensions." Yet in the context of the national election of 1969 the New Democratic Party returned to its earlier theme of age-group affirmation, as the party now pledged itself to work toward the goal of securing "additional specific income policies for groups such as senior citizens, farmers, fishermen unemployed etc. who may need additional income supplementation." Similar pledges in this vein were put forward by the New Democratic party throughout the 1970s and 1980s. For example, a platform statement of 1981 referred to Canada's over-sixty-five population using a variety of terms: Canada's senior citizens, the elderly, and pensioners. Likewise, in 1985 the New Democratic party manifesto referred to "the Government's cruel attack upon the elderly in particular upon elderly women."

And, finally, in regard to the United States, even though the platforms of the leading political parties in the 1950s had made frequent reference to the need to enhance social security benefits, it was not until the elections of 1960 and 1964 that platform writers began to regard the elderly as a distinct constituency, with interests that might possibly be separable from those of other categories of the national electorate. As I describe in an earlier writing,[19] the watershed for party thinking was the Democratic party's 1960 election effort, which included, for the first time by any national party, the establishment of a specific senior citizen arm, "Senior Citizens for Kennedy." Although in the short term the results of this attempt to make a direct appeal to senior citizens were disappointing—senior citizens ended up being *less* supportive of the Democratic candidate than was true of almost any other major grouping in the population—the results nevertheless had major impact on the thinking of leading politicians, who in the next presidential election, 1964, took it for

---

19. Henry J. Pratt, *The Gray Lobby* (Chicago: University of Chicago Press, 1976), chap. 5.

granted that a "Senior Citizens for Johnson-Humphrey" would be created and granted an important campaign role. The Republican party was somewhat slower to act on this front, but by the late 1960s it, too, was including age-targeted appeals in its election year platform statements.

It is apparent, therefore, that party platform writers now had abandoned their former assumption that the elderly are rooted in their voting preferences, and that winning over any large fraction of their number would be, as one party leader expressed it, "like fighting human nature."[20] In place of this traditional view, elderly voters now came to be viewed as reachable, at least at the margins, through group-targeted electoral appeals. By the early 1970s such references had become a standard feature of the quadrennial party platforms.

And it was not just that the elderly now came to be singled out for specific attention in party propaganda, but also that they and their younger-aged allies were beginning to occupy a place of singular importance in the overall content of platform pledges. In the Democratic and Republican platforms for election years 1976, 1980, and 1984 (six statements in all) the amount of attention—as measured by column inches of space—given in the platform to the elderly in all but one case (the 1984 Republican statement) exceeded that for any other designated grouping: handicapped persons, children, mothers, and racial and ethnic minorities. In Britain, a similar pattern: the Conservative manifesto for the 1983 general election singled out *no* particular group other than "the pensioner" for a special subhead (in a document of forty-seven pages). In the case of the British Labour party for the same election year, the manifesto singled out several different groups for special political appeals, but the amount of space devoted to what the manifesto termed "pensioners" was equalled only by one other group, namely the handicapped.

Policy Implications

The purpose of party manifestos and platform statements, and the way in which they are usually interpreted, is to express political parties' goals to the electorate. Yet in an important sense such statements are also statements by the party organization directed inwardly, toward its own activists and leaders. In this sense, a party platform becomes one of the cues that the party's elective officeholders take account of in arriving at choices on critical issues. In that sense, the fairly activist and positive image of aging and aged individuals contained in the partisan rhetoric of the 1960s, 1970s, and early 1980s was probably not viewed as a signal as to what steps must be taken, but more as

---

20. Ibid., p. 57.

what should at all costs be avoided. What the platform rhetoric clearly signaled was the elderly's emergence as an important electoral constituency—by
no means a unified bloc, but a grouping at least having sufficient cohesion as
to make it politically imprudent to offend its interests. The campaign rhetoric
was a message to officeholders to avoid any appearance of being at war with
existing age-benefit programs, to avoid proposing more than a token real-
dollar reduction or even the programs' possible elimination. Obviously, campaign promises and partisan images are no sure guide to politicians' behavior
in office. Yet, save for indicating the grave risks inherent in appearing to
threaten existing aging benefits, the rhetoric implicitly left open a broad area
for choice on the part of decision makers. They could expand, or refuse to
expand, existing benefits to the degree that their personal judgment and political instincts dictated.

Conclusion

The 1970s and 1980s opened up greater potential for possible enlargements in
government age-benefit programs than might have appeared likely on the
surface, given the constraining effects of recurrent economic troubles and
right-wing ideological dominance existing at this time. In economic terms,
these two decades saw changes in the prevailing fiscal picture, ones that at
first glance made it appear very unlikely that the newly elected governments
would propose, or enact, major program expansions in the field of aging. On
deeper analysis, however, it is apparent that fiscal resources were sufficient to
allow a margin for choice in this regard. And the normal tendency of right-
wing ideology, now in the ascendancy, would be toward solutions found in the
private sector and skepticism toward any and all public programs, especially
ones as vastly expensive as public pensions. Again, however, such ideological
thinking did not typically extend to government social insurance programs,
and especially not to ones of benefit to the elderly. Even the most conservatively inclined officeholders tended to become cautious in proposing drastic
changes in public pensions, which they generally declared to be both legitimate and necessary. And finally, the prevailing partisan political rhetoric did
not depict the elderly as now comfortably well-off and secure but instead
emphasized their newfound importance as an identifiable constituency within
the electorate, with significant needs still unmet.

All of this left open a wide scope for official judgment, not excluding
possible further expansions in existing old age benefits. The degree to which
policymakers would now exercise that choice in a manner congenial to the
interests of most seniors is a principal point of attention in the chapters to
follow.

CHAPTER 7

Phase Four in Britain

The present chapter and those that follow cover the final stage of pension policy development to be considered in this study. This fourth phase was no less distinct from what had immediately preceded it than was phase three from phases two and one, and in some ways more distinct. The far more detailed attention to be given to phase four—an entire chapter for each of the three countries—can be justified on the basis of its larger apparent impacts on interest group formation and group political behavior.

With respect to Britain, it was previously noted that the early 1960s and early 1970s saw fundamental changes in the country's wider economic, ideological, and partisan political setting. Taking such change as a given, the present chapter treats the changed content of pension policy during the 1970s, marking as it did the transition from phase three to phase four, and its apparent interest group consequences. Three developments of special importance serve as the focus of the following discussion: (1) the enlargement in scale of public pension benefits, (2) the enactment by Parliament of a major new statute, namely the State Earnings-related Pension Scheme, or SERPS, and (3) the consolidation of several pension-involved government ministries into a single ministry.

Pension Benefit Enlargements

Extending a pattern of development begun earlier, the scale and perceived importance of British old age pension benefits expanded significantly during the early phase four period. By 1984–85, spending on pensioners as a group amounted to approximately £19 billion, representing (as it had for a number of years) exactly half of Britain's total social security outlays. In the short space of a decade, 1969–79, social security outlays increased from £17.3 billion to £28.3 billion, representing a real growth in expenditure for this period—on a base of 100 for 1949—of from 264 to 431, or roughly 65 percent. Moreover, this expansion far exceeded that for other government programs, including housing, education, and health services.[1] Further evidence of government commitment in this area was the fact that the flat-rate

---

1. Nicholas Deakin, *The Politics of Welfare* (London: Methuen, 1987), pp. 128 and 114.

pension grew as a percentage of average earnings of male manual workers from 20 percent in 1969 to 22.3 percent in 1978,[2] and also that over the longer period 1951–81, pensioners' disposable income per head nearly tripled in real terms, whereas pensioners' income per person rose from roughly 40 percent in the earlier year to 70 percent in the latter.[3] This large outlay significantly affected the overall income security of Britain's elderly population, as was emphasized in a 1985 government report:

> Despite a marked increase in the number of persons of pensionable age, the incidence of low income for this age group fell dramatically. Taking all pensioners as a group, as many as 42 percent were in the bottom range of family incomes in 1971, but by 1982 the corresponding proportion had balled to 23 percent. Only about half as many pensioners had low incomes in 1982 and 1971.[4]

End of the Beveridge Era and the Coming of SERPS

The arrival in the late 1970s of the fourth phase represented the culmination of a long period of rethinking and reformulation that had been underway in Britain for a quarter century. Dissatisfaction with the existing set of benefits for old age pensioners began to be voiced in the immediate postwar era, and especially after parliamentary adoption of the National Insurance Act of 1946—a comprehensive scheme of social insurance designed to cover all contingencies.

The 1946 act carried into effect the basic principles laid down by Sir William Beveridge in his wartime policy paper, *Social Insurance and Allied Services* (popularly known as the "Beveridge Report"), and in his later book, *Full Employment in a Free Society.*[5] Although Beveridge's proposals were radical in some respects, especially in their insistence on treating Britain's social welfare programs in an integrated and comprehensive fashion, rather than piecemeal as had been the case, they were conservative in others, being largely a reshuffling of reform ideas already widely embraced in the prewar years by those of centrist political views.[6] The report proposed that

---

2. Government Actuary's Department, "Population and Pension Costs," annex B (background paper prepared for *Reform of Social Security: Programme for Change* [London: Her Majesty's Stationery Office, 1985]), p. 46.

3. Ibid., p. 40.

4. *Reform of Social Security,* vol. 3, p. 11.

5. William Beveridge, *Social Insurance and Allied Services* (London: Her Majesty's Stationery Office, 1942), and *Full Employment in a Free Society* (London: George Allen and Unwin, 1944).

6. Deakin, *Politics of Welfare,* p. 45.

Britain establish a unified benefit system responsive to a range of contingencies. Among these were certain fairly costly "risks," such as old age, and others of a less costly nature, including unemployment and maternity. In drafting his recommendations Beveridge was mindful of British public opinion. The public's strong aversion to the dole and other alleged give-away programs was a factor in his recommendation that old age pensions be included in the larger scheme of contributory insurance, thereby avoiding any close association between it and those social welfare benefits of a noncontributory character intended to benefit the poor and the destitute. There were limits, however, to Beveridge's deference to public sentiment. For example, his plan went contrary to the prevailing national mood in refusing to endorse, out of concern over potentially ballooning costs, the immediate grant of a full subsistence pension. He suggested instead that this benefit be phased in gradually over a twenty-year period.[7]

In enacting the 1946 National Insurance Act, Parliament essentially followed Beveridge's principles. Old age pensions were made part of a common social insurance scheme, their cost to be financed out of revenues from a flat tax on wages, and with benefit payouts to old age pensioners to be on a comparable flat-rate basis. The preexisting national assistance program, involving a means test, was maintained for those elderly unable to manage on the basic pension alone. Finally, the act followed Beveridge's lead in authorizing national administration of the new program, thereby doing away with the last vestiges of the Elizabethan poor law system under which care of the indigent had been defined as a local government responsibility.

The National Insurance Act set the course of Britain's pension policy for at least the next two decades, and certain of its distinctive features have remained operative to the present time. Yet a number of politicians, joined by some academics in the field of social policy (Richard Titmuss and Brian Abel-Smith especially), maintained from the beginning that the Beveridge system was flawed fundamentally, especially in its provision for elderly people. These critics insisted that any attempt to finance the scheme solely on the basis of a flat-rate tax on wages would have untoward consequences. It was argued that the Beveridge plan would constrain government's capacity to enlarge benefits to more socially adequate levels, given that the cost of any benefit enhancement would be financed out of a regressive form of taxation that would exact its heaviest burden upon the millions of low-paid workers who could least afford any added taxation.[8] Within a few years, parliamentary

---

7. B. E. Shenfield, *Social Policies for Old Age* (London: Routledge and Kegan Paul, 1957), pp. 96–97.

8. Michael O'Higgins, "Public/Private Interaction and Pension Provision," in Martin Rein and Lee Rainwater, eds., *Public/Private Interplay in Social Protection* (Armonk, N.Y.: M. E. Sharpe, 1986), p. 108.

debates on pension policy began to reflect the concern that the Beveridge-inspired system of social insurance was not satisfactory in alleviating hardship among Britain's elderly—a perception that came to be shared both among many pensioner advocates inside Parliament and also among many outside observers.

These concerns were soon reflected in the policy proposals put forward by Britain's major political parties. As early as 1951, the Labour party, then out of power and not destined to regain office until 1964, began a basic reexamination of its approach toward social welfare. Lengthy intraparty deliberation finally resulted in Labour's adoption in 1959 of a revised pension position, involving a proposed earnings-related superannuation scheme that sharply departed from Beveridge's flat-rate formula. The party's parliamentary leader, Hugh Gaitskell, declared that Labour would make pensions a major election issue in Britain's 1959 general elections. The governing Conservative party, not to be outflanked, quickly came forth with its own scheme for an earnings-related old age entitlement, and in the end it was this that eventuated in the 1959 National Insurance Act, to be implemented in 1961.

The 1959 enactment, as it turned out, was inadequately funded and insufficiently responsive to the mushroom growth of the nation's occupational pension schemes. Having failed to win full public acceptance, it remained on the statute books for only a little over a decade and then was superseded by a later enactment. During the 1960s pension policy as an object of political discussion and controversy entered a quiescent phase, even though it remained the object of vigorous behind-the-scenes discussion among policy intellectuals and study groups. In 1964, when Labour returned to power committed to a fresh look at pensions, it was widely recognized that the Beveridge revolution had essentially run its course.[9] Fashioning an alternative approach proved to be no simple matter, however, and it would not be until 1969, five years after taking office, that Labour would arrive at a fully fleshed-out position.

Policy views among both the leading parties represented in the House of Commons now began to crystallize, and there ensued a five-year period marked by political thrust and counterthrust. The new period began with a January 1969 white paper issued by the Labour government's secretary of state for social services, Richard H. S. Crossman. The Crossman white paper envisaged a completely new system of superannuation consisting of several tiers: the existing old age pension to be retained as the foundation, an

---

9. Maurice Bruce, ed., *The Rise of the Welfare State: British Social Policy, 1601–1971* (London: Weidenfeld and Nicholson, 1973), p. 276; Hugh Heclo, *Modern Social Politics in Britain and Sweden* (New Haven: Yale University Press, 1974), pp. 272–73.

earnings-related benefit to be added on top, and all benefits to be inflation-proofed by administrative adjustment every two years. Although influential in the long run, the Crossman report failed in the short run to reach fruition. Before it could come to a vote in the House of Commons the Labourites met defeat in the 1970 British general election. The newly installed Conservative government thereupon advanced its own superannuation proposal, and in the 1972 Parliament this scheme was formally enacted. Nevertheless, before it could be implemented the Conservatives were defeated in the next general election, and Labour thereupon used its parliamentary majority to cancel the Tory-passed measure.

Not until the middle 1970s would this era of pension policy uncertainty finally be brought to a close. In 1974 automatic adjustments in the pension benefit were introduced. And in the following year the Labour government introduced a fresh scheme to overhaul the state pension system, SERPS. As submitted for parliamentary consideration by the Labour cabinet in 1975, this scheme bore the heavy imprint of the new social services secretary, Barbara Castle. Castle's recommendations involved essentially a compromise between the more radical views of her Labour party predecessor, Crossman, and the 1972 Conservative plan as put forward by Sir Keith Joseph. The Castle plan's most important feature was the close integration that was to be forged between private sector and public sector pensions. Occupational pension schemes were allowed to contract out of SERPS provided they met certain minimum standards. Although the frequent turnovers of party control of government in the years prior to the adoption of SERPS in 1975 significantly delayed enactment of a state pension and social security reform programs that many regarded as long overdue, they appear to have had a stabilizing effect, in so far as they helped to foster a heightened degree of interparty consensus. Conceivably, if SERPS, or some Tory equivalent, had been enacted at some earlier point, while partisan conflict on this issue continued to rage, the result might not have been as securely based as has proved true of the legislation of 1975.[10]

The adoption of SERPS had at least two important consequences for the character and composition of Britain's age-political arena. Firstly, as Alan Walker persuasively argues,[11] it fostered the institutionalization of "two nations of old age." One "nation" consists of the relatively advantaged elderly whose working years are marked by steady employment with a firm of some

---

10. Alan Walker, "Pensions and the Production of Poverty in Old Age," in Chris Phillipson and Alan Walker, eds., *Aging and Social Policy: A Critical Assessment* (Aldershot, England: Gower Publishing, 1986), pp. 205–6.

11. Ibid., pp. 185–86.

size. (There are occasional cases of such advantaged individuals qualifying at retirement for no fewer than three pensions: the basic old age pension, a private occupational pension, and a SERPS top-up.) On the other hand, the other "nation" (consisting of those less fortunate individuals whose work experience was marked by irregular employment, or possibly by service in unwaged domestic labor) would face a retirement markedly more insecure and poverty-prone. A universal pension system might have avoided these disparities in retirement outcomes, but SERPS represented a rejection of that option. Moreover, the numbers of such at-risk individuals is by no means small, nor do they consist simply of those who have lived in poverty throughout their adult lives. Instead, as Walker points out, if one adds those below the poverty line to those with incomes only marginally above it (i.e., up to 140 percent of the supplementary benefit rate), fully two-thirds of Britain's elderly live in or on the poverty margin, compared to only a fifth of the nonelderly. Although some degree of cleavage between the better off and the less advantaged elderly has existed throughout modern history, SERPS appears to have further emphasized that distinction.

To the extent that the SERPS system has helped foster a duality within Britain's pensioner population, the scheme probably has enhanced the preexisting tendency toward the existence of two rather different forms of organized age advocacy in Britain. As documented more fully later on in this discussion, one of these is a set of interest groups, mostly fairly well financed and professionalized, which is oriented chiefly toward the concerns of pensioners not facing serious economic risk, whereas the second comprises a set of groups, rather less well financed and secure organizationally, that is more oriented toward persons of lower income, some considerable fraction of whom face severe economic hardship.

A second impact of SERPS, one perhaps not consciously intended by its framers yet implicit in its structure and mode of implementation, has been its contribution toward making the British pension system substantially more complex, opaque even, among its many beneficiaries. Writing in 1982, an informed student of British social policy remarks that "one point on which it is easy to obtain wide agreement is that the British system of social security is one of the most complex schemes in the world."[12] In place of the highly rationalized and coherent package proposed by Beveridge in 1942, Britain's pension benefit arrangement has since become fragmented and disjointed, resulting in problems for the clientele population as well as for civil servants in the Department of Health and Social Security (DHSS). Concern over this

---

12. John Creedy, "Comments on Chapter 4," in Michael Fogarty, ed., *Retirement Policy: The Next Fifty Years* (London: Heineman, 1982), p. 98.

was a factor underlying the Thatcher government's proposal to overhaul the state pension and social security system—as embodied in the green paper of May 1985 issued by the social services secretary, Norman Fowler—to strip away many of the existing system's special benefits and add-ons that had accumulated over the years. As Nicholas Deakin remarks, the green paper's "presentational emphasis was on the lack of clear guidance for users of the system, reinforced by the endless complications of the current rules and procedures, the creation of anomalies like the poverty trap, and the numbers of staff required to operate the system."[13] Indeed, a DHSS survey, taken for the 1983–85 social security reviews, presented evidence of distressingly low levels of public awareness about the system and its functioning. Fewer than half the respondents (45 percent) had even heard of SERPS, even though its elimination had been one of Norman Fowler's most highly publicized, and controversial, green paper proposals.

Reform efforts undertaken in the late 1980s aimed at correcting this difficulty proved only modestly successful. The 1983–85 social security reviews contributed to the enactment in 1986 of legislation that stripped away a number of the existing system's add-ons, discretionary payments, and special protections. The lawmakers were not prepared, however, to adopt Norman Fowler's original suggestion of eliminating SERPS entirely, or to diminish greatly the system's labyrinthine character. Thus, an observer reporting on the situation as of 1987 found evidence of continued administrative and public relations problems.[14]

Britain's intertwined and overlapping state pension system, to which SERPS added an additional dimension, has implications for age-advocacy and interest group behavior. As the following discussion reveals in more detail, this element significantly affects these groups in their dealings with government bureaus and ministries. It has encouraged them either (1) to develop their own policy-analytic and technical capability, a fairly costly option open to only a handful, or else (2) to rely upon outside institutions for this needed capability. Costs are entailed in either approach, and one can assume that the efforts on the part of seniors' organizations to adjust to the new era of program complexity has brought with it significant burdens not previously felt.

One cannot overlook the possibility that the marked complexity of Britain's public pension system is allowed to persist because having it so serves the interests of the Conservative party and Thatcherite ideology, now in the ascendance. Obviously, a system confusing to its beneficiaries and discouraging of full public understanding is likely to result, indirectly, in a lowering of

---

13. Deakin, *Politics of Welfare*, p. 141.
14. Ibid., p. 145.

the potential for senior citizen mobilization and protest—thereby enabling governance to occur more smoothly and with less disruption. It is impossible to test this notion on the basis of available data, but it is at least plausible.

Reorganization of the Social Security Bureaucracy

In addition to the expansion of pension benefits and the enactment of SERPS, a third important contributor to the emergence of the current fourth phase was the decision arrived at in 1968, and only fully implemented in the early 1970s, to merge the Ministry of Health with the Ministry of Social Security to form the current DHSS. Placed in charge of the new department, and given overall responsibility for its management, was the newly created post of secretary of state for social services. This development was reflective of a larger pattern of departmental restructuring and consolidation that commenced in the early 1960s and that ended up touching almost every area of British central government. Upon its completion around 1970, the government at Whitehall had fewer departments than had existed in 1914, notwithstanding that there now were over ten times as many civil servants.[15]

This step was rationalized by its sponsors essentially on managerial and programmatic grounds. In 1966, the government had established a Department of Social Security (DSS), as part of the overall effort to streamline operations. This name was adopted in the hopes of avoiding the stigma attached to existing units having titles containing the terms *welfare* and *assistance*. (These earlier programs for some years had been administered by, respectively, the Ministry of Pensions and National Insurance, and the National Assistance Board.) The administrative complexity that in the past had characterized governmental operations in this field was almost beyond description. In a typical year, 1943, age programs were diffused among no less than four national departments: the Ministry of Health, with responsibility for contributory old age pensions; the Assistance Board (later to become the *National* Assistance Board), charged with serving those elderly clients deemed as eligible for the supplementary, means-tested benefit; the Board of Customs and Excise, responsible for serving pensioners *not* in receipt of a supplement; and the Ministry of Pensions, whose work involved claims relating to the veterans of World War I and earlier wars. Although this confusing set of arrangements had been somewhat simplified by the mid-1950s—in the wake of abolition of the Ministry of Pensions and the removal of the Board of Customs and Excise from any pension involvement—there persisted a bifur-

15. Richard Clarke, "The Number and Size of Government Departments," *Political Quarterly* 43, no. 2 (April–June 1972), pp. 169–86.

cation between the National Assistance Board and the recently formed Ministry of Pensions and National Insurance. The merger of 1968 eliminated this last element of administrative diversity.[16]

Of primary interest for present purposes is, of course, these developments' indirect political effects. In these terms, the establishment of DHSS appears to have enhanced the relative visibility of state pension issues within the larger context of British domestic policy. The several individuals who have served in the post of secretary of state for social services have been accorded a level of cabinet prominence that was not typical of their predecessors, serving in the former post of minister of pensions and national insurance. Further enhancing the political prominence of DHSS during the Margaret Thatcher years was the decision to relocate the office of the social services secretary from its former unprepossessing site at the intersection of Elephant and Castle streets on the south side of the Thames River in London to an elegantly rebuilt structure on Whitehall Street in Westminster, within a few steps of all the chief ministries of government: the Treasury, Ministry of Defense, and Foreign Office among others. It is apparent, therefore, that this headquarters move represented a major gain in the ministry's symbolic importance.

It would appear that the high visibility accorded to DHSS eventually came to appear as a matter of concern to the Thatcher government, sensitive to the nuances of social welfare politics in Britain. In the middle 1980s Thatcher announced that her government was giving consideration to partitioning DHSS once again into its basic health and social security components. While the rationale for this proposal was not spelled out, it presumably related to a certain anxiety on the part of a conservative, free enterprise–oriented government toward this obvious increase in the stature of a major part of the national bureaucracy.[17]

In summary, Britain's fourth phase offered major incentives toward age-group mobilization and activism: (1) the enlargement of scope of the state pension system resulting from SERPS, (2) the continuing complexity of programs, capable of being comprehended through sophisticated interest group analysis yet beyond the grasp of most private individuals, and (3) the far more clearly defined bureaucratic target that DHSS now represented. For these reasons, the styles of political action that had come to typify old age advocacy organizations in earlier years might now no longer suffice, and basic reassessments on their part might now be required. The following section considers the extent to which that expectation was to become reality.

---

16. D. M. Chester and F. M. G. Willson, *The Organization of British Central Government, 1914–1956* (London: George Allen and Unwin, 1957), pp. 159–82.

17. "Partition of D. H. S. S.," *Pensioners' Voice* (NFRPA), September 1988.

Elite-Level Perceptions of Aging Organizations

In the late spring of 1988, I spoke individually with several policy-level civil servants in the DHSS. Those interviewed were selected for their particular concern with old age pensions and other income security programs, as well as with social service programs that include elderly persons as well as other client groupings. These informants were asked to describe the policy setting or environment within which the central government decides policy in this field. The responses given differed in several respects, but in one respect they were remarkably similar: in all cases, the first set of actors mentioned was age-advocacy interest groups. One of those interviewed, for example, began thusly: "My perception would be [confined] pretty much [to] pensions or income maintenance programs, because I am not involved in social services for the elderly—there would be a different set of actors there. In all of our most recent deliberations and struggles we had groups representing the elderly." Responding to the same query, another official spoke as follows: "I would begin with the pressure groups for pensioners themselves, even though 'grey power' seems to me less important here than in the United States." And still a third official, whose area of responsibility lies primarily in the field of social services, responded by elaborating at length on what he called the "elderly lobby," underscoring the high degree of collaboration that exists between his particular bureau and certain age-advocacy organizations.

One should not, obviously, overstate the significance of these responses. None of the informants was suggesting that Britain's age-advocacy groups are necessarily capable of determining policy outcomes, or that such advocacy deserves emphasis to the exclusion of other political forces. Still, there was no avoiding the pronounced stress placed by these informed individuals on the visibility and apparent influence of age-related nongovernmental groups.

The 1970s and 1980s were witness to an extraordinary wave of age-group formation in Britain. By the late 1980s there existed here a score or more of separately organized, age-active groups, not counting the hundreds of local chapters of such national organizations as Age Concern and the National Federation of Retirement Pensions Associations (NFRPA), formerly the National Federation of Old Age Pensions Associations (NFOAPA). (This group changed its name in the early 1980s by the substitution of *retirement* in place of *old age* in its original title.) Included within the wave are three groups that are Left-oriented: the Pensioners Rights Campaign, formed in 1989, whose membership within a year of its formation had reached ten thousand; the Greater London Pensioners Association, formed in 1973; and the National Pensioners Liaison Forum, formed in 1988. Another fledgling organization, the Association of Retired Persons (modeled on the American Association of Retired Persons [AARP]), displays a distinctly middle-class flavor. No full treatment of this widely diverse wave of organizational activity is possible within the limited scope of the present discussion. What is possible is to focus upon the largest and most politically active among them, viewed in the context of phase four policy developments.

There are presently five groups that stand out in these terms, some of them newly formed at this time, and others formed earlier but now undergoing a process of refocusing and redirection. They consist, firstly, of a set of three groups, all of which employ the common terms *age* or *aging* in their names, and, secondly, of two others where the common term of self-reference is *pensions* or *pensioners*. These choices of nomenclature in each case represent a clue toward a proper definition of its basic orientation and public policy outlook.

Britain's Age Coalition

Three organizations—Age Concern, Help the Aged, and Center for Policy on Aging (CPA)—comprise what may be termed the nation's "age coalition." During the 1980s these particular groups developed a collaborative relationship, one resting upon an accepted demarcation of roles and shared policy outlooks. Achievement of their respective jurisdictions did not come easily or quickly, as the following discussion reveals. Yet by the 1980s the long efforts to define their respective roles had reached fruition, as evidenced by their joint production of a pamphlet, *One Cause*, prepared in 1987 for general distribution. "To achieve their common aims," the pamphlet declares, "the three major agencies in the field—Age Concern, Center for Policy on Aging and Help the Aged—work closely together to change attitudes toward older people and to assure that their health, housing and social needs are not overlooked. Each organization, whilst working toward this common goal, contributes in a different way."[18] Further evidence of the three groups' interconnectedness was apparent from interviews that I conducted among their senior staff personnel in summer 1988. When asked to identify "other aging advocacy organizations that make a difference in Britain," these informants invariably mentioned one or both of the other two age-coalition groups, while only under prodding went on to discuss any of the interest groups outside that circle. The clear impression conveyed was that the leading pension groups are regarded from an age-coalition perspective as fairly distant cousins, and not at all as close relatives.

A leading study, by Robin Means and Randall Smith, deals with Britain's leading age-welfare organizations in historical perspective, and it is clear from this account that the presently harmonious atmosphere did not come

---

18. *One Cause*, pamphlet jointly printed by the three organizations, n.d. (circa 1987).

about quickly or at all easily.[19] The following account summarizes some of the more salient points from the Means-Smith study.

The National Old People's Welfare Council

The oldest of the three, Age Concern, was launched in the autumn of 1940 as the Committee for the Welfare of the Aged. After several early changes, the organizational name was fixed for a period as the "National Old People's Welfare Committee." (The word *council* was substituted for *committee* in the official name in 1955.) From its beginnings as the committee, and extending through its years as the council, this group remained under the protective umbrella of the National Council of Social Services (NCSS), which long provided it with generous patronage. The leaders of the National Old People's Welfare Council (NOPWC) developed close contacts with the Assistance Board, whose importance in aging policy was mentioned in the preceding, and which shared its special concern over the isolation and loneliness experienced by many thousands of Britain's elderly.

Even though the initial steps culminating in the committee's eventual formation occurred in May and June of 1940, prior to the launching of the wartime blitz of London and other metropolitan centers, the German air raids were nevertheless important to this group's development. By October of 1940, when the committee was formally chartered, the blitz had been unleashed on London, with attendant heavy loss of life and property destruction. Large-scale evacuation of London residents to remoter, less populous areas had begun. Elderly persons were among those most affected by these disruptions, with many having their homes bombed out and left without alternative accommodation. There was now an acute shortage of housing, and an insufficiency of needed inspection for damaged housing that might possibly be capable of restoration. Family members and other care givers often had died or been evacuated. In these circumstances the committee set for itself the task of ensuring that elderly people now remaining in London were properly looked after, a task that severely taxed its own meager resources and that was to remain a challenge in the later war years and even beyond that into the postwar era.

As previously noted, this organization during its first two decades, and even slightly beyond, remained under the tutelage of the NCSS. The parent organization provided its offspring with patronage in several forms: the free use of office space, payment of office and clerical salaries, provision of certain services, and assumption of a major proportion of the general expenses.[20] Yet,

---

19. Robin Means and Randall Smith, *The Development of Welfare Services for Elderly People* (London: Croom Helm, 1985).

20. Ibid., p. 342.

as the fledgling grew in stature, its early dependency relationship increasingly became a source of strain, as discussed in the following.

National Corporation for the Care of Old People

The wartime blitz of London also played a critical role in the formation of what would later evolve into a second major social welfare organization, one presently known as the CPA, but originally the National Corporation for the Care of Old People (NCCOP). While not formally chartered until August 1947, two years after the end of World War II, NCCOP also owed its formation in part to the wartime air raids and the stimulus these provided toward a fresh look at addressing the needs of elderly persons. The organization originally had two patrons: the Lord Mayor's National Air Raid Distress Fund and the Nuffield Foundation. (The Nuffield Foundation, a philanthropic organization established in 1943, identified as one of its original objectives the provision for "the care and comfort of the aged poor"—a concern stimulated in part by the wartime situation.) NCCOP took account of the fact that many old people in the immediate postwar years were living in situations of great hardship, especially in terms of housing, health, and spending money, with 110,000 London houses destroyed and 1 million seriously damaged. The organization's founders took up the challenge of first identifying, and then granting funds for the relief of, residential problems and other related requirements of the needy elderly.[21]

Help the Aged

In 1953 a group of charity-minded Christian businesspeople joined hands with several of the individuals who had earlier organized the Oxford Committee for Famine Relief (OXFAM), the British overseas charity and relief organization, to form the Help for Vital Causes Group (VCG). Expressing interest in the welfare needs of several categories of persons, the leaders of VCG from the outset regarded as one of their vital causes the generally depressed condition of Britain's elderly, and with time, they expanded their range of elderly-related programming. Soon, the possibility of separating off this particular facet of its larger organizational work began to appear attractive, and after a series of planning meetings held in 1960 and 1961, a decision was reached to continue such work through an autonomous body, Help the Aged.

By the 1970s Help the Aged had become a vast charity operation, employing a staff of hundreds in both Britain and abroad, and including a major fund-raising operation directed toward business firms and other potential do-

---

21. Eric Midwinter, "Commentary: Policies on Aging," in *Annual Report: Center for Policy on Aging* (London: CAP, 1988), pp. 7–15.

nors. The organization chose to avoid involving itself in direct service delivery, although it agreed to monitor elderly people's general situation and to offer policy recommendations relating to such matters.[22]

Overlapping Roles

By the mid-1950s the obvious overlapping of activity among these three organizations, plus the difficulty of justifying to contributors why such an apparent duplication of effort in a common field of action should be continued, had become a matter for serious concern. The problem was especially acute for two of these groups, the NCCOP and NOPWC (including the latter's parent body, NCSS), given their close similarities in names. In 1957 a joint working party consisting of representatives of these two bodies was set up and charged with more clearly demarcating their respective spheres of activity, and while little came of this effort, it set a precedent. A few years later, in 1964, NCCOP considered changing its name as one means of overcoming what an internal report referred to as "the confusion . . . in the minds of many people between [this corporation] and the National Old People's Welfare Council."[23] The establishment of Help the Aged around this same time probably contributed further to the confusion, there being now three, not just two, overlapping and competitive groups in the same specialized area of British social welfare.

While the precise manner in which these interorganizational problems were eventually resolved lies beyond the scope of this discussion, two points should be noted. First, the parental role played by NCSS relative to NOPWC had by the 1960s become a source of considerable internal disquiet and criticism. An outside study that was commissioned to investigate the problem concluded that the parent group was failing to provide the required coordination of outside activity, including governmental representation directed toward the Ministry of Health and participation in the ministry's policy-planning efforts.[24] A recommendation was put forward, and in the end agreed to, that the parent body should terminate its existing role and acquiesce to its fledgling's proceeding off on its own.

Secondly, there was growing support at this time for an increase in political activism on the part of voluntary associations generally, and this mood evidently had its effect on Age Concern's initial definition of its role. Underlying its fresh definition of objectives was the continuing expansion in

---

22. Kenneth Hudson, *Help the Aged: Twenty Years of Experiment and Achievement* (London: Bodley Head, 1982), pp. 18 and 30.

23. Means and Smith, *Development of Welfare Services for Elderly People*, p. 344.

24. Ibid., p. 341.

the scope of governmental programs and the increasing salience of government programs among the elderly. The Age Concern leadership was also aware of the extensive publicity given to certain newly formed interest groups operating in related fields of social policy: the Child Poverty Action Group, the Campaign against Racial Discrimination, and the Disablement Income Group—all of which had achieved credible reputations for political effectiveness and influence. Reflecting this new atmosphere, Age Concern asserted a decidedly more political mandate than had earlier characterized its predecessor.

Redefinition of Goals

Among all three of the voluntary organizations described in the preceding, the arrival of phase four was associated with redefinitions of goals, albeit in varying degree. While each of these groups had longstanding relationships with various ministries, extending back to their beginnings, this new phase was marked by a shift of emphasis toward a more systematic and deliberate approach to government. Typifying this reorientation was NCCOP. In 1980 this group renamed itself the "Center for Policy on Aging," thereby suggesting an increase in concern for policy issues, public policy as well as voluntary. Around this same time the corporation spelled out in its annual report a fresh sense of purpose:

> The basic approach is first to identify where it is that old people are at a serious disadvantage. This may be due to a lack of knowledge on the part of those responsible for their care . . . or it may be due to inadequate social policies on the part of [national] government or local authorities. . . . The Corporation will institute studies designed to find solutions, however tentative, to the problems it has identified . . . [and] will not rest until what it has found has been made known and discussed and tested.[25]

The CPA would leave to other, more advocacy-oriented, voluntary organizations the task of mobilizing public opinion and lobbying government, while emphasizing its own intention to serve as the "focus of consideration" of policy options relating to the elderly.[26]

With regard to Help the Aged, there was no such change of name or tangible shift in priorities, but an acceptance, informally, of public policy concern and political activism. This was implicit in the group's decision in

---

25. Quoted in Midwinter, "Commentary," p. 12.
26. Ibid.

1973 to publish a major study, *Pensions: A Challenge to the Nation*, which represented, according to Kenneth Hudson's semiofficial history, a "key document" in the group's collective life.[27] Moreover, in the following year the organization hired, as its head of public affairs, Mervyn Kohler, who came to Help the Aged out of a background as a former staff executive at the Conservative party central office. In his new post, Kohler has come to play a political liaison function, including linkages to both Whitehall and Westminster, and devotes well above half his time to government relations.

In none of the three organizations was the extent of political arousal quite so apparent as in the case of Age Concern under the leadership of its first director, David Hobman, who served from 1971 to 1987. Speaking for his organization, Hobman advanced a broadly defined mandate to promote the public policy interests of Britain's older and retired citizens. This outlook was evident in the titles of several Age Concern pamphlets of the 1970s: *Manifesto on the Place of the Retired and the Elderly in Modern Society* (1975), *Political Party Priorities for the Elderly* (1978), and *Modern Geriatrics—Modern Medicine* (1978). Hobman voiced the conviction that the elderly must assert themselves politically as an essential step toward ensuring a proper public response to their interests and aspirations.[28] He arrived at this conviction in part through an assessment of Britain's existing age-advocacy interest groups, especially the National Federation of Old Age Pensions Associations (NFOAPA), which the director regarded as having failed to make a very significant impact on the national government or to persuade leading politicians to become strongly identified with senior citizens and retirees. He compared the British situation unfavorably with that of the United States, where senators and members of Congress, under the impact of such powerful organizations as the American Association of Retired Persons (AARP), NCSC, and the Gray Panthers, were prepared to devote significant energies to serving on the committees on aging of Congress. "In the long run," Hobman continues, "it is the elderly themselves who must flex their political muscles, who must be heard in their own right without depending upon voluntary agencies, the leaders of the trade union movement, or individual politicians who may select them as a just or an expedient cause."[29]

Under Hobman's leadership, Age Concern increasingly took on the attributes of a pressure group, intent upon gaining access to the central govern-

---

27. Hudson, *Help the Aged*, pp. 109–10.

28. David Hobman, "Aging, Self-Help, and Political Action," in Frank Glendenning, ed., *Self-Help and the Over 60s* (a report of a seminar arranged by the Department of Adult Education, University of Keele) (Stoke-on-Trent, England: Beth Johnson Foundation, 1978), p. 16.

29. Talk reprinted in Hobman, "Aging, Self-Help, and Political Action," p. 16.

ment and achieving, if possible, the status of an insider organization. Beginning in 1978, his organization entered into an arrangement whereby it would pay the salary for the officer serving the All Party Pensioner Group in the House of Commons, a committee of back-bench legislators whose membership was (and remains) broadly inclusive of varying partisan and ideological persuasions. Launched initially on an experimental basis, this staffing arrangement was later made permanent. Age Concern currently employs on its staff an executive who in one capacity is subordinate to Age Concern's director and in another is accountable to the leadership of the All Party Pensioner Group. It is a dual role that has its counterpart in a few other areas of national government, for example, the Alcoholism Services and Policy Group and the All-Party Group on Civil Liberties. As A. G. Gordon and J. J. Richardson point out, the role played by Age Concern in the pension area is typical of all-party parliamentary committees generally, in that it is both stimulated and administered by a particular interest group.[30]

Areas of Policy Consensus

In the course of their common shift toward more explicit political and public policy awareness, Age Concern, Help the Aged, and the CPA have arrived at something of a consensus regarding the proper definition of the needs and interests of Britain's elderly. This agreed upon definition has at least two dimensions.

It includes, firstly, the belief that the needs of aging and aged individuals are multifaceted, and nonreducible to any single dimension, such as income security or pension adequacy. Illustrative of this outlook is a statement by Eric Midwinter, director of the CPA, made in a 1988 essay. After enumerating the diversity of his organization's elderly-related activities over the years—short-stay homes, day centers, chiropody schemes, laundry services for the incontinent, older persons' employment schemes, and large-print book services—Midwinter remarks:

> The fresh thoughts (within NCCOP and CPA) were, in chief, a response to changing times, with the increasing awareness that the whole of those in older age *and not just those rendered social casualties in older age*, were the fit focus for social and political analysis . . . . It was a tacit recognition that . . . social gerontology had an urgent need to *encapsulate all old people in all aspects of their life style*. . . . The 'care of old

---

30. A. G. Jordan and J. J. Richardson, *Government and Pressure Groups in Britain* (Oxford: Oxford University Press, 1987), p. 253.

people' now matters less [than before] . . . [and] responsibility must now be assessed in broader aspect of a huge retired population.[31]

The same conviction concerning the multifaceted character of aging was conveyed to me in the course of an interview with Mervyn Kohler of Help the Aged. After mentioning the age-related organizations, not ones part of the age coalition, Kohler remarked that, by comparison, his own organization has taken a more-varied approach, being "much more concerned with how you look after elderly people, the provision of care, the delivery of services, and most fundamentally the concept of what elderly people are all about in society."[32]

The second theme common to the three groups has been their shared belief in social policies that are grounded on the principle of elderly self-help and social participation. This is not to suggest that this age-participatory element is necessarily alien to the philosophies of other interest groups in aging, but only that the age coalition accords it exceptional emphasis. Instead of focusing on the government's obligations toward the elderly, its leaders are inclined to stress that social action should begin from an emphasis on what the aged can do for themselves. An executive of the CPA, Jillian Crosby, expressed this point cogently in my interview with her, observing that a central purpose of her organization is that of "seek[ing] to emphasize the more positive aspects of aging, *including options for active participation in retirement*. [We] do that through raising people's awareness."[33]

While the three organizations thus are congruent in their general social and political outlooks, this has not led them to openly collaborate in their dealings with government. Even though their officers and staff maintain close personal contact—facilitated by the close proximity of their national offices in London—their public relations have typically been separate and autonomous. Such autonomy has the dual benefit of encouraging continued support for each group on the part of its donors and members, and of allowing for separate contact with government when some separate need arises.

With respect to lobbying and pressure group activity, Age Concern is clearly the leading age-coalition actor. Evelyn McEwen, Age Concern division director for information and policy, directs a staff of ten full-time professionals—a number that does not include either the previously mentioned staff aide to the All Party Pensioner Group or the organization's director, Sally Greengross, even though both these individuals have important

---

31. Midwinter, "Commentary," pp. 11–12 (emphasis added).
32. Mervyn Kohler, interview, June 1988.
33. Jillian Crosby, interview, June 1988 (emphasis added).

government relations roles. In addition, over 60 other staff professionals are employed at the Age Concern headquarters, assigned to such widely diverse programs as policy analysis and research, field staff, publishing, information, and fund raising. (And this headquarters staff is exclusive of the additional 150 full-time employees assigned to Age Concern's employment training program.) Even though these more than 200 London-based employees do not engage for the most part in lobbying activity, their existence, when added to Age Concern's over one thousand local offices distributed throughout Britain, obviously enhances the organization's visibility and political presence; it would be a rare member of Parliament who does not have one or more Age Concern local offices in his or her constituency.

It is partially a consequence of these large resources that Age Concern has managed to secure for itself an immediacy of access to government that is probably unequaled among British interest groups involved in aging. In response to my question on the extent of Age Concern informal contact with government, Sally Greengross offered this interesting response:

> The bureaucracy at Whitehall is not all faceless to us. I mean we had two quite senior members from the DHSS down here [at our offices] just this week. They come from time to time to talk with us, and I go there a lot too. You must realize that we carry out programs either on behalf of the Department or ones that the Department is very much interested in—for example, through the Age Concern Institute of Social Gerontology at the University of London. This was founded by Age Concern England in collaboration with King's College, and between us we underwrite its core expenses. For the Department we carry out programs such as a current hospital discharge. . . . It is part of my job, therefore, to know the Department officials well. This also suits both sides.[34]

The Pensions' Coalition

As pointed out, Britain's age coalition is linked together by the close, informal ties among its component interest groups, stemming from their similarities in origin, internal structure, and method of approach to elderly people's needs and aspirations. The same could be said of the array of groups that have, as their common designation, the word *pensioner* or *pensions*. Here again, a commonality of group beginnings, structural arrangements, and definitions of need is apparent.

---

34. Sally Greengross, interview, June 1988.

National Federation of Retirement
Pensions Associations

The first of the pensioner organizations to emerge was NFRPA, formerly NFOAPA, whose importance is discussed in earlier chapters. In press releases and in other publicity the organization commonly refers to itself as "Pensioners' Voice," the name used for many years for its monthly house organ, even though not its official name. In the phase four era this group has for the most part continued its traditional mode of behavior: regular, prearranged visitations by its representatives to the offices of pensioner-relevant ministries at Whitehall, efforts made toward mobilization of seniors at the local as well as the national level, and dissemination of the group's public policy views through various propaganda outlets.

Yet, while the traditional approaches continue to be employed, the organization has seen a decline in its former level of political influence. Contributing to this have been certain developments in its wider environment. The federation now faces competition from other politically active groups, especially the better-funded, more centrally located, and more professionally staffed Age Concern England. Also involved has been the growing complexity of aging programs in Britain, to which NFRPA has had difficulty adjusting given its lack of strong policy-analytic capacity. And in addition to such external developments, its leaders have been obliged to confront various internal problems. In the space of a decade beginning in the 1970s its number of constituent local associations contracted markedly. Whereas in 1978 the federation had more than fifteen hundred local branches, by 1988 the number had plummeted to slightly over eight hundred. In accounting for this, federation leaders point in part toward government-funded urban redevelopment projects, which have razed many of the neighborhood halls upon which the branches were reliant for holding their meetings. Also emphasized is the decline in rank-and-file enthusiasm for the federation's traditional branch ideal—a development related to television and other forms of mass entertainment that have displaced the federation's shared social activities and age-group fellowship. Even where the local branches survive, moreover, there is evidence of a lessened sense of shared purpose, in contrast to the situation of former years with its strong element of purposive solidarity. Whereas the branches had once contributed all but a small fraction of the revenues required for national operations, such branch support by the late 1980s represented only around 60 percent of total revenues.[35]

These developments have been a source of anxiety for the national leadership. Speaking before the federation's annual conference in 1977, the gen-

---

35. George Dunn, interview, June 1988.

eral secretary, George Dunn, voiced alarm over what he termed the growing rank-and-file "apathy." Dunn went on to remark that "many of our Branches are so concerned today with tomorrow's outing, the size of next week's jackpot, that members never give a thought to next year's pension or how it is that in the last thirty-eight years their pensions have risen from ten shillings to fifteen pounds thirty."[36]

As government policy during the 1970s and 1980s became increasingly complex, the advantages of an interest group's possessing a strong policy-analytic component became ever more apparent. Yet, given its financial stringency, NFRPA was unable to develop such a capacity on its own, or to open a London office where its officers could be in intimate day-to-day contact with government ministries. The federation's offices remain situated in Lancashire, six hours by train from London, the national capital.

Union-Affiliated Pensioner Groups

Britain's trade union movement in recent years has confronted a wider social environment that in many respects is as threatening, and potentially as disruptive to traditional modes of political action, as that described for NFRPA. This has compelled the labor movement to reappraise its traditional approaches and to explore new strategies and tactics.

Such fresh thinking was in large degree responsible for the success of an upstart group, militant in its outlook and composed mostly of residents of inner-city London and one or two other larger cities: the British Pensioners Trade Union Action Association (BPTUAA). This group began with the expulsion in spring 1973 of the Camden branch (London) of the NFRPA, and its members' subsequent decision to reconstitute themselves as the Camden Pensions and Trade Union Action Committee. In September of that year, at the national meeting of the Trades Union Congress (TUC), the Camden group joined forces with like-minded unionists from Merseyside in BPTUAA's formation. The new group depended on a degree of patronage from the unions and the Left of the Labour party and managed to establish branches in areas where the older pensioners' organization had not had much success. Its successful launching soon became a rallying point for radical elements in the pensioner movement whose members shared a dissatisfaction over the moderate approach long attributed to NFRPA; it grew as much from such dissatisfaction as for any other reason.[37]

---

36. "Report of the General Secretary," *Proceedings of the Thirty-eighth Conference* (Blackburn, England: NFOAPA, 1977).

37. John Miles, personal correspondence, March 1992. (Miles is an activist in Britain's pensioner movement.) See also C. Phillipson, *Capitalism and the Construction of Old Age* (London: Macmillan, 1982), pp. 137–38.

Even though such community-based activism had implications for the British labor movement in general, the TUC and other trade union organizations were slow to acknowledge its existence. Despite the TUC's century-long support for the cause of state pensions, its leaders mostly remained convinced that pension-related lobbying efforts in this field were best channeled through regular union structure, as opposed to spontaneously by senior activists. The prevailing view for many years was that union policy on state pensions is properly a matter for determination by actively employed union members, with retirees filling at most a subordinate role.

This early view did not long endure, however, as the TUC and its member bodies came to accept the need for union retirees to be organized on some separate basis. Acting in part in response to the ferment stirred up by BPTUAA, the British labor movement after 1973 began to encourage the formation of trade union retired member associations. A survey conducted in 1987 by the TUC revealed that after a decade of evolution 6 of its affiliated unions had now established such units, of which two now employed full-time staff. And an additional 40 unions reported making formal provision in their constitutions for retiree participation, including limited voting rights and/or the right to attend and be heard at union meetings. (Among the 54 unions surveyed, only 8 had thus far failed to take positive steps in this field.) The survey also reported some intriguing findings on the functions being fulfilled by existing retired member associations or anticipated in the case of ones still in the planning stage. From a list of several possible retired member associations' functions that union leaders were asked to consider, the one most frequently checked as important was political advocacy. "It is clear," its authors note, "that lobbying is not only the most important area of [retired member] activity, but is likely to become even more so in the future."[38] The survey findings were underscored by a TUC staff executive, who remarked to me in an interview that the retiree movement within the labor movement has a pronounced political and public policy character. While the extent of genuine retired member associations' autonomy within unions remains unclear, the presence of this element does seem to have augmented the pension-related pressure applied by TUC on the Labour party, and also BPTUAA's efforts to lobby unions on behalf of pensioner concerns. In short, trade union policy on pensions is no longer decided on a strict top-down basis, by elective union officials and senior staff, but instead has become at least partly a bottom-up process, wherein union-retiree thinking must be taken account of.

---

38. Social Insurance and Industrial Welfare Department, *Pension Committee Survey Report*, mimeo (London: TUC, August 1987).

Reappraisal of Union Pension Advocacy

In addition to witnessing the early stirring of retiree activism in the labor movement, the middle to late 1970s also was a time of questioning of traditional union strategy aimed at influencing public pension debates. The enactment of SERPS by a Labour government soon proved itself ambiguous from a trade union standpoint: on the one hand, it promised long-term improvement in retired workers' income security, yet on the other, it offered little or nothing for presently retired workers already drawing pension benefits. With respect to the latter, government officials acknowledged a degree of hardship but insisted that lack of resources prevented anything much by way of a remedy. The TUC, despite its favorable access to Labour governments in the 1960s and 1970s, was given little satisfaction upon voicing its demand for a 40 percent increase in the size of the pension, which it estimated would cost the Exchequer roughly £four billion.

TUC representatives found themselves unable to penetrate the government's seemingly solid wall, as was brought home to its representatives in the course of meetings at Whitehall. When a delegation from the labor organization met with the social services secretary in November 1977 to present its demand for the 40 percent pension boost, the secretary's response was one of agreement that in principle an increase might be justified, but that "the cost involved . . . [is] so substantial there [is] no possibility of its being achieved in the near future."[39] A second TUC delegation at around the same time was given similarly unwelcome news by the secretary of state for social security. After listening to the group's plea that SERPS would provide little or no benefit to many persons already in receipt of a state pension, and that the government should therefore use its discretionary authority to provide some immediate relief, the minister reacted that he was not committed on the issue, and that considerable administrative difficulties stood in the way of providing more than a very limited benefit boost. What little action the government was prepared to take in this area was viewed by organized labor as wholly inadequate. Thus, responding to an uprating in pension benefits, as announced by the chancellor of the exchequer in April of 1978, the TUC General Council the following month voted to deplore the move as inadequate and went on to lament what it termed the "small progress made toward [the TUC's] pension demands."[40] Whitehall remained cool to all of this.

Given this environment, the TUC felt obliged to reappraise its basic state pension political strategy. In spring 1978, the TUC General Council agreed

---

39. *TUC Congress Report, 1978* (London: TUC, 1978), p. 99.
40. Ibid., pp. 99–100.

to sponsor the following September a Trafalgar Square, London, national demonstration in support of higher retirement pensions, and to employ its energies and resources toward ensuring the large-scale involvement of union retirees. In a subsequent appraisal of this mass demonstration, union leaders were impressed by the large-scale participation of union retirees. This helped to increase the TUC's receptiveness toward proposals of an organizational nature and in turn prompted the labor federation's general council, toward the end of 1978, to pass a resolution for the TUC to "organize and convene" a new, union-related pensioner organization, the National Pensioners Convention. While the convention's principal purpose would be to support efforts to increase the base retirement pension to the level long considered as essential by organized labor, it also would serve to address a larger range of pension-related issues.

The steering committee appointed to organize the convention thereupon drafted a "Declaration of Intent" to be submitted for conference-delegate consideration. It emphasized that the new group's founding meeting would keep to the forefront the problem of economic insecurity. Thus:

> The Convention declares that every pensioner has the right to . . . an adequate State retirement pension. There must be an immediate commitment to a pension level of not less than one half of the average gross earnings for a married couple and not less than one third of average gross earnings for a single person, uprated at six monthly intervals.[41]

Following months of planning, therefore, the convention held its founding meeting on June 14, 1979, at a hall in central London with over two thousand persons in attendance. Among other actions, the delegates approved the declaration and the establishment of the National Pensioners Convention as an ongoing age-advocacy organization.

While the TUC's action in agreeing to sponsor this interest group partially reflected labor leaders' frustration at the perceived pension policy failures of Labour governments under Harold Wilson and James Callaghan, there was also a second consideration. At precisely this moment, Jack Jones, the longtime general secretary of the Transport and General Workers Union (TGWU)—the largest constituent body in the TUC—reached the mandatory age of retirement as defined by his union. In the 1950s and 1960s, Jones had become among the most prominent labor leaders in Britain, having led the TGWU in a series of highly publicized transport strikes. A figure of considerable stature in the labor movement, Jones for some years had actively pro-

---

41. Quoted in *TUC Congress Report, 1979* (London: TUC, 1979), p. 89.

moted the interests of retirees, both within his own union and elsewhere in the labor movement. With Jones's retirement now at hand, the TUC leaders began to view the proposed National Pensioners Convention as a logical outlet for his energy and talents.

During the first ten years of the National Pensioners Convention's existence its top office, that of chairperson, was reserved for the TUC general secretary (in the late 1980s an office held by Norman Willis), while Jack Jones was given the post of vice-chair, a position that made him the most prominent figure in the National Pensioners Convention's affairs. It was Jones, for example, who for many years delivered the major address at the convention's annual rallies in central London and then led a delegation of convention notables to Ten Downing Street for an arranged meeting with the prime minister. Jones's name came up repeatedly in the course of my interviews, both within and outside the Labour movement, whenever the National Pensioners Convention was under discussion.

Yet labor leaders had reason for concern that this new organization, however energetic and well supported, might not in itself prove sufficient for overcoming the daunting difficulties in the pension area that the labor movement now confronted. Throughout the 1970s and 1980s trade union membership in Britain declined, a trend attributable in large part to the ascendancy of Margaret Thatcher. Thatcher became prime minister for the first time following the British general election of 1979, and subsequently, her highly publicized quarrels with labor leaders augmented her popularity with the British electorate. Since the Conservatives remain in office at the present writing under the leadership of Thatcher's protégé, John Major, it is apparent that the National Pensioners Convention has spent its entire organizational life in a political atmosphere dominated by Thatcherite thinking. It is scarcely surprising, therefore, that when I enquired of a TUC staff member involved in pension matters what the extent was of the National Pensioners Convention's influence over public policy the informant voiced doubt that there had been any impact whatever.

And the prevailing partisan political climate has not been the sole barrier confronting the convention since its formation. While the convention claims to speak for pensioners generally, it is well known that a shrinking minority of British voters are Labour-identified. This poses an obvious problem for an organization whose leadership consists in large part of present and former union officials, whose budget is TUC subsidized, and that is widely perceived, incorrectly perhaps, as Left-leaning and Labour-oriented. A National Pensioners Convention's opening toward the center and center-right of British politics, in the form of a coalition with the national federation (i.e., NFRPA), thus had obvious appeal.

The Pensions' Coalition Emerges

From its beginnings in the late 1930s, the NFRPA maintained tenuous link-ages with the TUC and certain of its constituent national unions. The connec-tion reflected their roughly parallel views on key issues of pensioner concern. On several occasions federation leaders reached out to union leaders, appeal-ing for a joining of hands on particular issues. In 1952, for example, the NFOAPA general secretary informed his constituency that "for the past two years we have made a determined effort to enlist the support of Trade Unions for our cause. . . . It is gratifying to know that we have met with the warmest response from practically every union."[42]

Still, despite the occasional coalitional efforts, it was several decades before anything much developed by way of an ongoing, substantive political collaboration. Despite their broad agreement on an array of pension related concerns, the two movements for many years diverged in terms of preferred style of action and class composition. As was pointed out to me by a federa-tion leader, "In the early years our leaders pressed long and hard for support from the TUC and from individual unions, and met with only very little support. . . . At that time the unions felt that they had no responsibility once their members had ceased to work." A measure of suspicion and mistrust was felt on both sides. An informant within TUC recalls that many union leaders were of the opinion that the NFOAPA's largely middle-class membership made impossible its having a proper understanding of the British working class or maintaining friendly feelings toward trade unions.

Yet the shared adversities of the late 1970s and 1980s helped to dispel this atmosphere of mistrust; leaders in both camps now reevaluated their former positions and began to consider the possible payoffs from joint action. A new relationship was implicit in the joint NFOAPA and TUC sponsorship of the National Pensioners Convention. A number of NFOAPA activists were present at the convention's founding meeting in 1979, and one of their number was selected to serve as a principal speaker. This meeting was later hailed as an important symbolic event at the NFOAPA's annual convention the follow-ing year.[43] Moreover, in the lead-up to the launching of the National Pen-sioners Convention the federation's general secretary, George Dunn, met several times with Jack Jones to work out the details of the convention's constitution. More recently, the federation has had representation on the con-vention's steering committee, while its national president has participated in

---

42. *Old Age Pensioner*, October 1953, p. 1 (available at NFOAPA headquarters, Black-burn, England).

43. "Report of the Publicity Officer," *Proceedings of the Forty-first Annual Conference* (Blackburn, England: NFOAPA, 1980), p. 7.

the convention's delegations that have met with the prime minister. Contributing to this more harmonious atmosphere has been the two groups' agreement on a key point of public policy, including the demand that government fix the state pension at some substantial fraction of the average weekly wage in British industry—a view that the government, for its part, has adamantly refused to accept. These various linkages have been mostly left implicit and not strongly emphasized in the reports rendered by leaders to members, and in each group's public statements and pronouncements.

It would be misleading to suggest, however, that intergroup harmony and cooperation represent the total picture. Beginning in the middle 1980s the pensions' coalition was confronted with an increased level of distrust among age-active interest groups. This was implicit in the formation at this time of regional groupings like the Pensioners Protection party and the Pensioners Rights Campaign, outside the structures of the NFRPA, the TUC, and the BPTUAA. These fledgling groups were indicative of a grass roots upsurge, to which the more-established pensioner organizations now struggled to respond. The new wave of organizational activity benefited greatly from the expansion of funding to the voluntary sector by local councils across Britain, as well as by Britain's Department of the Environment—funding for which local pensioner groups are eligible to apply, and have done so with considerable success.[44]

The Two Coalitions: Variations in Governmental Access

This chapter brings out some of the ways in which the two coalitions differ in their definitions of elderly people's political interests. Although the pensions' coalition seeks to avoid committing itself to any single conception of elderly people's welfare, its component groups do strongly emphasize the adequacy of retirement income as an overriding concern. They hold strongly to the view that, absent an acceptable level of state pension income, no other governmental benefits, neither singly nor in combination, can serve as an acceptable substitute. On the other hand, the groups comprising the age coalition are less inclined to stress the purely economic dimension and instead are inclined to underscore the wide diversity of old people's needs, opportunities, and capacity for social participation, while also emphasizing the importance of maintaining needed social services for the frail elderly and the handicapped. For them, income adequacy is but one aspect of a proper definition of need, and not necessarily the most important.

In light of the preceding, a source of particular frustration for the pen-

---

44. John Miles, personal correspondence, March 1992.

sions' coalition has been that Britain's basic pension has only barely kept pace with the cost of living in recent years: over the ten-year period from November 1978 to April 1988 the pension rose from £19.50 to £41.15, an increase in real terms of just 2.4 percent.[45] While this level of benefit exceeded that of most other national programs, most of which declined in real terms, it was not the sort of increase from which a pension organization could derive great satisfaction. The age coalition, on the other hand, with less immediate stake in the pension as such, has found in this less cause for alarm.

The strong emphasis of the pensions' coalition on the perceived inadequacy of the existing pension benefit levels almost certainly contributed to its difficulty in gaining favorable access to the Thatcher government. While none of the interest group leaders interviewed for this study in 1988, whatever their coalitional affiliation, were approving of the Thatcher government's basic approach (all, for example, voiced displeasure over the government's 1986 social security reforms that abolished a number of age-related state benefits and scaled back the level of anticipated benefits under SERPS), there was still a marked contrast in outlooks. Whereas the leaders of the age-coalition groups expressed considerable satisfaction regarding their degree of access to the bureaucracy and to cabinet ministers (as illustrated by the previously quoted statement of Sally Greengross, the Age Concern director), no such satisfaction was found to exist among the pensions' coalition leaders. Illustrative of the latter was the following remark made to the author by George Dunn, the executive director of NFRPA ("Pensioners' Voice"):

> We still manage, as in past years, to arrange meetings with top officials, but there are more barriers and impediments than before. Since the Thatcher government assumed office we have not had access to the Treasury. We wrote a letter recently to the Prime Minister on a certain matter, and the first response we got back was from her private secretary informing us that "the prime minister, unfortunately, is unable to respond personally to enquiries from private individuals." That was infuriating, and we had to write to her a second time before a more satisfactory response was forthcoming.[46]

It is clear from this, as well as other evidence, that since the early 1970s the NFRPA has to a considerable degree relinquished the insider status in national government it enjoyed as recently as the 1950s, including regular, even bureaucratized relations with government departments involved in social welfare. As two leading observers have noted, such insider status tends to be

---

45. "Parliamentary Spotlight," *Pensioners' Voice*, August 1988.
46. George Dunn, interview, June 1988.

one of the distinguishing features of influential pressure groups in British government.[47]

A similar remoteness from the center of power in Parliament was apparent in the remarks of TUC staff executives interviewed for this study. One TUC official admitted that the National Pensioners Convention's access has been diminished by a Thatcherite perception of the convention as being Labour and leftist dominated.

Organizational Constraint

This present discussion of Britain's fourth phase should not close without giving some attention to the problems of organizational maintenance that have resulted, directly or indirectly, from alterations in policy content. Even though the predominant effect of such alteration is the stimulation of existing seniors' organizations, this has not been the case entirely. Already mentioned in this context has been the case of NFRPA, with its recent decline in membership and local-chapter shrinkage. And the constraint element probably has extended, to one extent or another, to most other voluntary organizations in this field, although not always with such obviously negative results. To no small extent, such constraint inheres in the unusual complexity of British pension programs, and in citizens' difficulty in comprehending the existing set of eligibility standards and its interconnections. In the words of one observer:

> The complexity means that there are often clear conflicts of interest between different categories of beneficiary. Movement leaders face a difficult task in working with ideas held by the rank and file membership. These ideas are often only crudely related to the realities of pension finance. [Pensioner] campaign priorities end up facing the principle of improvement rather than of reality. Below the surface there lurks a fatalism.[48]

Conclusion

Britain's fourth phase of pension politics, as brought into existence by some major changes in public policy and public administration, has been associated with a significant change in the nation's age-political arena. A number of new interest groups have been formed, and later on have flourished, whereas others less fortunate have been put under stress and obliged to alter their

---

47. A. G. Jordan and J. J. Richardson, *British Politics and the Policy Process: An Arena Approach* (London: Allen and Unwin, 1987), p. 189.

48. John Miles, personal correspondence, March 1992.

traditional lobbying and group-maintenance modes. Age-group coping strategies have taken several forms, especially efforts made to adjust potential intergroup tensions through the formation of inclusive coalitions. Yet, such strategies have varied in their effectiveness, and no aging organization is presently as powerful or as influential as its leaders probably would prefer.

CHAPTER 8

Phase Four in Canada

An observer informed about the Canadian public pension situation and imaginative in making projections could well have anticipated, at the close of the decade of the 1960s, the elements that would serve to distinguish this field over the coming two decades. Such an observer might have foreseen, for example, the extent to which Canadian social welfare in general, and aging policy in particular, would depart from its European antecedents. As K. G. Banting observes,[1] Canada's welfare state, unlike that of Britain or of the United States (or, indeed, of almost any other industrial country), is a bifurcated system, in which the federal government is dominant in the area of income security, while the provinces are preeminent in establishing policy in education, health, and social and community services. With Canadian governments becoming increasingly involved in all these fields, one could have reasonably anticipated that public programs would continue their existing tendency to reflect the warp and woof of Canadian federalism, and that the federal and provincial governments would become increasingly interdependent in fulfilling their program responsibilities.

The imaginary observer also might have anticipated that the next two decades would see an increasing political assertiveness on the part of Canada's ten provinces—at the expense of the federal government in Ottawa. This trend, already apparent at the end of the 1960s, was (and remains) reflective of the nation's two official languages, Quebec's "quiet revolution" combined with the growing assertiveness in the West, a thinly spread national population across an enormous landmass, and Canada's unique consociational character.[2] Given the provinces' growing political importance, the observer might therefore have correctly foreseen that the provinces would demand, and would receive, a major role in the administration of aging benefits of all kinds, public pensions included. Yet certain developments were now impending that even the best informed and farsighted observer probably could not

---

1. K. G. Banting, *The Welfare State and Canadian Federalism* (Kingston, Canada: McGill-Queens University Press, 1982).
2. Arend Lijphart, "Consociational Democracy," *World Politics* 21 (January 1969): 207–25.

have anticipated. Chief among them was the transformation that was now about to occur in the number and visibility of political actors in the aging field, interest groups included. Nothing in the situation at the close of Canada's third phase would have led one to expect such a development. As was brought out in the preceding chapter, the political functions whose successful fulfillment was required in this field were then performed in all cases by one actor, or in some cases a bare handful. Thus, the National Pensioners and Senior Citizens Federation (NP&SCF) and the Canadian Labor Congress, each working from a slightly different perspective, largely fulfilled the functions of policy articulation and outcomes monitoring. A set of recognized seniors' advocates in the federal Parliament was critically important in regard to the decision-making function—one involving the drafting of legislative proposals, the erection of age-supportive policy agendas, and the persuading and cajoling of parliamentary peers. Thirdly, a cluster of senior civil servants in the treasury and the Department of National Health and Welfare performed important policy analysis and technical advice-giving functions. Finally, Canada's provincial governments were significant in the necessary role of policy legitimation, given the special position of the provinces under Canada's decentralized brand of federalism. It was, overall, a system marked by considerable tidiness and predictability.

Yet, particularly with respect to the interest group aspect, such relative simplicity was soon to be superseded by a policy arena of considerable complexity. What factors produced this significant change? What were its overall dimensions? And what problems, if any, were to ensue once its full impact was felt? The following discussion provides answers to these questions.

The Changing Content of Pension Policy

Canada's transition from phase three to phase four of pension and income-security policy took place over the six-year period 1965–71. This span of time encompassed several fairly far-reaching policy developments that involved both the expansion of existing programs to unprecedented levels and the introduction of new programs based upon fresh approaches. Four parliamentary enactments were involved: the Canada/Quebec Pension Act of 1965, the Guaranteed Income Supplement Act of 1966, the indexation of the Old Age Security (OAS) pension to the cost of living (enacted in 1965 and taking effect in 1968), and the New Horizons Program of 1971. Canada's transition obviously arrived earlier than was true in Britain, given that it began not around 1970 but five years previously. In addition, Canada's time frame was narrower, in the sense that phase four commenced only fourteen years after the onset (in 1951) of phase three. In Britain, on the other hand, these same two points were separated by almost half a century, 1925 and 1970. This pecu-liarity of the Canadian case was largely attributable to the fact that pension issues did not deeply divide the nation's two leading political parties, as was true in Britain, and that pension reforms in Canada therefore could be enacted fairly easily and quickly as the situation seemed to require.

From Universal to Contributory Policy

Unlike Britain, with its exceptional complexity of present-day state pension policy, and also the United States, where the Social Security Act represented a sudden, dramatic break with past policy, which has since endured with re-markably little alteration as the basis of government action in this field, the Canadian pattern has been one of successive "waves of political initiative," with old programs discarded and new ones added in a fairly logical, ordered manner based on experience.[3] As made clear in a previous chapter, the bed-rock upon which Canada grounds its present-day policy is the Old Age Secu-rity Act of 1951.

Although this old age security system had been supported by all three of Canada's leading political parties, only a few years would elapse before political pressure began to build in favor of its fundamental overhaul. The principle of *universality*, upon which OAS originally had been grounded, was soon called into question by various influential persons, and demands were now voiced for altering the existing system so as to include benefits based on the *contributory* principle. The latter approach soon gained broad acceptance, brought about by its appealing cost-containment element (given that expendi-tures under a contributory system would be limited by the nation's prevailing rate of employment and general economic health), and also by its promise of increased benefit enhancement (given that benefit increases of substantial scale now became more affordable, at least for certain types of recipients). Furthermore, under a contributory pension system the Old Age Assistance Act of 1951—twinned with OAS at the outset but always much less popular because of its means-tested aspect—could be eliminated without producing undue hardship.

Such considerations in the end proved decisive. The adoption of the Canada/Quebec Pension Act in 1965 introduced an important earnings-related element into Canada's existing system of federally funded benefits for the elderly. And in the same year eligibility under the existing OAS benefit was

---

3. On the topic of waves of political initiative, see Christopher Lehman, "Patterns in Policy Development: Social Security in the United States and Canada," *Public Policy* 25, no. 2 (Spring 1977): 261–91.

lowered from age seventy to sixty-five, and indexing against inflation was introduced, limited to 2 percent.[4]

Despite the importance of this legislation, pension politics in one form or another would continue for several years as a leading topic of national debate, and the focus of widespread public interest. It was initially anticipated by the Liberal government under Prime Minister Lester Pearson that enactment of the Canada/Quebec Pension Plan (CPP), coupled with the other changes mentioned, would serve to push the issue of public pensions out of the arena of partisan political conflict. While that expectation was partly fulfilled, given that in the years that followed the CPP portion of the pension system was accepted into the Canadian political consensus and then largely disappeared as a focus of political debate and controversy,[5] it was also true that a new Liberal government elected in 1968 under Pierre Elliott Trudeau lost little time in making clear its desire to deemphasize further the principle of universality, and to stress instead that of selectivity and personal contribution—a move fraught with controversial overtones.

The principles of selectivity and contribution underlie a 1970 government white paper, *Income Security for Canada*. Acting upon its assumptions, the government proceeded to freeze the OAS benefit at $80 a month and to increase the required residency period before eligibility could be established.[6] The basic OAS "demogrant," while remaining in place, would no longer be as central to the Canadian pension system. These changes aroused misgivings among the elderly's advocates, who saw them as posing an obvious threat to a needs-based definition of old age entitlement.

Controversy over the correct course of pension policy was brought to a head during, and just following, the October 1972 Canadian elections, where pension issues figured prominently. The election produced a major setback for the Liberal government, involving the loss of the Liberal party's parliamentary majority. In the wake of the election results, Prime Minister Trudeau succeeded in retaining office, but only by entering into a coalition with Canada's third party, the New Democrats. In exchange for their votes, New Democratic party leaders demanded that Trudeau accept several of their priorities, including a promise that government backtrack at least somewhat from its 1970 white paper assumptions. Thus, in the middle 1970s Ottawa twice boosted the universal OAS benefit, raising it finally to $100 a month, and at the same time adjusted the Guaranteed Income Supplement (GIS) by increas-

4. Kenneth Bryden, *Old Age Pensions and Policy-making in Canada* (Montreal and London: McGill-Queens University Press, 1974), p. 131.

5. Helen Ann Nancy O'Donnell, "A Diagnosis by Ideology: Ideological Perspectives on the Formation of Pension Policy in Canada" (Ph.D. dissertation, McMaster University, Hamilton, Ontario, 1984), p. 329.

6. Ibid., pp. 333–34.

ing its base level while simultaneously indexing it to the cost of living, as had been done for the OAS in 1968.[7]

Pension Issue Prominence in the 1970s and 1980s

Pension issues continued to figure in national debates throughout the 1970s. For example, in the middle years of the decade the Canadian women's movement for the first time achieved strength sufficient for it to exert an influence on decisions relating to retirement pensions. The movement's leaders were made aware of the large numbers of wives, aged 60–64, of male OAS beneficiaries who failed to qualify for a pension benefit, having had no previous paid employment, thus forcing the couple to eke out an existence on the husband's pension benefit alone. Many such women were unprotected against the very real risk of ending up in poverty or near poverty. On the basis of such concerns, women's movement representatives in Ottawa began pressing the Trudeau cabinet to provide such older wives with improved protection. The special adviser on women in the Department of National Health and Welfare, a post then newly created, became a key player in persuading the government in June 1975 to implement the spouse's allowance as an adjunct to OAS.[8] (This program has since become a permanent fixture, with spending levels exceeding $40 million annually by the middle 1980s.) The importance attached to pension issues was also reflected in the 1979 federal election, where pension policy was vigorously debated between the Conservative leader, Joe Clark, the eventual victor in the election, and Trudeau, the prime minister and Liberal party leader. (Trudeau was turned out of office only for a few months. Save only for this brief interlude he served continuously as Canada's premier from 1968 to 1984.)

In a climate of economic instability, fiscal downturn, and ideological swing to the Right in Canadian politics, nothing done by government in the 1970s and 1980s represented a stronger signal to senior citizens that policy choices by government leaders might adversely affect Canada's elderly pensioners than did the decision taken by the government of Brian Mulroney in May 1985 to propose a partial deindexation of the federal OAS pension. The political furor that erupted in the wake of this proposal throws an interesting light on the character of senior citizen political action in present-day Canada. A later section of this chapter describes that controversy as a leading example of senior citizen political activism in the fourth phase of policy development. The Mulroney proposal represented a signal to senior citizens and their

7. Bryden, *Old Age Pensions and Policy-making in Canada*, p. 177.

8. Henry J. Pratt, "Aging Policy and Process in the Canadian Federal Government," *Canadian Public Administration* 30, no. 1 (Spring 1987): 66–67.

younger-aged allies that they did not have the luxury of regarding Canada's existing old age security system as impervious to possible cost cutting and program reduction. Such persons were now forced to recognize that officeholders were prepared, given certain conditions, to scale back and even possibly eliminate key parts of the nation's public pension system. Such awareness presumably served to increase the willingness of seniors and their younger-aged allies to coalesce in support of political advocacy in this field.

New Horizons

While the pension policy initiatives discussed here were all characterized by fairly high levels of public interest and comment, other state actions in the same general field occurred in a less-publicized, less conflictual, atmosphere. Little noted at the time, but potentially important in terms of seniors' mobilization, was the enactment in 1971 of the New Horizons program. Beginning with the initial awards made in 1972, grants under this program could be used in communities across Canada to help launch and maintain senior citizen clubs and community organizations. New Horizons owes its existence to a belief among policymakers in Ottawa that many elderly persons experience loneliness and isolation in old age; it was their belief that a program consisting of both federal dollars and federal expertise could be effective in breaking the pattern of withdrawal among the elderly, fostering significant expansion in such persons' emotional security and scope of friendships. Within ten years of its launching New Horizons had proved itself instrumental in helping to form seniors' groups by the hundreds; estimates were that approximately one-third of Canada's retired population of 2.5 million were being served by the program.

One interesting aspect of New Horizons is that it is among only a handful of Canadian social welfare programs that are both federally funded and federally administered. Provincial leaders might ordinarily have resented the apparent intrusion on their administrative prerogatives that this program represented, given that social services are ordinarily defined as falling under provincial jurisdiction. Yet any such perception on their part was successfully avoided through the program's stress on involving seniors in worthwhile activities, and the related minimizing of the social services aspect. It was also helpful that in dollar terms the program was not especially large, and moreover that its grants were restricted to programs nonpolitical in character. Whatever the reasons, provincial distrust of New Horizons never in fact materialized.[9]

9. Ibid., pp. 67–68.

Enlargement of Age-Defined Benefits

At least equally important as the government's policy changes, and probably more so from the standpoint of the average Canadian, was the steady, and in time very substantial, enlargement of benefits authorized by Ottawa to the base of existing age-benefit programs. One can offer a reasonably precise figure on the magnitude of federal old age expenditures by combining into a single number the published figures on federal outlays for OAS, GIS, and other programs that are elderly-specific with estimates (provided to the author by a senior civil servant informed in this area) for the elderly's share of programs that include the elderly along with other client populations. The resulting total for 1983 was $17.6 billion. (This figure, it should be pointed out, combines relevant items in the main federal budget and the separately maintained social insurance budget.) This large sum represented 18.1 percent of all federal spending—general fund and social insurance combined—for that fiscal year.[10]

While these large figures are impressive on their face, they take on full significance only in light of long-term patterns of federal expenditure. By 1984 Canada's elderly received nearly half of all federally financed income transfers, about $16 billion, even though such persons accounted for just over 10 percent of the total population. These expenditures had a major impact on the nation's elderly population, as is pointed out in a jointly authored study by two economists, one at the Economic Council of Canada and the other on the staff of the Department of National Health and Welfare. These authors remark:

> Poverty among [elderly] couples, in 1984, was virtually eliminated, and for [elderly] singles, even though the poverty rate remained high (44.5 per cent for females and 27.1 per cent for males), the poverty gap was reduced by nearly 90 per cent. [OAS and GIS] provided the elderly with a basic guaranteed income equivalent to 99 per cent and 76 per cent of the average poverty threshold for couples and singles respectively.[11]

The report went on to point out that the longer-term outlook for the economic well-being of the elderly looks increasingly positive as higher labor force participation rates increase coverage under the Canada and Quebec pensions,

---

10. Ibid., p. 58.

11. Hans Messinger and Frank Fedyk, "The Impact of Government Income Transfers on Poverty in Canada," paper delivered at the annual meeting of the Canadian Economics Association, June 1988, p. 30 (available from Department of National Health and Welfare, Ottawa).

and as elderly persons, encouraged by recent changes in the tax code, increasingly save for their own retirements.[12]

The full scope of such benefit increases is apparent from the following brief survey of Canada's income security programs, in which special attention is paid to long-term patterns. OAS, the oldest of Canada's present-day federal entitlements, first became fully operational in fiscal year 1952–53, at which time expenditures amounted to $323 million. Although this figure was to rise steadily over the next decade and a half, it was not until fiscal year 1966–67 that it crossed the symbolically important $1 billion barrier (to $1.03 billion), roughly triple the original figure. While this spending level probably appeared as substantial in the context of the late 1960s, it would be dwarfed by the level reached subsequently. By fiscal year 1985–86 spending under OAS had soared to $8.9 billion—an almost ninefold increase over 1966–67. Individual benefits under OAS reflected the same pattern. The maximum monthly OAS benefit was fixed at $40 when the program first went into effect in 1952. It took twenty years, to January 1971, before this figure was to double, to $80 monthly. But at that point there began a dramatic surge, such that in only fifteen years time, by 1986, it had reached a monthly level of $294, quadruple the figure for 1971.

The pattern was the same with the GIS, which Parliament tacked on to the OAS framework in 1966. Upon first becoming fully operational, in fiscal 1967–68, its expenditure level was $234,000. By fiscal year 1970–71, GIS spending had risen to $280,000—again, a rise of only modest proportions. At this point, however, the rate leapt, reaching $1 billion in fiscal 1976–77, and triple that a decade later, 1985–86, when it stood at $3.3 billion.[13]

Finally, there is the CPP, for which one should count only its retirement portion so as to exclude those pension benefits that are not defined by age. Contributory retirement benefits from this source were a mere $612,000 in calendar year 1967 when payouts began. This figure then rose to $57 million by 1971, a large change in percentage terms but modest, absolutely, by comparison with what was to come. Truly substantial CPP increases came only during the 1970s and 1980s, reaching $1.5 billion by 1981 and $3.6 billion by 1986. Average CPP benefits rose accordingly: from a mere $19.79 monthly in 1970 they soared to $127.00 monthly in 1980 and then to $250.00 in 1986, more than *twelve times* their 1970 base.[14]

Two distinct kinds of incentives are pointed out in this discussion of old

---

12. Ibid., p. 35.

13. Minister of National Health and Welfare, *Historical Statistics on Old Age Security* (Ottawa: Health and Welfare Canada, 1986), pp. 1 (table 1) and 18 (table 7-H).

14. Minister of National Health and Welfare, *Historical Statistics on Canada Pension Plan* (Ottawa: Health and Welfare Canada, 1986), pp. 30 (table 8-G) and 311 (table 39-A).

age policy, each of them contributing independently to the enlargement of Canada's political arena on aging. On the one hand, the New Horizons program, with an annual budget in the 1980s in the range of $10 million to $15 million, represented explicit incentive, deliberately intended by its sponsors to foster senior citizen organizational development. On the other, a much larger, though more indirect, incentive was implicit in the expansion of old age entitlements. Such outlays, totaling in the hundreds of millions of dollars, cannot be ignored in the context of subsequent age-related organizational development. Since incentives of both the explicit and implicit types became available at precisely the same historical moment, one cannot easily disentangle their respective impacts or say with any certainty which was the more important from the standpoint of interest group development. My own view is that the burgeoning of voluntary age-based organizations in the 1970s and 1980s was chiefly attributable to the latter of these factors, and that even though grants from New Horizons made a contribution, their relatively small size and restriction to nonpolitical purposes resulted in their being secondary in importance as compared to rising public pension expenditures.

The Political Context of Age Policy

Mushrooming of Seniors' Organizations

Writing in 1974, and reflecting on the political environment for Canadian state pensions as it existed as of, approximately, 1972, a leading student of Canadian public policy, Kenneth Bryden, draws a distinction between primary and subsidiary actors in the pension field. In the former category he places the following political actors: selected members of the federal Parliament, trade unions, political party organizations, senior civil servants, and the larger commercial and manufacturing associations. In the latter, or subsidiary, category Bryden lists three types, one of them "pensioner organizations." Of these, three are singled out as especially important: the National Pensioners and Senior Citizens Federation (NP&SCF) (formed in the 1940s), Canadian Pensioners Concerned (CPC) (formed in 1970), and Pensioners for Action Now (formed 1972). (A handful of provincial-level seniors' groups also are mentioned by Bryden, but only in passing.) Although persuaded that one of these, namely NP&SCF, "was unquestionably a factor" in pension policy struggles in 1963–65 and again in 1970–71, Bryden does not consider pensioner organizations in general as major players.[15]

Yet, the picture was changing. Writing less than a decade later after Bryden, in 1983, Kenneth Kernaghan and Olivia Kuper in a jointly authored

---

15. Bryden, *Old Age Pensions and Policy-making in Canada*, pp. 194–97.

monograph devote a major section to the topic of nongovernmental organizations active in this field.[16] These authors identify five political interest groups as having an age-specific focus, plus an additional six whose concern for the elderly represented one aspect of some larger definition of organizational purpose. While again pointing out the importance of the two national groups on Bryden's list, NP&SCF and CPC, these authors add three others: the Canadian Association on Gerontology (CAG) (founded in 1971), the Canadian Institute of Senior Centers (formed in 1977 under its original name, "Senior Centers Organization of Canada"), and the National Advisory Council on Aging (1980). (The last-named of these is in some respects a voluntary organization, being governed by a board of laypeople drawn from across Canada, but also can be considered a governmental agency, being staffed by civil servants, having its headquarters in the edifice that houses the Department of National Health and Welfare, and having its funding entirely derived from the federal treasury.) The Kernaghan-Kuper commentary differs from Bryden's earlier assessment in more than just numbers, however. It attributes to these organizations an enhanced level of political importance, seeing them as not mere subsidiary actors, but as a consequential political force that was exerting an increasing "influence [on] government policies and programs."[17]

A still more recent enumeration of national seniors' organizations, a spring 1989 survey carried out by the National Advisory Council on Aging, confirms, and also expands upon, the enlargement in seniors' advocacy organizations.[18] The survey identifies eight nationally active seniors' organizations: the five listed by Kernaghan and Kuper plus three others: the Canadian Council of Retirees (formed in 1975),[19] the Canadian Association of Retired Persons (CARP)(1985), and One Voice Seniors Network, which is usually referred to simply as "One Voice" (1987).[20] The survey does not seek to measure these groups' level of activity or effectiveness but rather to identify

---

16. Kenneth Kernaghan and Olivia Kuper, *Coordination in Canadian Governments: A Case Study in Aging Policy* (Toronto: Institute of Public Administration of Canada, 1983).

17. Ibid., p. 37. (emphasis added).

18. "List of National Seniors Organizations," derived from unpublished survey of Canadian seniors' organizations conducted by the National Advisory Council on Aging (NACA), March 1989 (available in NACA Office, Brooke Claxton Building, Tunney's Pasture, Ottawa).

19. It is not surprising that the Kernaghan and Kuper 1983 enumeration should have omitted any mention of the Canadian Council of Retirees. This organization is nonincorporated and has no general membership base. Although it has achieved some degree of visibility within the Canadian labor movement—its headquarters is located in the Ontario headquarters of the Canadian Labor Congress—it has but low visibility outside of labor circles. On the other hand, there is every reason to include it in a listing of nationally based age-advocacy organizations. Its secretary-treasurer, William Corns, is a member of the board of One Voice, and Corns visits Ottawa "five or six times a year" to advocate politically on behalf of seniors' issues. William Corns, interview, Toronto, July 1989.

20. This group was federally chartered in 1976, but its real organizational existence dates from 1985. Murray Morgenthau, CARP national president, interview, Toronto, July 1989.

those that are presently active, as well as to gather information on such points as their size and date of founding.

An assessment that does attempt to do just this is offered in one of my own published writings from this same approximate period. My study begins by surveying major federally financed programs in aging and proceeds to analyze them from the standpoint of the political forces that initially brought them into existence. There is no presumption that senior citizen groups were important in any of these governmental actions, although the analysis is open to that as one possibility. The study's major conclusion is that while the shape and content of the federal government's present array of programs on aging probably owes slightly more to the combined weight of senior civil servants than to senior citizen groups, that ascendancy is not very marked. In short, while interest groups must compete with other political actors in seeking to influence the scope and content of political agendas, their influence nevertheless has been (and remains) fairly considerable.[21]

Summing up, three studies appearing in the 1980s lend support to the view that Canada's fourth phase has seen a transformation in the scope and character of organized senior citizen advocacy in Canadian government. In place of the rather simple pattern characteristic of phase three, the more recent period has been marked by rather considerable complexity and diversity. While differing assessments are possible regarding the overall political importance of this increased activity, most observers would probably agree that the new setting has involved an increase in seniors' organizational clout in Ottawa.

Differing Styles, Differing Domains

Unlike their British counterparts, Canada's senior citizen and age-advocacy interest groups have not arranged themselves into coalition clusters. While some coalition behavior, or networking, has occurred, most of the larger interest groups have tended to avoid such ongoing joint efforts. Instead of classifying groups on the basis of ongoing intergroup effort, therefore, a more fruitful approach in the Canadian case is one that arranges these organizations on the basis of organizational form and mode of leadership. Two such modes are presently apparent: the fully staffed, or professionalized, type and the volunteer-led, or amateur.

The Volunteer Style

Four of the eight organizations mentioned previously—the NP&SCF, CPC, Canadian Council of Retirees, and Canadian Institute of Senior Centers—

---

21. Pratt, "Aging Policy and Process in the Canadian Federal Government," p. 75.

display the characteristics associated with the volunteer style of organization. This mode of operations consists of the following elements: (1) primary reliance on volunteers to perform vital organizational functions, (2) a tendency to shift the site of the national headquarters from time to time so as to meet the convenience of the elected officeholders, and (3) solicitation of needed revenues chiefly from members in the form of dues, as opposed to reliance placed on outside patronage or on income derived from various direct member services. In table 1 this model is applied to each of the particular cases.

The volunteer mode finds strong defenders among activists in Canada's senior citizen movement. Such defenders are inclined to view it as beneficial in screening out careerists (persons more interested in the job for its own sake than in achievement of the group's social and political objectives) while at the same time maintaining spontaneity. The point was forcefully expressed to me by an officer of the Canadian Council of Retirees: "[My group] is a voluntary effort, and that should not surprise you considering that volunteerism in Canada is quite prevalent. *I like it that way.* If you get a professional staff, they always want to have it their way. Professionalism is creeping in here in Canada, and that's a bit alarming."[22] Secondly, defenders of the volunteer mode view it as diminishing greatly the potential for the organization to be coopted by government, an ever-present danger when a professionally staffed national office is situated close by the leading federal ministries and departments in Ottawa.

Although the volunteer style does not necessarily diminish a given group's overall capacity for influence, a group of this type is likely to be constrained in its efforts to deal effectively with the civil service, which the Canadian system vests with considerable discretionary authority. Interest group lobbying of the bureaucracy typically requires special abilities, particularly technical competency, policy-analytic capacity, and program sophistication. The bureaucracy does not easily open itself to interventions by groups that are lacking in what one analyst has termed "privileged status,"[23] and such status has yet to be achieved by interest groups of the volunteer type. This may explain, in part, why such groups tend to disregard the bureaucracy and instead concentrate their energies on the achievement of access to elective politicians.

Characteristic of the volunteer style of governmental involvement is the adoption of formal resolutions at annual conventions, and the conveying of these in the form of a brief to Ottawa for prearranged meetings with key federal ministers, and less formally with back-bench members of Parliament.

---

22. William Corns, interview, Toronto, July 1989.
23. Robert Presthus, *Elite Accommodation in Canadian Politics* (Toronto: Macmillan, 1975).

TABLE 1.   Amateur-Style Retiree and Senior Citizen Organizations

Name	Year Founded	Site	Staff Type
		Headquarters	
National Pensioners and Senior Citizens Federation	1945	Toronto	Volunteer and part-time paid
Canadian Pensioners Concerned	1969	Toronto	Volunteer
Canadian Council of Retirees	1977	Toronto	Volunteer
Canadian Institute of Senior Centers	1977	Windsor/Toronto	Volunteer

As revealed by interviews with informants, members of the House of Commons and other politicians typically regard such annual visitations as occasions for improving their feel for grass roots opinion.

Such heavy reliance on the legislative side of government is reflective of volunteer groups' basic character. The incentive systems that sustain them as organizations, while prodding them into identifying areas of policy need and into putting forward legislative remedies, do not in general produce the level of revenues that is necessary for the achievement of full carry through or intimate involvement in the governmental process. Their representatives tend to be distant from the day-to-day functioning of government, and especially so from the federal bureaucracy, whose workings are generally beyond their capacity to influence or even fully to comprehend.

In a slightly different category than either the professionalized or the volunteer-led organizations is CARP. This group obtained its federal charter in 1976 but did not become organizationally active for almost a decade (1985). Making use of an aggressive promotional campaign and a wide array of available member benefits—for example, insurance, travel plans, and discount products—CARP's membership has risen to a 1990 figure of thirty-five thousand. The organization takes its name and basic orientation from the American Association of Retired Persons (AARP), formed in 1958, although relationships between the CARP leadership and AARP have not been especially close or supportive.[24] It seems valid to exclude this organization from further attention in this study, since it does not hold membership meetings, does not adopt stands on public issues, and makes only sporadic efforts to influence the federal government.[25]

---

24. Murray Morgenthau, interview, Toronto, July 1989.
25. *CARP News* (official publication of CARP), September 1991.

The Professional Style

The remaining three groups, CAG, the National Advisory Council on Aging, and the One Voice Seniors Network, display the characteristic features of the professionalized organization. These features include (1) the employment of a full-time paid director, who is recruited on the basis of organizational expertise and experience and is not typically a senior citizen, (2) maintenance of a well-staffed headquarters office, for which the organization alone is responsible and that is shared with no other voluntary organization, (3) location of the national office in Ottawa, if not from the group's very outset, then as soon as resources permit,[26] and (4) member dues, if any, are but one source of organizational revenue (and usually not the most important), with heavy reliance placed upon various forms of external patronage.

The last of these elements, relating to patronage, has been a factor of critical importance in the emergence of professionalized senior citizen organizations in recent years. For example, the One Voice organization has depended, since its inception in January 1987, on funding provided by the Samuel and Saidye Bronfman Family Foundation. The level of Bronfman funding to this organization has been substantial. Likewise, the CAG, a scientific organization devoted to the generation and dissemination of age-related research, depends only 30 percent on the dues provided by members. Instead, its revenues are derived mostly from outside sources: government grants, sale of CAG publications, and surpluses realized out of its annual meetings. The opening in 1979 of the CAG's Winnipeg headquarters was made possible through a $50,000 grant from the J. W. McConnell Foundation of Montreal.[27] In all three of these cases, therefore, the patronage element has been critical in enabling the organization to realize its present scale of operations, including its professionalized aspect.

Professionalism and the New Advocacy Style

The recent wave of Canadian seniors' organizations has brought with it a change in the traditional mode of senior advocacy in Ottawa. Lobbying activity on behalf of seniors in Ottawa has traditionally consisted of two types: firstly, private individuals appointed to serve on government advisory bodies such as the National Council on Welfare and the Canadian Council on Social

---

26. Informal arrangements were worked out for the removal of the CAG headquarters from Winnipeg, where it had been since 1979, to Ottawa, and the decision was formally approved at the organization's fall 1989 annual convention. Norman Blackie, CAG director, interview, Winnipeg, July 1989.

27. Ivan Hale, One Voice, interview, June 1989; Norman Blackie, interview, Winnipeg, July 1989.

Development[28] and, secondly, volunteer activists representing seniors' organizations, especially NP&SCF and CPC. The increased visibility of professionalized interest groups in recent years has to some extent altered this traditional picture, as organizations such as CAG and One Voice have begun to assert themselves politically.

Such groups' Ottawa headquarters locale has facilitated the professional groups' new methods for approaching government. Unlike their volunteer counterparts, the Ottawa representatives of these groups, such as Ivan Hale, the director of One Voice, and Norman Blackie, director of CAG, make it a point to cultivate connections with the federal bureaucracy involved with age-related social concerns. Such contacts tend to promote common public policy outlooks and shared definitions of senior citizen needs and concerns.

Case Study of Volunteer-Style Political Action

One can obtain a clearer sense of the difference between the professionalized and the volunteer modes of political action by devoting attention to a recent controversy in Ottawa whose high-stakes outcome had major senior citizen implications. The case involved mostly organizations of the volunteer type, with a heavy emphasis on elective officeholders and a related capacity to function effectively in that setting.

No other issue of the 1970s and 1980s surpassed the intensity of controversy that erupted in the wake of the government's 1985 proposal partially to deindex the federal OAS pension. Pierre Elliott Trudeau had been out of office only a few months at the time, having yielded the office of prime minister a short time prior to the 1984 Canadian elections. The election itself produced a massive Conservative victory, under the direction of the party's leader, Brian Mulroney. This large parliamentary majority provided little by way of cover or protection, however, when late in May 1985, Michael Wilson, newly installed minister of finance in the Mulroney cabinet, tabled his first budget in the House of Commons. Reflecting on the nation's economic vicissitudes, including a soaring federal deficit and official anxiety over Ottawa's capacity to meet its expenses, Wilson announced the government's intention to alter the indexing formula under OAS in such manner that pension benefits would no longer be fully protected against inflation. Henceforth, in response to any increases in the price level, OAS benefits would be raised only up to a set maximum, with pensioners themselves expected to absorb any additional cost-of-living increases.

Recognizing that the Wilson-Mulroney policy, if allowed to stand, would

---

28. For a brief discussion of these organizations' role in age-related matters see Pratt, "Aging Policy and Process in the Canadian Federal Government," pp. 69–70 and 72.

represent an important shift in pension policy, opposition forces in the House of Commons in Ottawa were quick to react. The leaders of both the Liberal party, John Turner, and the New Democratic party, Ed Broadbent, soon voiced impassioned opposition, and deindexation now became headline news in the print media as well as on radio and television. Canada's television networks were particularly important in shaping the political setting as the controversy played itself out. As an NP&SCF leader later remarked to me in an interview, "We have to give real appreciation to the [television] media because they kept heat on; if they hadn't kept the issue right up front, we might have lost the support of the people."[29] Television reporters sought out and interviewed senior citizen leaders in cities across Canada, thereby indirectly helping to mobilize opposition to what the finance minister had proposed.

Two weeks went by, but still the Conservative government remained steadfast in its resolve, refusing to back down in the face of a mounting chorus of criticism and abuse. At this juncture, Liberal and New Democratic party spokespersons fanned out across the country aiming to arouse grass roots support for their cause.[30] It is likely, however, that the Mulroney government had already anticipated such partisan political protest but largely discounted its fervor.

Not so predictable or so easily discounted, however, was the fierce opposition that began to be heard from Canada's senior citizens and from their younger-aged sympathizers. Orchestrating that sentiment, while at the same time adding to it, was a broad array of established interest groups. Some of these, such as the Canadian Chamber of Commerce and the Business Council on National Issues, spoke for constituencies not normally inclined toward support of high social welfare expenditures. Two others, namely the Canadian Council on Social Development and the National Advisory Council on Aging, were both dependent on patronage from Ottawa (the former group partly so, the latter entirely) and yet became fully involved in the cause. Obviously, this was a situation in which the usual political logic no longer fully applied.

Among all the interest groups that spoke out on the issue, none was more vocal or more aroused than the NP&SCF. Acting in concert with its provincial affiliates across the country, especially the three hundred thousand-strong United Senior Citizens of Ontario, this group lost no time in issuing a statement condemning the deindexation scheme and making clear its intent to mobilize a national protest. When the early efforts in this vein failed to elicit a response from Ottawa, the organization intensified its drive, making clear its willingness to participate in a Toronto rally called by the Ontario Senior Citizens Coordinating Council.

---

29. Les Batterson, president, NP&SCF, interview, July 1989.
30. *Toronto Star*, June 6, 1985, p. A4; June 16, 1985, p. A6.

When this Toronto gathering took place, twenty-six interest groups were represented, most prominently the NP&SCF, but also numerous others—for example, the Ontario division of the CPC. The delegates voted to approve a resolution of protest, and a delegation was charged with seeing to it that it was properly conveyed to Ottawa. In response to a request from this delegation to meet with the finance minister, Michael Wilson signaled his acceptance, but only on condition that the meeting not be made public and that the press be excluded. These terms were agreed to, and the meeting ended up lasting longer than expected, two hours, suggestive that the minister now was in a mood to listen. At the same time, NP&SCF arranged for bus loads of seniors to journey from Toronto to Ottawa to voice their protest.[31] In addition, other senior citizen groups, especially the Federation de l'Age d'Or du Quebec (FADOQ) (Golden Age Association of Quebec), Seniors' Action Now of Saskatchewan, and CPC, issued statements and took steps needed to ensure their being properly publicized and received in Ottawa.

Mass protest demonstrations began to occur in the national capital, and these were not always of an orderly, deferential character. At one point a group of placard-carrying old age pensioners brought the prime minister's limousine to a halt, whereupon one elderly woman, identified as a constituent in the prime minister's own riding (parliamentary district), taunted him, declaring, "You made promises that you wouldn't touch anything, You lied to us!"[32] The television cameras, hungry for telegenic events, found such incidents irresistible.

No prudent government could long afford to resist such an outpouring of mass protest, and in the end the prime minister and his cabinet accepted the inevitable and backed down. On June 26, two days subsequent to the meeting with pension group leaders, Wilson announced in the House his government's decision to withdraw the deindexation proposal. Several hours later, the prime minister held a press conference during which he apologized to Canada's elderly for having put the proposal forward in the first place.

Columnists in certain of Canada's newspapers sensed in this incident something unique in the long history of Canadian pension politics. For example, a column in the *Toronto Star*, published at a time when the controversy still raged, spoke of the "coming of age of gray power in Canada" and stressed the upsurge in "political sophistication" on the part of NP&SCF.[33]

The deindexation episode is suggestive of certain essential characteristics of the NP&SCF, Canada's prototypical volunteer seniors' organization.

31. *Toronto Star*, June 22, 1985, pp. A1 and A10. Also, Les Batterson, interview, July 1989.
32. *Toronto Star*, June 20, 1985, p. A1.
33. Val Sears, "Gray Power: Coming of Age," *Toronto Star*, June 15, 1985, p. B1.

Firstly, the incident serves to emphasize the pronounced linkage between the organization's lobbying priorities and its policy preferences as embodied in convention-adopted resolutions and policy statements. A review of the organization's *Annual Convention Report* in a typical year, 1988, reveals a strong emphasis on the concerns of elderly persons in modest circumstances, the elderly poor included.[34] Thus, the 1988 report underscores the need to maintain the purchasing power of the OAS pension, to guarantee elderly persons' health benefits, to ensure that taxes laid upon the low-income elderly do not pose an unreasonable burden, and to ensure that government provides state-assisted housing at affordable rates. Given such an orientation, it is clear that the deindexation issue fitted nicely into this group's enduring public policy concerns and priorities. Secondly, the incident illustrates the dependency of the national leadership of NP&SCF on the organization's affiliated provincial federations, another indication of the importance of provincial government in the Canadian governmental system and the value for a national organization in having a solid base of support at that level. Thirdly, and perhaps most importantly, the NP&SCF was in a position to adopt a stand that went directly against a policy position of the Mulroney government, notwithstanding the fact that seniors in large number had voted for the Progressive Conservatives in the recent federal election. Clearly, NP&SCF on this occasion demonstrated a capacity successfully to oppose a recently elected and still-popular government in office. In short, the federation on this occasion demonstrated its ability to mount a political effort of singular scope and intensity, pulling together and orchestrating what otherwise could have been but scattered opposition to the proposal.

Turf Wars

The mushroom growth of Canadian pensioner and senior citizen organizations during the 1970s and 1980s, including both professionalized and volunteer-led groups, was associated with considerable rivalry and disagreement over turf. Although sharing a common outlook on most public policy issues, these interest groups were also driven by their maintenance needs to emphasize their distinctiveness within the larger picture. A leading observer, C. G. Gifford, has pointed with concern to the variance in public statements and opinions that has resulted from such diversity. "Creating a united voice to represent all interests is a challenge for the movement in the 1990s," Gifford writes, and he goes on to lament the absence of "any ongoing universal coalition in Canada, like the Leadership Council of Aging Organizations in

---

34. NP&SCF, *Annual Convention Report*, for the convention held at Niagara Falls, Ontario, September 1988 (Toronto: NP&SCF, 1988).

the U.S."[35] While one should be cautious regarding any assumption that the council, or any other organization, has succeeded in creating unity of senior-group expression in the United States, there is little question that the absence of any such body in Canada exacerbates the potential for embarrassing inter-group disagreement and friction.

Canadian interest group competition in aging can be dated from at least as far back as the early 1970s, when a cleavage opened up between Canada's established seniors' organization, the NP&SCF, and an upstart group, CPC. At this early period, the CPC was highly expansive, its leaders committed to mounting a challenge to the legitimacy and support base of its more-established rival. The CPC's effort to create affiliate organizations in all ten provinces was viewed by NP&SCF leaders with alarm, as involving a direct threat to its status as a nationally based seniors' organization.

While intense for several months, however, this particular rivalry was to prove short-lived. CPC survives to the present writing, but not on the grand scale envisioned by its early leaders. It presently has provincial affiliates in but three of Canada's ten provinces, namely Nova Scotia, Ontario, and Alberta, and even there has managed to define areas of concern that do not substantially overlap those of the provincial federations affiliated with NP&SCF; the two national organizations have developed a fairly clear demarcation of roles, thereby in large part dissipating their earlier competitiveness.[36]

A second interorganizational cleavage, dating from approximately this same period but more enduring over time, has separated the NP&SCF from the largest francophone seniors' group, namely the two hundred thousand-member Golden Age Federation of Quebec (Federation de l'Age d'Or du Quebec, commonly referred to by its acronym, FADOQ). FADOQ lays no claim to a national base of support, instead asserting its provincial identity. While eligible for membership in NP&SCF as a provincial affiliate, it has consistently refused such affiliation since its beginnings in 1970. From the standpoint of NP&SCF such refusals constitute an obvious embarrassment, considering the national group's absence of a genuine Quebec support base, and the fact that francophones comprise roughly 25 percent of Canada's senior citizen population. FADOQ did cooperate with NP&SCF and other groups in the 1985 crisis, but it remains the case that Canada's senior citizen movement is bisected along ethnic and linguistic lines, in much the same manner as is Canada as a whole.

Although obviously troubling, these cleavages do not directly threaten the unity of Canada's politically aware seniors' activists, the bulk of them

---

35. C. G. Gifford, *Canada's Fighting Seniors* (Toronto: James Lorimer, 1990), p. 253.
36. Doreen Fraser, CPC national president, interview, Halifax, July 1989.

anglophone. Of more serious concern has been the recent rift opened within the anglophone community. Its origins and present manifestations are clearly of importance and therefore bear close attention.

For a number of years Canada's Samuel and Saidye Bronfman Family Foundation has been known for its special interest in the problems and concerns of elderly persons. Although not the largest of the nation's private foundations—it actually ranks tenth in terms of both resources and grants given out—Bronfman's $50 million in 1988 assets still makes it a substantial presence in the general field of Canadian philanthropy.[37] Interested observers have realized for some time that if the foundation were to direct a large share of its available resources toward the funding of a senior citizens organization, the consequences could prove quite significant.

The foundation deliberated for some time before deciding on this significant matter. Out of a sense that it should more fully inform itself regarding the real-life circumstances of Canada's elderly, the foundation in 1984 dispatched two of its officials—one of them Ivan Hale, who was to figure prominently in later developments—to undertake a cross-national fact-finding tour. All ten of the provinces, in addition to the two territories, would be included. During its journey, the team was everywhere warmly received, and its attention was repeatedly called to various senior-related needs that purportedly were being met neither by the federal or provincial governments nor by the NP&SCF or the other established seniors' organizations. These needs included, particularly, the allegedly unmet challenges in the areas of transportation, adult literacy, and social exclusion of the elderly. In the course of this tour, and also later in phone conversations and in follow-up regional meetings held in various cities, the possibility was explored of Bronfman foundation funding to assist in the establishment of a new voluntary organization—one structured more along caucus lines than general membership. It was further proposed that such an interest group, in undertaking political action, should favor a low-key, nonconfrontational approach, in contrast to what some considered as the highly assertive, even abrasive, style of NP&SCF. Finally, strong emphasis was placed on the need for such a group to reach out to other age-advocacy organizations, including some, like the Canadian Legion, that are not formally age based but whose memberships are now predominantly senior citizen. Indicative of the strong emphasis to be placed on this coalition function was the name suggested for the new group, "One Voice Seniors Network."

Although the Bronfman foundation leaders displayed interest in these discussions, they kept the matter under advisement for some months while

---

37. *Canadian Directory of Foundations* (Toronto: Canadian Center for Philanthropy, 1989).

making no formal commitments. During this time, the foundation was approached by a delegation representing NP&SCF. "When Charlie McDonald [the then NP&SCF president] and I heard that the Bronfman foundation was first thinking about this," the current president, Les Batterson, told me in an interview, "we arranged to have a meeting with Ivan Hale and the foundation's director to discuss the problem of [their] deciding to set up another organization that didn't have any representation from seniors. [We proposed that] they should fund our group instead. But they rejected that. I don't know why."[38]

McDonald, Batterson, and others within NP&SCF were keenly disappointed at the foundation's eventual decision to direct its support elsewhere. Their reaction was more than a simple matter of money, given their aim to alter certain of their organization's traditional features. These reform-minded leaders were engaged in an effort to recast their group along more professionalized lines, and achieving that would require significant external funding. As Batterson told me later in our interview, NP&SCF might become more effective politically if it had the resources needed both to maintain a properly staffed Ottawa office and to allow its national executive to assemble and decide policy on a fairly frequent basis, as opposed to just twice annually as has long been the case.

Already at the time of the meeting with the Bronfman people, Batterson was seeking, despite considerable internal opposition, to correct what he saw as NP&SCF's chronic lack of funds. With the approval of then president Charlie McDonald, he submitted a proposal to redraft the federation's constitution so as to provide for a per capita dues structure. This would make the federation in his words "more like a labor union" and would require that the constituent provincial federations should contribute dues proportionate to their memberships. Such income would serve to supplement the fairly modest dues revenue already obtained from the organization's roughly five thousand directly contributing individual members. Although this proposal was debated on the convention floor, the per capita dues scheme was, to Batterson's dismay, voted down. Secondly, around this same time Batterson and others were instrumental in having the NP&SCF's board approve a request to the federal government for the organization to be granted charitable status under a provision in the Canadian tax code making donations to approved charitable organizations tax deductible. Such charitable designation was considered essential if NP&SCF was to attract significant funding from Canada's private sector. Again, however, this initiative resulted in disappointment for Batterson and his allies. The federal ministry responsible for deciding on charitable status twice turned down the requests from this source for such designation, the first time toward the end of the Trudeau era in 1984 and the second at the begin-

---

38. Les Batterson, interview, July 1989.

ning of the Mulroney government the following year. The justification given for the decision was that the organization was ineligible for such classification by virtue of its extensive lobbying role and campaigning on issues considered politically controversial. The negative ruling from Ottawa was all the more difficult for NP&SCF to accept, given that certain other age-advocacy organizations, One Voice included, were successful in achieving charitable status designation.

Conceivably, NP&SCF might have responded to the emergence of One Voice with equanimity, viewing it as a welcome asset to Canada's seniors' movement, and not a rival. Such an attitude on its part was never very likely, yet this has not prevented One Voice from actively promoting its seniors' network concept. And at least two of the preexisting national aging groups have responded by joining in the network, having come to regard One Voice not as a competitor but as an ally. Thus, the president of One Voice at the close of the 1980s, Jeanne Woodsworth, served simultaneously as president of the Ontario division of CPC; likewise, William Corns at this same time was both the secretary-treasurer of the Canadian Council of Retirees and an active One Voice board member. Similar close involvement on the part of NP&SCF was never a possibility given its traditional claim, stretching back for many years, to be the chief representative of Canada's senior citizen and retiree population.

The unease on the part of NP&SCF has clearly been augmented by One Voice's meteoric rise, leaving little time for the older organization to accommodate itself to the changed situation. The Bronfman foundation decision to fund One Voice, at a level sufficient to guarantee it a successful launching, was rendered in 1986, and the new organization opened its Ottawa headquarters in January of the following year. Thus, the new group sprang into existence, fully fledged, in a matter of a few months. Its headquarters accommodations were on a scale that far surpassed those of other interest groups in Canada's age-politics arena and included an office suite situated on an upper floor of a modern high-rise building, directly in sight of Parliament Hill and the principal ministries of government.

In financial terms, the Bronfman foundation's action in providing funding to this fledgling organization was unprecedented in Canadian pension group history. The One Voice financial statement for 1988 listed contributions from this source at roughly $200,000, which, coupled with the earlier subventions from the same source, placed the foundation's total contribution at well above $500,000—a substantial figure by Canadian lobby group standards. Moreover, the published figures do not include the national director's salary, which in the late 1980s the foundation continued to pay. Even assuming, moreover, that Bronfman foundation subsidies were one day to be terminated, a by no means remote contingency, the organization would still be well positioned to obtain patronage from other governmental and nongovernmental sources, given that it has been granted a charitable status designation by the federal government.

Conclusion

Canada's fourth phase of public pension development was ushered in by a series of fairly dramatic public policy changes. These included, firstly, a series of age-related enactments by the federal government and, secondly, substantial enlargements in the level of pension benefits. The effect of these developments was indirectly to raise the relative visibility and perceived importance of age benefits. Furthermore, the events of 1985 evidently produced considerable public anxiety lest the existing benefits be substantially scaled back. These developments, augmented by New Horizons grants, facilitated the process of seniors' coalescence, thereby augmenting the strength of provincial seniors' federations as well as national organizations. As the public policy changes were more widely felt, seniors' organizations of both the amateur/voluntary and the professional/caucus varieties were enabled to enlarge their levels of visibility and perceived importance. Indeed, by the end of the 1980s this proliferation of interest groups was being viewed by disinterested observers as something of a problem, given the numbers of groups presently active and their potential for overlap.

One should be wary of overgeneralizing or exaggerating the significance of incentives arising directly or indirectly from government, since the formation of seniors' clubs and other forms of organized age advocacy would probably have occurred to some extent in any case, given population aging and an increasingly self-conscious retiree community. The shared desire among seniors for group activity and companionship, and for fuller participation in the life of the wider society, would have been sufficient in themselves to produce some movement along these lines. Nevertheless, absent the increased governmental presence, such a development most probably would have been on a much smaller scale and been far less productive.

CHAPTER 9

Phase Four in the United States

In a wider international perspective the United States emerges as, perhaps, the most dramatic example of the transition from phase three to phase four of pension policy, so substantial have been its recent increases in aging expenditures and related expansions in individual benefit levels. In 1987 entitlement and other mandated federal programs represented the largest single category of U.S. government outlay (44 percent). In the period leading up to 1987, moreover, entitlements were the most important contributor to the overall enlargement in federal outlays, with spending in this area rising almost $300 billion since 1970, and by over $460 billion since 1962. This category of spending is one of four employed by analysts to describe federal outlays, and among these its rate of growth has been exceeded only by that of interest on the national debt, and the latter, it should be noted, was from a smaller base. Thus, the rate of change in entitlement spending has far exceeded that for either of the other two categories, namely "nondefense discretionary" and "national defense."

The elderly loom large in the overall context of entitlement spending. Seventy percent of outlays in the category "entitlement and other mandatory spending" are for programs that chiefly benefit older Americans: Social Security, Medicare, military and civil service pensions, and a number of smaller programs. (The remainder of entitlement spending consists in roughly equal parts of non–means-tested programs—chiefly agricultural price supports and unemployment insurance—and means-tested, chiefly Medicaid and food stamps, both of which partly benefit the elderly.) By the late 1980s Social Security had come to represent 30 percent of all federal outlays, and a 1987 study by the Congressional Budget Office predicted that this proportion would reach 36 percent by the middle 1990s, assuming that no policy changes intervened to arrest the trend.[1]

Entitlements during the fourth phase have not only become large as a share of total federal outlays but also significant in the context of the entire U.S. economy. Federal outlays in a particular field are usefully expressed as a

---

1. Statement of Nancy M. Gordon (assistant director of the Congressional Budget Office) in U.S. Congress, House, Committee on the Budget, *Hearings before the Task Force on Income Security*, 100th Cong., 1st sess., 1987, pp. 121–23.

percentage of gross national product, and such percentages therefore can serve as an index to society's commitment to the particular field in question. Federal entitlement spending as a percent of gross national product changed but little in the 1950s and 1960s, remaining within the narrow range of between 5 and 6-plus percent; likewise, during these same two decades elderly-targeted programs remained fixed in the defined range of between 1 and 2-plus percent.[2] In the period to follow, however, the picture altered. During the 1970s and early 1980s "entitlement and other mandatory spending" soared from a 1970 level of just over six percent of gross national product to 10-plus percent in 1986, and in the recession year of 1982 it reached 12 percent. For all elderly-targeted programs, the rate of growth was more marked still, rising from 2-plus percent in 1970 to 7 percent of gross national product sixteen years later. Among the other large objects of federal expenditure, only interest on the federal debt claimed a similarly high rate of increase—from 1-plus to around 3 percent. (Spending on national defense and nondefense discretionary programs both declined in relative terms—the former rather sharply from 10 down to 6-plus percent, the latter more marginally.)[3] By the 1980s, therefore, Social Security and Medicare, and to a lesser extent all federal entitlements, came to be regarded as a major fiscal challenge, both in the narrow context of the federal budgeting process and in a larger macroeconomic context.

Having in mind these fiscal realities, policy analysts by the middle 1970s began to question whether the decidedly pro-aging thrust of recent government decision making could long continue, especially in light of other urgent priorities. As early as 1978, one observer, Robert B. Hudson, anticipated an early redirection in federal spending priorities, with its effects to be felt in the "severe limits" that might soon be imposed on "the ability of government to embark on new [elderly-related] initiatives."[4] For the first time one heard discussion in Washington concerning the possible reduction in Social Security benefits as a means of ensuring that the elderly would assume a more proportionate share of the fiscal burden.

Factors in the Large Outlays

The increases in federal outlays in the field of aging reflected several considerations. One factor was demographic, namely the aging of the population and resulting expansion in the number of Americans made eligible for benefits

---

2. Calculations based on figures reported in Bureau of the Census, *Historical Statistics of the United States: Colonial Times to 1970* (Washington, D.C.: Government Printing Office, 1975).

3. U.S. Congress, *Hearings before the Task Force on Income Security*, fig. 3, p. 124.

4. Robert B. Hudson, "The 'Graying' of the Federal Budget and Its Consequences for Old-Age Policy," *Gerontologist* 18, no. 5 (October 1978): 435 (article reprinted in Robert B. Hudson,

under various age-targeted programs. As pointed out in a previous chapter, the U.S. population aged sixty-five and above has increased steadily in recent years, reaching well over 11 percent of the national total by the 1980s. Given the country's longstanding commitment to maintaining the integrity of Social Security (i.e., Old Age, Survivors and Disability Insurance [OASDI]), population aging on this scale inevitably had major implications for overall age-related federal outlays.

But more than simply population aging was driving the change. Writing in 1981,[5] two economists, Robert L. Clark at North Carolina State University and John A. Menefree at the Social Security Administration (SSA), undertook to account for the Social Security benefit increases of the recent past, and to predict the likely trend of future benefit changes. Their analysis disaggregates elderly-related spending increases into three categories: qualitative improvements stemming from deliberate policy choice, inflation, and growth of the aged population (i.e., population aging). These authors' overall conclusion is that the rise in federal spending in this field had occurred chiefly from deliberate choice, particularly by lawmakers in Congress who voted the liberalizations into existence. Without discounting population aging and inflation as contributory factors, they are of secondary importance; instead, "much of the past graying of the federal budget has occurred due to explicit policy changes by the federal government."[6]

The federal expenditure increases translated directly into enlarged individual benefits, as is apparent in the following inflation-adjusted figures on OASDI dating back to 1955.

Average Monthly OASDI Benefits, by Year, in Constant 1982–84 Dollars

1955	$231
1960	276
1965	266
1970	299
1975	385
1980	414
1985	446
1987	451

---

ed., *The Aging in Politics: Process and Policy* [Springfield, Ill.: Charles C. Thomas, 1981], pp. 261–80).

5. Robert L. Clark and John A. Menefree, "Federal Expenditures for the Elderly, Past and Future," *Gerontologist* 21 (1981): 132–37; see also Ken Judge, "Federal Expenditures for the Elderly: A Different Interpretation of the Past," *Gerontologist* 22, no. 2 (1982): 129–31, and "Reply" by Robert L. Clark, *Gerontologist* 22, no. 2 (1982): 131–33.

6. Clark and Menefree, "Federal Expenditures for the Elderly," p. 135.

Obviously, the increase in OASDI benefits began well before the commence-ment of phase four, but their rate of increase did not diminish once that period began.

Various analysts have probed the political dynamics involved in this large commitment of government resources, and the prevailing consensus is that it was largely a reflection of an increased congressional awareness of elderly voters as an electoral constituency. Hudson reports, for example, a pervasive belief on Capitol Hill that the elderly are uniquely "deserving" (i.e., legiti-mate) and also uniquely "useful" (i.e., capable of serving as the core constitu-ency around which other interest groups can rally in pursuit of their own political agendas).[7]

Impacts of Policy Change on the Elderly

While the findings of pension policy analysts are suggestive, they are insuffi-cient to convey fully the impacts of the spending increases on elderly people. The impacts have come in several forms. In the first place, there has been a dramatic reduction in the extent of old age poverty. In the 1950s the federal government had not yet established its official definition of "poverty," but later estimates, done retrospectively for that period, have placed the rate for persons aged sixty-five and above at about 35 percent.[8] That figure markedly contrasts with the poverty rate for the same age grouping in the 1980s. By then, as a consequence of an increase in inflation-adjusted Social Security outlays from roughly $50 billion at the end of the 1950s to $200 billion in the late 1980s, the proportion of poverty-stricken elderly persons had declined to a mere 12.4 percent—slightly below that for the nonelderly U.S. population.[9] SSA data further reveal that in the absence of Social Security benefits, the poverty rate among all elderly persons would have been 50 percent in the late 1980s, and that among elderly blacks, instead of an actual rate of 33 percent, the rate would have been 70 percent. Moreover, as of 1986 Social Security represented the major source of income (i.e., 50 percent or above) for two-thirds (62 percent) of all those in receipt of such benefits.[10]

A second impact concerns average household incomes. For the U.S.

7. Hudson, "'Graying' of the Federal Budget and Its Consequences for Old-Age Policy," pp. 428–30.

8. Budgetary Review of Income Security Programs (testimony of Nancy M. Gordon, Congressional Budget Office), in U.S. Congress, *Hearings before the Task Force on Income Security*, p. 5.

9. Ibid.

10. U.S. Department of Health and Human Services, *Income and Resources of the Popula-tion 65 and Over* (Washington D.C.: Department of Health and Human Services, September 1986), p. 10. It should be pointed out, however, that while the elderly have experienced a dramatic decline in their rate of poverty in recent years, many of them are still not especially well-

population as a whole, household incomes did not change in real terms between 1970 and 1986; the figure for both years was approximately $25,500 in constant 1982–84 dollars. Yet, among households that were senior citizen headed, these years saw a rise in incomes of more than 20 percent, from just under $14,000 to almost $17,000.[11]

Thirdly, the heavy federal outlays for Social Security, Medicare, and other age-targeted federal programs contributed to an enhanced propensity among seniors to choose retirement as opposed to remaining actively employed. Whereas in 1960 25 percent of Americans over sixty-five were still employed full time, by 1980 this figure had dropped to just 15 percent.[12] Admittedly, factors other than simply government policy contributed to this trend, including technological change and the actions of business firms, labor unions, and other employers. Yet, if changes in government policy did not represent the total picture, they were nevertheless fundamental.

A final impact of federal policy change is its strongly stimulative effect on the nation's private pension system. Two federal enactments stand out in this connection: the Self-Employed Individuals Tax Retirement Act, the Keogh Act of 1962, and the Employment Retirement Income Security Act of 1974. The former of these provided tax incentives for individuals to establish individual retirement accounts, whereas the latter regulated corporate pension schemes so as to ensure that retirees would in fact receive the pension benefits to which their work experience entitled them. (The Employment Retirement Income Security Act also defined certain other worker rights, relating to such matters as pension vesting and portability.)[13] These congressional enactments were a factor in the doubling of income from private pensions as a proportion of all retiree income, from 3 percent in 1962 to 6 percent in 1984.[14] The acts contributed to the increasing scale of pension fund assets, whose combined real value rose from $389 billion in 1970 to $1,403 billion in 1987. Affected in the same way were individual retirement accounts, whose real value, over the period 1981–87, rose nearly tenfold, namely from $31.2 billion to 309.5 billion.[15]

---

off. Elderly people, to a greater extent than the nonelderly population, tend to cluster around the poverty level and just above it. (See U.S. Congress, *Hearings before the Task Force on Income Security*, p. 6.)

11. U.S. Bureau of the Census, *1989* (Washington, D.C.: Government Printing Office, 1989), *Statistical Abstract of the United States*, table 712, p. 440 and table 716, p. 443. The Bureau of the Census does not report on household incomes for the sixty-five-plus population for the pre-1970 period.

12. John E. Schwartz, *America's Hidden Success: A Reassessment of Twenty Years of Public Policy* (New York: W. W. Norton, 1983), p. 128.

13. Ibid., p. 3; U.S. Congress, *Hearings before the Task Force on Income Security*, p. 5.

14. *Income and Resources of the Population 65 and Over*, p. 3.

15. Calculations based on U.S. Bureau of the Census, *Statistical Abstract of the United States, 1990* (Washington, D.C.: Government Printing Office, 1990).

In summary, the actions of the federal government impacted the nation's elderly population in a variety of ways. Among the direct impacts was the reduction in poverty levels among the elderly, the significant rise in disposable household income, the increasing preference for retirement among the over-sixty-five age group, and the expansion in the share of personal income represented by private pensions. More indirectly, the government helped to augment the tendency for persons who are old on a chronological basis to identify themselves in those terms, accepting such labels as "senior citizen" and "retiree," and thereby enlarging the pool of citizens who are potentially receptive to membership appeals from senior citizen and retiree organizations.

Transition from Phase Three to Phase Four

While the shift in U.S. aging policy was evolutionary, encompassing a period of twenty years and more, one still can offer a fairly precise date for the transition from the U.S. phase three to phase four. A strong case can be made that it occurred between late 1971 and early 1973. The basis for this is as follows: (1) the increase at this time in the visibility and public acceptance of the nation's aging agenda, (2) a series of important legislative changes occurring on Capitol Hill; and (3) a shift in the character of the nation's gray lobby. Each of these developments merits brief attention.

Increased Age Visibility and the 1971 White House Conference

No event of recent times was of greater immediate or long-term significance than was the November 1971 White House Conference on Aging. Although similar in some respects to the earlier-held White House Conference on Aging of 1961 and also to the President's Conference on Aging of 1950, this conference was unique in terms of its impact on subsequent federal legislation and in the legitimacy it helped confer on the nation's gray lobby.[16] Speaking from the perspective of one whose career in old age advocacy spanned more than twenty years, Peter Hughes, the longtime government relations director at the American Association of Retired Persons (AARP), remarked to me in an interview in 1989 that the 1971 White House conference was "the real turning point . . . the obvious milestone," marking the transition from an earlier

---

16. Henry J. Pratt, *The Gray Lobby* (Chicago: University of Chicago Press, 1976), pp. 140–44, 149–53; Henry J. Pratt, "Symbolic Politics and White House Conferences on Aging," *Society* 15, no. 5 (July-August 1978): 67–72; Dale Vinyard, "White House Conferences and the Aged," *Social Service Review* 53 (December 1979): 655–71; Andrew W. Dobelstein, *Serving Older Adults: Policy, Programs and Professional Activities* (Englewood Cliffs, N.J.: Prentice-Hall, 1985), pp. 81–82.

period of fairly circumscribed policy making in aging—of concern to only a handful of policy specialists—to the subsequent era, which saw an "explosion" of Capitol Hill interest in this field.[17] Hughes's assessment lends support to my own previously published analysis of this same period. Writing in 1976, I point out that in the wake of the 1971 White House conference, and partly in response to conference-adopted resolutions, Congress in June of the following year adopted H.R. 15390, which involved dramatic and fundamental changes in the Social Security system: raising the Social Security tax and wage base, authorizing an automatic cost-of-living adjustment, and providing an across-the-board 20 percent benefit increase—the largest single-time increase ever.[18] Taking these Social Security amendments into account, and also certain other measures adopted in the same year, the Senate Special Committee on Aging later concluded that older Americans could look back on the year 1972 "as ranking only behind 1935, when Social Security was enacted, and 1965, when Medicare became law."[19]

Another key congressional enactment, and likewise related in part to a strongly worded 1971 White House Conference on Aging resolution, was the 1973 Older Americans Act amendments. This legislation devolved upon the Administration on Aging (AOA) substantial new authority, especially the mandate for it to oversee the establishment across the United States of local-level Area Agencies on Aging (AAAs). These would operate within defined planning and service areas and oversee a broad range of social services but would not themselves directly provide such services. Congress at the same time appropriated funding to enable the expansion of areawide planning in aging. Although the AOA had been led very ably by its first director, William Bechill, who served in this post from 1965 to 1969 and had successfully steered the agency through an often hostile political environment, the agency up to this point had achieved little in the way of bureaucratic power or autonomy. The 1973 amendments conferred upon the agency an enhanced measure of authority and stature, and this in turn facilitated AOA's forging a strategic alliance with a politically influential source of external support, the Association of Area Agencies on Aging (N4A). (The latter organization had been formed in 1975, and given that it was and is entirely composed of local public officials, it soon came to be looked upon as a force to be reckoned with in the field of elderly-targeted social services.) This federal agency and interest group coalition soon proved itself effective, especially in its successful promotion of "legislation that would preserve and strengthen the AAA

17. Peter Hughes, interview, McClean, Va., August 1989.

18. Pratt, *Gray Lobby*, chaps. 9 and 10 and especially p. 154.

19. U.S. Congress, Senate, Special Committee on the Aging, *Developments in Aging 1972 and January-March 1973*, 93d Cong., 1st sess., 1973, p. ix.

structure under Title III of the Older Americans Act."[20] Even though the AOA since its inception had never lacked for some measure of political and bureaucratic influence, its importance was now significantly augmented.

The question may be raised as to why the period 1971–73 has been selected to define the transition into phase four, and not 1965, the year in which Congress enacted three pieces of breakthrough legislation on aging: Medicare (added to the Social Security system as Title XVIII), Medicaid, and the Older Americans Act. (The last of these authorized the establishment of the AOA.) While a case could be made in favor of this earlier date, several considerations militate against it. Although Medicare, Medicaid, and the Older Americans Act were all obviously important in symbolic terms, their tangible impacts for several years were fairly limited—a fact attributable to their meager funding levels and the limited staffing authorized for their respective administrative agencies. In contrast, the enactments of 1972–73 resulted fairly quickly in large new outlays, and these in turn produced, and were perceived as producing, some immediate policy impacts.[21]

Increase in Age-Organization Numbers

It is now appropriate to consider the apparent impacts of pension policy changes from the standpoint of political interest groups, beginning with the quantitative aspect before moving on to the qualitative. The 1970s and 1980s witnessed at least two important changes in the array of age-advocacy organizations in Washington. Firstly, a considerable number of such groups were now formed. Their focus, for the most part, was not so much on aging but on some particular aspect of that field that allegedly was being ignored, or insufficiently addressed, by existing voluntary organizations. While some question can be raised regarding the extent of these newly formed organizations' level of influence, their wide diversity is undeniable. In purely numerical terms, the organizational wave occurring in the 1970s and 1980s was extraordinary, its scale probably

---

20. Dobelstein, *Serving Older Adults*, pp. 79–80.

21. Although this discussion primarily stresses the transforming effect of federal policy change, it is worthwhile taking note of other developments that contributed to the more favorable atmosphere for senior citizen and retiree organizing efforts in these years. For example, the 1970s and 1980s saw the perfection of new member-recruitment technologies, especially direct mail, which have greatly facilitated the targeting of particular groups in the general population. Direct mail appeals give national organizations the option of directly appealing for a large mass membership while bypassing any need for local organization. These technologies have been fundamental in the emergence of at least two of the presently active seniors' organizations. Another development has been that of the plethora of organizations, both public and private, that collectively comprise the so-called aging enterprise. While this development is traceable in part to changes in federal policy, it also has other roots. See Carroll L. Estes, *The Aging Enterprise* (San Francisco: Jossey-Bass, 1979).

TABLE 2. Constituent Organizations of the Leadership Council of Aging Organizations, by Year of Founding

Founding Decade	Organization
1920s	National Association of Retired Federal Employees (1921)
1940s	Social Security Department/AFL-CIO (1942)
	Gerontological Society of America (1945)
1950s	National Council on the Aging (1950)
	Western Gerontological Society (1954)
	Retired Workers Department, United Auto Workers (1957)
	American Association of Retired Persons (1958)
1960s	American Association of Homes for the Aging (1961)
	National Council of Senior Citizens (1961)
	National Association of State Units on Aging (1964)
1970s to May 1982	Concerned Seniors for Better Government (1970)
	National Caucus and Center on the Black Aged (1970)
	Gray Panthers (1970)
	National Indian Council on Aging (1972)
	National Interfaith Coalition on Aging (1972)
	Urban Elderly Coalition (1972)
	National Senior Citizens Law Center (1972)
	National Association of Meal Programs (1973)
	Association for Gerontology in Higher Education (1974)
	Associacion Pro Personas Mayores (1975)
	National Association of Area Agencies on Aging (1975)
	National Association of RSVP Directors (1976)
	National Foster Grandparents Program Directors (1976)
	National Indian Council on Aging (1976)
	National Association of Nutrition and Aging Services Programs (1977)
	National Pacific/Asian Resource Center on Aging (1979)
	Older Women's League (1980)

Source: Organizations: Bennett M. Rich and Martha Baum, *The Aging: A Guide to Public Policy* (Pittsburgh: University of Pittsburgh Press, 1984), p. 21; dates of founding: *Encyclopedia of Associations, 1990* (Detroit: Gale Publishing Co., 1990), and by direct contact with the group.

exceeding that of any previous wave of its kind in American history. This is evident from the dates of formation of many present-day political organizations, for example those comprising the Leadership Council of Aging Organizations, as noted toward the bottom of table 2.

As shown by this listing, a majority of the council's member organizations as of 1982, fourteen out of twenty-seven, were established after 1971. The same observation applies to the several aging-involved groups that presently maintain a Washington, D.C., headquarters, as identified in the *Encyclopedia of Associations, 1990*, under the rubrics "aging," "senior citizens," and "retired persons," and as listed in table 3. Only those groups having

TABLE 3. Aging Groups with Washington, D.C., National Headquarters

Founding Decade	Organization
1940s	Gerontological Society of America (1945)
1950s	National Council on the Aging (1950)
	American Association of Retired Persons (1958)
1960s	American Association of Homes for the Aging (1961)
	National Council of Senior Citizens (1961)
	National Association of State Units on Aging (1964)
	National Institute on Age, Work, and Retirement (1968)
	(affiliated with National Council on the Aging)
1970s	National Caucus and Center on the Black Aged (1970)
	National Alliance of Senior Citizens (1974)
	National Association for Human Development (1974)
	National Association of Area Agencies on Aging (1975)
	Leadership Council on Aging Organizations (1978)
	Affiliated Groups with National Council on the Aging:
	National Institute of Senior Centers (1970)
	National Institute of Voluntary Organizations for Independent Living for the Aging (1971)
	National Center on Arts and Aging (1973)
	National Center on Rural Aging (1978)
	National Institute on Adult Day Care (1979)
1980s	Association of Informed Senior Citizens (1981)
	Villers Foundation (1981)
	American Association for International Aging (1983)
	Americans for Generational Equity (1984)
	Affiliated Groups with National Council on the Aging:
	National Institute on Community-Based Long Term Care (1984)
	National Center for Health Promotion and Aging (1985)

Source: Encyclopedia of Associations, 1990 (Detroit: Gale Publishing Co., 1990).

Note: This listing excludes membership groups composed of special categories of retirees (e.g., retired military officers). Also excluded is Gray Panthers, which opened a Washington, D.C., office in the 1980s, but whose national headquarters remained in Philadelphia.

national capital offices are here listed, on the assumption that such a Washington, D.C., locale is reflective of a desire for national governmental access. Of chief interest in table 3 are the various dates. They reinforce the earlier observation of phase four as powerfully fostering age-group formation.

Politicization of Existing Organizations

Moving from the quantitative to a qualitative perspective, the change in the interest group environment associated with phase four is best comprehended under five headings: (1) the increased centrality for seniors' organizations of all kinds in Washington, D.C., (2) the increased politicization of preexisting groups, (3) the formation of seniors' groups of a type rarely seen in the past, (4) internal factionalism and cleavages associated with enlarged membership and size, and (5) incipient struggles over turf, and the resulting desire to establish coordinating structures.

Headquarters Sites and Expanded
Public Policy Concern

In the late 1960s, at the close of the third phase of policy, only the National Council of Senior Citizens (NCSC), among the U.S. age-advocacy organizations, was concerned broadly with federal policy on aging and with achieving access to government. With respect to the other national organizations occupying this field, political action appears to have occurred only spasmodically and on a more narrowly defined range of issues. Reflective of this was the fact that at this time only the NCSC, among the voluntary organizations that fit this description, maintained its headquarters in the national capital.

For the most part, the leading organizations on aging located their national headquarters in some regional city, remote from Washington. Thus, the National Council on the Aging (NCOA), founded in 1950 as the National Committee on Aging of the National Social Welfare Assembly, originally chose New York for its headquarters, in whose vicinity resided its founders Ollie Randall, Albert J. Abrams, and Geneva Mathiasen. NCOA was chiefly involved at the time in the social service area, and this role required only occasional lobbying forays to Capitol Hill. Likewise, the Gerontological Society of America (GSA), an organization of scholars, researchers, and planners in the aging field, established its original headquarters in St. Louis, where its founders mostly resided. Vincent Cowdry, an early GSA president, arranged for the organization to have free office space at Washington University in St. Louis, where Cowdry was dean of the medical school; the core of its leadership—Robert Kleemeier, Herman Blumenthal, and James Kirk (editor in chief of the association's official journal)—all held faculty appointments at the same university. The GSA's scholarly and scientific purposes evidently left but little space for public policy activity. The AARP, founded by Ethel Percy Andrus as an offshoot of the National Retired Teachers Association (NRTA), which itself had been founded by Andrus (1947), initially made use of its western regional office located in Long Beach, California, as its center of operations, Long Beach having been for many years Andrus's place of residence. (NRTA and AARP did establish a national office in Washington, D.C., but this was not initially the association's organizational center.) Finally, the site chosen for the headquarters of the Gray Panther organization upon its formation in 1970 was Philadelphia, home to the founder, Margaret ("Maggie") Kuhn.

Yet with time these organizations would become in varying degrees politicized, as indicated by their decisions subsequently to relocate their headquarters to a national capital venue. NCOA made this headquarters shift in 1960, while at the same time changing its name from *committee* to *council* and enlarging its mandate so as to encompass a more-pronounced emphasis on governmental relations. In the case of AARP, the Washington office came into its own as the real center of the group's operations around 1967, following Andrus's death in that year and the appointment of Cyril Brickfield as her successor—Brickfield being a man of quite considerable experience in government. The GSA relocated its headquarters to Washington in 1970 in the course of an expansion in its perceived political mandate. The Gray Panthers shifted its center of operations to Washington in 1985. (The Philadelphia office is still listed formally as the headquarters, and it continues to perform certain functions, among them publication of the official *Network Newspaper*, but Philadelphia has ceased to be the main center of Gray Panther operations.)[22] It is noteworthy that none of the age-advocacy groups here, or any other visible organization on aging, has ever abandoned Washington for another locale.

Clearly, all but one of these headquarters relocations occurred during the 1960s, suggesting that the advantages of a Washington venue had become apparent well prior to the beginning of phase four. There are indications, nevertheless, that it was not until after the arrival of the new phase of policy in the early 1970s that the redefinitions of organizational goals, implicit in the change in headquarters locales, reached their full fruition. In the case of AARP, for example, governmental access had been problematic up through roughly the end of phase three. The association's first director of governmental relations, Ernest Giddings, who served in that post until 1969 when he was replaced by Peter Hughes, found himself unable to gain very much by the way of visibility and acceptance on Capitol Hill—notwithstanding that by this time the combined membership of AARP and NRTA exceeded one million and was growing.[23] At the point that Hughes stepped in to replace him, AARP's governmental relations program was run by just two persons: the director and a single secretary. Yet, a decade and a half later AARP's work in this area had expanded almost beyond comparison. It was now a major enterprise. The number of staff personnel engaged in federal and state lobbying,

---

22. Frances Humphreys, Gray Panther executive director, interview, September 8, 1989.

23. Peter Hughes, interview, McClean, Va., August 1989. Giddings was a Michigan Republican and a longtime friend of his fellow GOP stalwarts from that state: John Martin—the first commissioner on aging during the Nixon administration—and Gerald Ford, then the GOP House minority leader and later (1974–77) the U.S. president. Giddings was not a genuine political presence on Capitol Hill, and his approaches there were concentrated on the minority, GOP, side as opposed to the majority Democrats.

combined with the numbers assigned to the AARP "Vote Project" and the AARP Policy Institute, yielded an overall government relations complement for 1986 of between 150 and 160 employees.[24] One should guard against any presumption that this increase in AARP lobbying capacity necessarily translates into enlarged political power, especially in light of certain findings to be presented in the following. Still, the change in its scope of operations at least made AARP a potentially consequential actor on age-related policy matters, something that few, if any, observers would have said of it in 1970.

Politicization of Existing Groups:
The Case of the Gray Panthers

The Gray Panther organization offers an interesting case study of how the changed political atmosphere associated with phase four has helped to produce an increased politicization among existing age-active organizations. Although the particulars of the following account are obviously unique to this group, the general pattern probably applies, to one degree or another, to most of the established organizations in this field.

The Gray Panthers was founded in 1970 by Maggie Kuhn, then a sixty-seven-year-old social activist who insisted that the new group should see itself not as a senior citizen organization but instead as a coalition of old and young united in common cause. The Gray Panther slogan "age and youth in action" reflected this orientation. On the occasion of its founding and for several years subsequent, the Gray Panthers occupied themselves with the politics of culture to the virtual exclusion of aging programs financed and administered by government. Thus, for example, the Panthers staged guerrilla theater skits outside the 1974 American Medical Association convention in Chicago to protest the alleged heartlessness of the American health care industry. The national leadership was largely unresponsive at this time to the potential organizational benefits inherent in governmental access. Such aversion to direct governmental involvement reflected the unique goals and internal structure of the Gray Panthers, coupled with the group's dubious attitude toward age-targeted federal programs, which were viewed for the most part as a rip-off of the elderly.

In its formative stage, the Gray Panthers experienced a remarkable enlargement in membership, from a bare handful of activists at the outset to more than ten thousand members in its local networks by 1975. Its early organizational ethos incorporated much of the spirit and organizational thinking embraced by the social movements that typified the 1960s: the anti–

---

24. Peter Hughes, interview, McClean, Va., August 1989.

Vietnam War protest, black liberation, women's rights, and the consumer movement. Following these examples, Gray Panther leaders determined to avoid a hierarchical governing structure, and instead to develop a shared leadership arrangement. In addition, formal membership, dues structure, and specific qualifications for membership (including age) were all rejected. Emphasis was placed on the movement's grass roots character and the need to foster networks of autonomous local affiliates, and there was corresponding deemphasis on bureaucracy or anything resembling a large headquarters staff. (As late as 1981, the national staff in Philadelphia consisted of only six persons.) The organization thus came to embrace a philosophy that political scientist Jo Freeman, in analyzing the women's movement, referred to as the "myth of structurelessness."[25]

Radical in organization structure, the Gray Panther movement was equally so in terms of its social and economic goals. Its celebrated "Goal Five," adopted at the first Gray Panther National Convention and reaffirmed in 1979 after some controversy, committed the organization to "transcending the profit motive" and eliminating "the concentration of corporate power" in America. The clear implication of this was that the Gray Panthers would emphasize radical social change rather than incrementalist politics and would place themselves to some extent outside the moderately reformist orientation that typified more mainstream political organizations. Existing federal programs on aging were viewed as mostly nefarious, and destructive of seniors' dignity and self-respect. Thus, while its representatives did participate in the 1971 and 1981 White House Conferences on Aging, its manifestos expressed wariness over what these conferences appeared to signify, regarding the conferences not as a step toward seniors' liberation but as still another way in which some people sought to legitimize elderly people's oppression. In an article appearing in the *Gray Panther Network* shortly before the 1981 conference began, Maggie Kuhn warned that the coming gathering was "in synch with the entire aging network [which] assumes that the problems of the old will be solved through benefits and services for the old. This thinking, and the legislation stemming from it, segregates the elderly from the rest of American society, thereby enhancing hostility between generations."[26]

In addition to parting from the more mainstream age-advocacy organizations with respect to the aging enterprise, the Gray Panthers also were distinguishable on the basis of political goals. The organization, refusing to limit

---

25. Jo Freeman, *The Politics of the Women's Liberation Movement* (New York: W.W. Norton, 1975). See also "Gray Panthers First Decade," *Gray Panther Network* (July-August 1980), p. 5.

26. Henry J. Pratt, "The 'Gray Lobby' Revisited," *National Forum: The Phi Kappa Phi Journal* 62, no. 4 (Fall 1982): 32.

itself to policies of direct concern to retirees and senior citizens, took keen interest in issues that transcend age groupings like poverty, nuclear arms reduction, and the U.S. transportation industry.

In time, nevertheless, the expanding scale and perceived importance of government programs on aging impacted the organization's general outlook. There was an acknowledgment of the potential benefits inherent in orthodox pressure group activity and lobbying, even for an organization radical in its inclinations. In place of the early structurelessness, formal procedures for becoming and remaining a Gray Panther member were accepted as necessary to the furtherance of organizational objectives. The necessity for employing a full-time paid staff was likewise embraced. To a degree, these shifts in outlook were reflective of the values and attitudes of the newly recruited members, many of them individuals concerned over the need to enhance old people's status and power, and less so with the needs of economically vulnerable persons regardless of age, as had been true of Panther activists at the outset. As a consequence, certain goals, such as nationalization of transportation and of the oil industry, have come to enjoy less than wholehearted support among the rank and file. According to a leading study by Ruth H. Jacobs and Beth Hess, there has developed a lack of internal consensus on this, and most other, Gray Panther radical objectives.[27]

In addition, the organization's initial despairing attitude toward the federal government as having little or no positive potential in regard to the needs and aspirations of elderly people has since been largely superseded by a guarded hopefulness. The group has taken stands on a number of national legislative concerns, including participation in the campaign (ultimately successful) to amend the Age Discrimination in Employment Act so as to outlaw mandatory retirement, the movement to end sex discrimination under Social Security, the campaign to enact Congressman Ronald Dellum's national health insurance bill (H.R. 2969), and the effort to lift the federally mandated ceilings on savings accounts interest rates. Moreover, articles appearing in the *Gray Panther Network* make it apparent that Gray Panther leaders have come to embrace the necessity for collaboration with other like-minded interest groups, including seniors', organizations, as a means of securing desired legislative outcomes. While claiming tax exemption under section 501 c(3) of the Internal Revenue Code, as an organization only incidentally involved in lobbying and political action, the Gray Panthers nevertheless decided to relocate its main base of operations from Philadelphia to Washington.

The preceding is consistent with the view that the increased scale and importance of aging benefits associated with phase four have been fundamen-

---

27. Ruth H. Jacobs and Beth Hess, "Panther Power: Symbols and Substance," *Long Term Care and Health Services Administration Quarterly* 2 (Fall 1978): 238–44.

tal in causing the Gray Panthers to reevaluate its initial political posture, and to embrace the necessity for securing and maintaining access to the national government.

Politicization of Existing Groups: AARP and the Nonmandatory Retirement Struggle

An equally telling example of how the recent phase of policy development has impacted existing aging organizations is the experience of AARP in the area of mandatory retirement legislation. AARP's goals have always included a public policy dimension, and legislative outlawing of mandatory retirement has been one of its legislative objectives, but prior to phase four the association had seldom, if ever, succeeded in becoming a consequential political actor in this or any other area of interest on Capitol Hill. The association's exceptional size and resource base, while conveying certain political advantages, also proved to some extent an impediment, in the sense that size entailed an increased risk of internal discord and factionalism. Yet, in recent years, the organization has developed the capacity, assuming relative unanimity among its constituency, to exert considerable influence on selected issues of aging concern, and it is on that basis that it has achieved rather substantial political influence among members of Congress. An account of the association's drive for nonmandatory retirement legislation—involving from its standpoint the protection of certain basic constitutional rights—should prove informative as a means of demonstrating how the present policy setting has impacted this largest of present-day seniors' organizations.[28]

The association was not yet a year old when its founding president, Dr. Ethel Percy Andrus, declared in a speech, "It would be difficult to conceive of a more vast waste of manpower and/or production than that caused by mandatory retirement."[29] (Andrus's consciousness on this point obviously had been raised by her own earlier experience of forced retirement at age sixty as principal of Lincoln High School in Los Angeles, Andrus having had the distinction of becoming the first female high school principal in California.) There were other indications of AARP concern on this matter prior to Andrus's death in 1967, even though, as suggested previously, it is unclear that the organization could muster much in the way of political influence, or ensure that its message got across to federal policymakers.

---

28. The following discussion is based on the author's article "Uncapping Mandatory Retirement: The Lobbyists' Influence," in Karen C. Holden and W. Lee Hansen, eds., *The End of Mandatory Retirement: Effects on Higher Education*, New Directions for Higher Education Series, no. 65 (San Francisco: Jossey-Bass, 1989), pp. 15–32.

29. Quoted in *AARP Bulletin*, June 1978, p. 6.

This picture began to change in the early 1970s. In 1971, with the White House Conference on Aging approaching, AARP published a book of essays in which scholars and former government officials, including anthropologist Margaret Mead, economist Juanita Kreps, and Wilbur Cohen, former secretary of the Department of Health, Education, and Welfare, called for an end to mandatory retirement.[30] At the conference itself, AARP fought for passage of a resolution declaring mandatory retirement to be in violation of rights guaranteed under the U.S. Constitution. Unwilling to endorse the AARP position, the conference instead adopted a statement on the need for greater enforcement of existing federal, state, and local anti–age-discrimination laws. A subordinate clause of this "better enforcement" theme did suggest the need to eliminate the age limit of sixty-five in age-discrimination legislation, as well as a possible expansion of the Age Discrimination in Employment Act to cover all employees in the public and private sectors. Moreover, another resolution affirmed that "chronological age should not be the sole criterion for retirement. A flexible policy should be adopted . . . [and] employment opportunities after age sixty-five must be made available."[31] While not a ringing victory for the AARP position, it was an important step.

In the years to follow, AARP continued to press its case, although for a time with no great success. It filed an amicus curiae brief in the case of *Weiss v. Walsh* supporting a philosophy professor at Catholic University who alleged that Fordham University, having offered him a prestigious humanities chair, withdrew its offer when it learned that he had passed his sixty-fifth birthday. The case was later decided against the plaintiff and against the position favored by AARP.

The prevailing political climate on Capitol Hill finally took on a more favorable aspect when in 1977 Claude Pepper took over as chair of the House Select Committee on Aging. Pepper promptly made clear his intention to use the committee-sponsored hearings as a forum from which to promote the nonmandatory retirement cause, thus giving AARP a substantial and highly reputed ally within the government. The details of how Pepper manipulated the legislative process over the next year and a half so as to secure the enactment of the 1978 amendments to the Age Discrimination in Employment Act outlawing mandatory retirement at age seventy need not concern this discussion. What is presently significant is the finding reported by Laura C. Ford, on the basis of an in-depth study, to the effect that "there is no question that the needed spark was provided by the political activism of the American

30. M. Abrams and B. Robinson, eds., *Forty-six National Leaders Speak Out on Options for Older Americans* (Washington, D.C.: NRTA/AARP, 1971).

31. U.S. White House Conference on Aging, *Section Recommendations on Employment and Retirement* (Washington, D.C.: Government Printing Office, 1971).

Association of Retired Persons, the National Retired Teachers Association, the Gray Panthers, etc."[32] Clearly, the AARP leadership could look with some satisfaction on this 1978 success. Its leaders nevertheless remained dissatisfied. Of grave concern to the association, as reflected by pronouncements appearing in its annual legislative policy statements of this period, was the fact that the enactment only postponed the permissible age of mandatory retirement in American life, and thereby failed to confront the allegedly "civil rights" issue of forced retirement, including employees' right to have full consideration given to their capacity for continued successful performance of their duties.

The Republican victory in the 1980 election, coupled with the GOP capture at the same time of control in the U.S. Senate, changed somewhat the political environment for proposed changes in the Age Discrimination in Employment Act. In past years, age discrimination legislation had been generally regarded as a Democratic issue, in view of the fact that the Democrats had been in the majority in both houses of Congress and a Democrat occupied the White House both when the Age Discrimination in Employment Act was adopted in 1967 and again in 1978 when its most important subsequent amendments were adopted.

As it turned out, however, the 1980 election results did not retard the movement for positive legislative change in this field and indeed may have helped to accelerate the process. (The GOP's 1976 and 1980 party platform statements had both called for an end to this widespread industry and government practice.) AARP leaders had long collaborated closely on this matter with Claude Pepper, a liberal Democrat, and now its leaders were in a position to enlarge the pro-uncapping coalition to include equally close ties with the GOP leadership. AARP's huge membership base, which in the early 1980s exceeded twenty-five million, helped to facilitate this process.

Nevertheless, despite the combined strength of AARP, the Reagan White House, Congressman Pepper, and spokespersons for both political parties, powerful forces in Washington remained opposed to full uncapping of the retirement age, and their support was sufficient to ensure that, for the moment, proposals of this type would not make it out of committee. Chief among these were two political forces, the U.S. Chamber of Commerce and the American Federation of Labor and Congress of Industrial Organizations (AFL-CIO). The former of these interest groups had consistently opposed the proposal whenever it came up on Capitol Hill. In the case of the AFL-CIO, the announced position was somewhat equivocal. While labor leaders generally affirmed the validity of nonmandatory retirement in principle, the feeling now

---

32. Laura C. Ford, "The Implications of the Age Discrimination in Employment Act Amendments of 1978 for Colleges and Universities," *Journal of College and University Law* 5 (1978–79): 178.

was, in light of the serious recession afflicting the U.S. economy, that this was not the appropriate time to strip away established mandatory retirement practices that might work to the disadvantage of unemployed younger workers. During Ronald Reagan's first term in office (1981–85), therefore, the matter remained stalled on Capitol Hill.

Providing the momentum needed once again to fire up the legislative steamroller was a combination of a reviving national economy and the entry into the picture of a new political force, namely the organized police and fire fighter unions. These unions asserted themselves not out of any desire to uncap mandatory retirement but rather to preserve that established practice as it applied to police officers and fire fighters. Most public safety officers were content to accept forced early retirement if, in exchange, they could be granted an enhanced early retirement package. With the issue thus reopened on Capitol Hill, Congressman Pepper could again apply political leverage for his (and AARP's) objectives. And it was these, more so than the activity of the police and fire unions, or of the other affected interests, that were most fully embodied in the final legislative outcome of 1986.

Again, the details of how total uncapping was finally adopted into law by Congress need not concern this discussion. What does bear emphasis is the fact that at a critical juncture on Capitol Hill, with the relevant legislation stalled in the Senate (having previously passed the House), it was the outside pressure on Congress provided by AARP coupled with inside pressure on the part of pro-uncapping senators, especially John Heinz of Pennsylvania, that were key to eliminating the blockage. Senator Heinz and AARP employed their legislative skills to the maximum in ensuring that the House-passed bill went directly to the Senate floor, bypassing the regular committee structure. Standing in the way of such a procedure were a series of holds previously placed on the bill by anti-uncapping senators (stimulated by the U.S. Chamber of Commerce), the effect of which was to prevent the measure's coming to a vote under the Senate's unanimous consent rule. This left open only the established standing-committee route for achieving a floor vote on the proposal. The Chamber of Commerce believed that it had this avenue effectively closed off as well, but on this it miscalculated. Throwing the full weight of its legislative muscle into the struggle and working in collaboration with the organization's affiliates in selected states, AARP's national lobbying staff succeeded first in identifying the particular senators who had placed the holds (despite Senate secrecy rules designed to prevent such information becoming known) and, second, in applying pressure aimed at persuading those senators to withdraw their holds, thereby permitting the legislation to move forward. In the end, the holds were withdrawn one by one, until at last none remained. In this manner a group of very conservative senators, including Jesse Helms of North Carolina among others, displayed their instincts for political survival, recognizing the logic of not appearing to oppose what one AARP lobbyist later characterized to me in an interview as the greatest civil rights legislation for the elderly of recent times. When the Senate vote finally came, the measure passed overwhelmingly, and on November 1, 1986, President Reagan signed it into law.

In conclusion, it would be erroneous to attribute AARP's increased legislative clout, as illustrated by the nonmandatory retirement case, entirely to the changed policy environment associated with phase four. The association's expanding size and fiscal resources most probably would have enlarged its capacity to influence public policy outcomes even in the absence of the increased visibility and perceived importance of government aging benefits associated with the decisions that launched this new era of public policy. Having said that, however, it seems more than coincidental that the association should transform itself from what was essentially a Capitol Hill nonentity as recently as the late 1960s into a Washington political force of compelling significance by the late 1970s, and that this should occur in the immediate aftermath of the policy breakthroughs and expanded aging benefits identified as marking the transition from phase three to four. Clearly, government policy shifts were not the only factor involved here, directly or indirectly, but there is every reason to believe that they were second to none in their importance.

Formation of Single-Issue Groups

In addition to the formation of increasing numbers of age-active interest groups and behavioral changes on the part of preexisting groups, the fourth phase of policy development has been distinguished by the emergence of seniors' organizations of a type not commonly found at earlier periods. The organizing wave of the 1970s and 1980s involved the formation of interest groups of fairly defined constituencies. In place of seniors' organizations formed on the mass membership, general purpose model, as had typified the preceding era, the new wave consisted for the most part of ones more of the caucus type and somewhat narrower in focus. Illustrative of the latter have been the National Indian Council on Aging, the Older Women's League, and the Urban Elderly Coalition, to name but a few. To a far greater degree than formerly, the organizations formed at this time owed their existence to sponsorship by some older, established organization (the NCOA has been especially active in this sponsoring role). Another specialized basis for organization has been occupational role, namely groups consisting of professional workers involved with the elderly, for example the National Association of RSVP Directors. While there is presently no membership organization at the national level that devotes itself primarily to the concerns of the poor, or welfare dependent, elderly, such people have at least indirectly participated in the recent organizing wave, given the special concern with that population category manifested by the Villers Foundation.[33]

Even the recently formed organizations that might appear, on the basis of name, to be of the broadly based, general membership type are found on closer examination to be essentially single-interest. The leading cases in point are the National Committee to Preserve Social Security and Medicare (NCPSSM) and the National Alliance of Senior Citizens (NASC). The former group was founded in 1982 by former congressman James Roosevelt, at the height of the national debate over the funding crisis in Social Security. Making aggressive use of direct mail solicitations warning that Social Security was in grave danger, this organization succeeded within a short time in signing up more than half a million members. Also a heavy direct mail user was the NASC, formed in 1974 by a twenty-seven-year-old political entrepreneur, C. C. Clinkscales. While some question can be raised regarding this group's subsequent claim of having two million members, it at least succeeded in gaining a measure of visibility. Despite their own claims of being committed to broad mandates, Christine L. Day is almost certainly correct in classifying both NASC and NCPSSM as single-issue groups, on the basis of their relatively narrow foci and insistence on recruiting members entirely through mail solicitations and thereby avoiding establishment of local chapters or holding membership meetings or conventions.[34]

Both these groups, it should be mentioned, have a marked ideological focus: NCPSSM leaning decidedly to the Left, NASC equally so toward the ideological Right. In announcing the formation of NASC, for example, C. C. Clinkscales explicitly stated that it should serve "in order to give older adults who did not fit under the liberal umbrella a conservative voice." And his name for the organization, "National Alliance of Senior Citizens," was deliberately chosen "in an effort to neutralize the radically left-wing National *Council* of Senior Citizens."[35] And the Rooseveltian sponsorship of NCPSSM not only calls to mind the liberalism of Franklin D. Roosevelt, but also the no-less-liberal views of James, his son.

It would appear, then, that, once the potential for new interest group formation that was inherent in phase four of U.S. policy development had made itself felt, there remained but few categories of the nation's elderly population that remained entirely without an organized national voice. The combination of the general interest groups, mostly formed during phase three,

---

33. Christine L. Day, *What Older Americans Think: Interest Groups and Aging Policy* (Princeton: Princeton University Press, 1990), p. 29.

34. Ibid., pp. 27–28.

35. Quoted in the *Senior Guardian* (official publication of the NASC, Arlington, Va.), March/April 1991, p. 1.

and the single-interest groups, mostly arising during the period following, has produced in Washington an unprecedented array of age-related political interest groups. This should not be taken as suggesting, necessarily, that all these groups—whether acting singly or in combination—are influential politically to the degree that their numbers and size might seem to indicate. It is, rather, to suggest that by the end of the 1980s one could speak of an apparent saturation of age-based and/or age-advocacy organizations in the nation's capital.

Fundamental to the surge in single-issue and narrowly focused interest groups typical of this period has been the increased anxiety felt by many senior citizens (and their younger allies) over the preservation of existing federal benefits. Such a mood is explicit in the name chosen for one leading group, namely the "National Committee to Preserve Social Security and Medicare." It also underlies, if less explicitly, certain others. Apparently, it was not until the 1970s that elderly persons in large numbers came to regard existing federal programs as so vitally important to their personal well-being as to justify and necessitate their supporting mass membership and age-advocacy organizations in all their number and diversity. In contrast to the strong phase three emphasis on the need to establish new federally funded aging programs, the mood of the more recent period has been more one of defending benefits already in existence. Thus, Day aptly remarks, "Now that [older people] have such a large stake in government, and are accustomed to the benefits they receive, [they] are more responsive than ever to purposive incentives [from various voluntary organizations"].[36]

Elements of Weakness and Potential Discord

Up to this point in the discussion, phase four has been viewed as essentially positive in its impact on seniors' organizations. Among the beneficial effects mentioned have been the growth in organizational memberships and financial base, the enlargements in staff, the enhancement of governmental access, and the proliferation of specialized groups responsive to the wide diversity among elderly Americans. Yet a close examination reveals that these various changes, whether taken separately or together, have also entailed new elements of risk and potential disadvantage. Despite evidence to indicate that the nation's gray lobby has realized growing influence in Washington since the onset of the present era of public policy,[37] such strength has not been equivalent to what might have been expected, given the large resources and high

36. Day, *What Older Americans Think*, p. 69.
37. Ibid., p. 96ff.

reputation for legitimacy of seniors' organizations. In treating the downside of the developments occurring over the past two decades, therefore, the following discussion begins by examining the changed internal dynamics of one fairly representative group, namely AARP, and then moves on to discuss the often-disrupted relations between the various seniors' organizations.

AARP in the Context of the Medicare Catastrophic Coverage Act

In analyzing the forces involved in the 1983 struggle over Social Security reform, Paul Light emphasizes the AARP's rather surprising lack of influence and assertiveness.[38] Light points out that AARP found it impossible to mobilize for effective political action in this struggle, notwithstanding its "huge membership" and "$41 million budget [which] included a complete team of lobbyists."[39] Whereas on the one hand the leaders of the NCSC "had no doubts about the organization's political agenda . . . [which] meant that [it] had more lobbying weapons," this did not apply to AARP, whose trustworthiness on this issue was considered as suspect by some on Capitol Hill, and where the group's fundamental position remained obscure.[40] Direct evidence is lacking, but this indecisiveness seems reflective in part of the association's internally complex, cross-class character, causing one major sector of its constituency to become pitted against another, with resulting organizational stasis. If true, the 1983 struggle can be regarded as a foretaste of a subsequent Capitol Hill struggle, in which internal dynamics were unquestionably a major factor, namely the 1988–89 struggle over catastrophic coverage legislation. Here, as the following discussion suggests, AARP's vast size and inclusiveness, while beneficial initially, ended up working to its disadvantage and ultimate political defeat.

In June of 1988, after eighteen months of difficult legislative work, the House-Senate conference report on the Medicare Catastrophic Coverage Act was passed, and in the following month the measure was signed into law by President Ronald Reagan. The legislation provided for the largest expansion of Medicare since the program was established in 1965 and was designed to protect beneficiaries from having their life savings wiped out by huge medical bills. The terms of the legislation provided that after a modest annual deduct-

---

38. I am indebted to my former Wayne State University student, Ann Petty, whose research on the Medicare Catastrophic Coverage Act underlies much of what appears in the following section.

39. Paul Light, *Artful Work: The Politics of Social Security Reform* (New York: Random House, 1985), p. 76.

40. Ibid.

ible was paid, all remaining hospital costs would be covered. One of its unique features, which contributed both to its initial ease of passage and later to undoing, was the funding of expanded benefits by the beneficiaries themselves. Financing would be from a roughly 15 percent surcharge on federal income tax payments—to be levied on the 40 percent of Medicare beneficiaries who pay at least $150 in federal income taxes. (The remaining 60 percent would be exempt from program-related taxation.) The wealthy elderly would pay a larger share: the maximum surtax—set at $800 for a single person and $1,800 for a couple—would typically be paid by those whose incomes exceeded $70,000. The new tax schedule was to take effect in April 1990 when 1989 income taxes would become due.

The measure passed with bipartisan support during a time of fiscal austerity, and represented a major expansion in a social program. Its acceptance by the White House was therefore surprising, considering the conservative ideology of the Reagan administration. Such acceptance was in part explainable on the basis that it offered something for members of both parties: congressional Democrats could satisfy their desire to enlarge social programs without adding to the federal deficit, whereas congressional Republicans were attracted by its budget-neutral aspect. Spearheading the effort to move the catastrophic costs issue onto the national agenda had been the secretary of Health and Human Services, Otis R. Bowen, a physician and former governor of Indiana whose wife had spent the last months of her life in a hospital before dying of bone cancer.

Early on in the legislative process, AARP made known its strong support for the Medicare Catastrophic Coverage Act, and later saw to it that its Capitol Hill lobbyists remained actively involved as the process moved forward. The measure as it emerged from Congress did not please many in the Reagan administration, and pressures were applied for him to veto it. AARP helped to block these efforts and persuade the president to sign the measure into law. Accounts in the press and statements in the *Congressional Record* make it apparent that the White House, and most members of Congress, believed that AARP spoke for the majority of senior citizens on this. For example, when the House version of the act was coming up for a vote, Representative Henry A. Waxman (D-California) declared, "As long as the AARP and the National Council of Senior Citizens continue to support it, I think Congress will too."[41] Likewise, when congressional staff members began feeling the intensity of opposition, and tried to convince the senators and House members that there seemed to be a serious political problem, a com-

---

41. Julie Rovner, "Catastrophic-Costs Conferees Irked by Lobbying Assaults," *Congressional Quarterly*, March 26, 1988, p. 777.

mon initial response was that the staff must be overreacting and that AARP's strong support was a better indicator of grass roots opinion than was the small vocal group of opponents. The association's reputation for political credibility, as built up over a number of years, obviously served it well during this initial stage of the legislative struggle.

Within a matter of weeks of the adoption of the act, a series of seismic shocks, emanating from the grass roots, made it clear to Capitol Hill lawmakers that the measure was by no means as universally supported by the elderly as had been originally supposed. A flood of mail opposing the measure began reaching congressional offices from angry constituents. Senator Pete Wilson (R-California), for one, received three thousand letters, fifteen thousand postcards, and uncounted thousands of phone calls opposing the surtax, and one of Wilson's aides told an interviewer, "There is a genuine grass-roots outpouring of opposition."[42] And Congress was not alone as a target of criticism; AARP also soon found itself placed on the defensive. From his retirement home in Las Vegas, Daniel Hawley, a sixty-four-year-old former airline pilot, was instrumental in organizing a protest group, Seniors Coalition against the Catastrophic Coverage Act, whose fire was directed in no small part against the association. "They [AARP] thought retired people were sitting around doing their ceramics and their little aerobics classes in senior centers and wouldn't give any fight," he told the *Chicago Tribune*. "Well, they found out differently."[43]

As the protest mounted in intensity, senators and House members turned their wrath against AARP. Representative Harris Fawell (R-Illinois), for one, remarked to a reporter that "AARP is out of this one. They've clearly lost touch with their membership. Maybe they're too worried about selling prescription drugs to pay attention to costs and to duplication of services. People have lost faith in this law."[44] And an unnamed congressional staffer was quoted as saying, "Maybe we have to rethink the idea that this lobby [AARP] really does speak in the name of all these seniors."[45]

Further embarrassment inhered in press publicity regarding the disciplining by AARP officials of local- and state-level activists in the organization who had dared to voice their support for the position taken by the elderly protesters. Under headlines such as "Seniors Wrath Stings Lobby," the association's internal struggle received wide public airing. A volunteer who headed AARP's Vote Project in seven California districts was reported as

---

42. *Los Angeles Times*, May 6, 1989, p. 21.
43. *Chicago Tribune*, September 3, 1989, pp. 1, 14.
44. Ibid., p. 14.
45. Ibid.

having been fired for having supported repeal legislation, and an AARP chapter president in Tallahassee, Florida, was forced to withstand two attempts by state AARP officials to oust him after adopting the same position. Clearly, the passage of the bill had "torn the fabric of AARP."[46] In the wake of this incident, AARP's director of legislation, John Rother, affirmed that "people [were] forming opinions on the basis of gross misinformation."[47] Yet, Rother also admitted that "we didn't give our members a great enough sense of participation."[48]

When Congress acted in 1989 to repeal the act, it did so in the face of continued AARP support for the legislation, and with an increased conviction on the part of many members that the association was not entirely trustworthy as an expression of elderly persons' opinions. From the association's perspective the incident was, to say the least, politically costly.

Various interpretations are possible concerning the larger significance of this incident. My own view is that the debacle is best understood as a result of AARP's extraordinary size. At thirty-three million members, this group now encompasses a major fraction of the entire U.S. older population, with all its incipient cleavages and potential conflicts. By lending its support to the act, the association obviously served the class interests of one sector of its constituency, namely its less-advantaged members, many of them in urgent need of catastrophic health care protection, but not so the interests of its wealthier, more affluent members who, to a disproportionate degree, would now have to bear the cost, and with little to offset that by way of personal gain. This latter group, while smaller numerically, was more politically mobilizable, given its members' higher disposable incomes and typically higher levels of education and verbal skills. Consequently, this subgroup of AARP members was in a better position to make known its views regarding the stands adopted in the name of the association, while also more effectively putting pressure on Congress. A smaller interest group than AARP might not have confronted such an internal cleavage, or at least not to the same embarrassing extent. The association conceivably could have remained silent on catastrophic coverage, thereby avoiding embarrassment, but to do that would have opened it up to the charge of irresponsibility, given that the act was clearly in the interest of a majority of its members. Given AARP's cross-class character, it is by no means inconceivable that this same internal cleavage could manifest itself again on some other issue at a future point.

---

46. Ibid.
47. *Los Angeles Times*, May 6, 1989, p. 21.
48. *Wall Street Journal*, December 27, 1989, p. A8.

Coping with Interest Group Rivalry

An equally problematic aspect of the new realities associated with phase four has been the enlarged potential for intergroup discord. While the gray lobby's increased diversity has been a source of strength in some respects, it has also introduced novel dangers from the standpoint of governmental access and political effectiveness. The growing numbers of groups and the increased diversity of agendas carries with it an inherent risk of increased internecine strife. While impossible to eliminate entirely, such risk at least can be mitigated through the establishment of consultative mechanisms whereby policy differences can be aired, and possibly ironed out, before becoming an embarrassment in the wider political arena. To what extent, then, have serious efforts in this direction been undertaken, and with what degree of success?

Efforts aimed at achieving consensus on elderly related public policy issues have been a feature of senior group behavior in Washington since roughly the outset of phase four. In 1972, six such organizations, acting in the wake of the 1971 White House Conference on Aging, joined hands to form a consultative body, the Conference of Interested Agencies in Aging (CIAA). The six, with but one exception, had combined forces the previous year to form an ad hoc collaboration, the purpose of which was to influence the resolutions adopted by the 1971 White House Conference.[49] This early consultative body lacked staying power, however, and had ceased to function by the middle of the decade.

The absence of any consultative forum where the interest groups in aging could meet to discuss their shared concerns was widely perceived at the time as a source of shared vulnerability. In reflecting, for example, upon recent strife between the two largest seniors' organizations, NCSC and AARP, one observer, Robert Binstock, remarked in 1976 that "some of our most dismal failures come when the two mass membership organizations are at odds and there is no clear articulation of needs from the other groups . . . . It will be a continuing struggle to get the aging groups to realize that we are part of a broader brotherhood."[50] Such thinking was one of the factors enter-

---

49. A few years previous to this, in the middle 1960s a series of informal meetings had been held, attended by the representatives of a handful of age-related interest groups. These meetings lacked any central focus, however, and were soon suspended. The six groups comprising the CIAA, at the time of its formation in 1972, were the National Association of Retired Federal Employees (NARFE), NCSC, AARP, NCOA, the National Caucus on the Black Aged, and the National Conference of Homemakers and Home Health Aides. See Pratt, *Gray Lobby*, pp. 130, 152.

50. Quoted in Linda E. Demkovich, "There's a New Kick in the Step of Senior Citizen Lobbies," *National Journal*, October 2, 1976, p. 1388.

ing into President Jimmy Carter's January 1977 decision to appoint Nelson Cruikshank as his White House adviser on aging, a post newly created at this time. Cruikshank was highly qualified for the post—solid Democratic party credentials, a career in the labor movement (having been named in 1942 the director of the newly formed Social Security Department of the American Federation of Labor [AFL]), and former president of the NCSC. The high esteem in which he was held was not confined to the liberal wing of the Democratic party but extended somewhat across party lines. Cruikshank, for example, was highly esteemed by the senior Republican serving on a committee on aging, Arthur Flemming, the chairman of the 1971 White House Conference and a former secretary of Health, Education, and Welfare. The friendship between these two men extended back to their shared undergraduate experience at Ohio Wesleyan University.

Cruikshank applied himself assiduously to his new duties. Rather than permit the continuance of internecine strife among leaders of the seniors' movement, the presidential adviser arranged a series of unity luncheons at the White House, attended by himself and a few other key players. Based on the positive atmosphere there engendered, a larger meeting was arranged at a hotel near Dulles International Airport attended by representatives of all the important groups on aging, roughly twenty attenders in all. Cruikshank's message to this gathering was blunt: if he was going to be successful as an advocate for the elderly within the Carter administration, intergroup conflict and sniping must end, and an atmosphere must be established of at least outward harmony. This message was received positively, and the delegates ended up agreeing to establish a new body, the Leadership Council on Aging Organizations, to begin operations in 1978. In a departure from earlier efforts in this same vein, the person selected to chair the new group, David Crowley, was not identified with one of the big three groups on aging (AARP, NCSC, and NCOA) but rather represented one of the smaller and less prominent organizations in this field, the American Association of Homes for the Aging. A man respected for his charm and force of personality, Crowley was well positioned to play the neutral broker role among the various parties.

In the months to follow, the Leadership Council on Aging Organizations succeeded in establishing itself, and it has since endured as a low-visibility presence in Washington. The initial member organizations have mostly stayed on board, and additional groups have since accepted membership.

And within one year of the council's formation, a second coalition, decidedly more politically activist in its basic objectives, emerged under the banner "Save Our Security" (SOS). Initially constituted with the intent of fighting President Carter's proposed cutbacks in certain Social Security benefits, this coalition has since varied over time in terms of its level of activity. Intensely active at the beginning, it later lapsed into relative quiescence, only to be revived in response to the Reagan administration's May 1981 proposal to slash Social Security benefits, including the cost-of-living adjustment. At the peak of the 1981–83 struggle SOS had the active support of 125 affiliated groups with a combined membership of thirty-five to forty million persons.[51] At the present writing, it again has become relatively quiescent, with the diminishment of the earlier perceived threats to the Social Security system.

These coalitions represent an obvious response to the proliferation of age-advocacy organizations in Washington. Their greatest success probably has consisted in giving to the smaller aging-involved organizations the capacity to combine forces and thereby to achieve a measure of political access lying beyond their separate capacities. The coalitions have exerted some impact politically, especially in serving to augment the gray lobby's defensive capacity in holding off large-scale reductions in aging benefits.

However, the extent to which the two present-day coalitions have succeeded in enhancing the senior movement's unity and cohesiveness remains unclear. The 1980s witnessed several struggles on Capitol Hill in which the larger seniors' organizations were visibly divided, including the 1983 controversy over the Social Security bailout package and also the 1988–89 catastrophic health care struggle wherein AARP and NCSC took one side and the NCPSSM the opposite. If one of the intended purposes of these coalitions was that of the elimination of intergroup dissention over matters of public policy, it is difficult to find the evidence for that in the recent record.

Conclusion

The political arena associated with phase four in the United States differs fundamentally from that earlier associated with phase three. The most visible difference consists in the substantial increase in the number of seniors' organizations, and the resulting expansion in organizational agendas. In place of the bare handful of organizations that had characterized phase three, most of them of the general membership type and committed to strategies emphasizing private, nongovernmental approaches, the more numerous groups characteristic of the present period have manifested a strong gravitational pull toward the federal government, and an increased desire to achieve and maintain political influence. The internal dynamics of seniors' organizations also have been altered substantially, if not in every case at least in some. Furthermore, efforts to resolve intergroup rivalries, while energetic, have not entirely succeeded in preventing embarrassment and public displays of rivalries and turf disputes.

The data presented give reason to question the usual assumption that the perceived power of seniors' organizations has increased in direct proportion to

---

51. Light, *Artful Work*, p. 82.

their growing numbers and tangible resources. Phase four has seen some increase in the gray lobby's reputed political influence, but close investigation reveals that such increase has not been commensurate with what might be assumed on the basis of objective indicators such as wealth and membership size. The growing size of individual interest groups, and the increased diversity among groups as a whole, carry elements of political vulnerability that are as significant in some ways as the more tangible indicators of group political power.

CHAPTER 10

Conclusion

This book's introductory chapter offers a thesis intended to account for some intriguing problems relating to interest groups in the field of aging. The thesis suggests that programs initiated by governments over the course of this century have been indirectly productive of incentives that proved helpful, if not critical, in the formation and maintenance of voluntary organizations in the old age security field. It is hypothesized that the statutory enactments that authorized those programs, coming at various times and at differing dates depending on the country in question, were of fundamental importance in the subsequent expansion in the number and size of interest groups in this field, and likewise in the tendency for such groups to form in waves, as opposed to randomly over time. A corollary hypothesis is that such national organizations, having once formed and become reasonably stable, then developed the capacity to participate in the subsequent reform and restructuring of existing old age security schemes, thereby suggesting a reciprocal relationship between aging organizations and government.

The data developed in the course of this study broadly support the hypotheses. Yet, they also call attention to some needed modifications, given that various complexities, not anticipated in the initial formulation, have made themselves apparent in the course of the investigation. This chapter begins, therefore, by recapitulating the phases of age-policy development, with special attention paid to comprehending their significance more fully in the light of theory.

Theoretical Implications

Phase One

Foreign models emerge from this study as a major input in the initial adoption in Canada, Britain, and the United States of old age pension legislation. Pension-advocacy groups, aware of such models and intent on their adoption domestically—possibly in modified form—devoted themselves to lobbying government, and often with considerable success. The distinctiveness of phase one consists largely in its absence of any genuine reciprocal relationship between age-advocacy interest groups and government. And no real possibility existed for any ongoing reciprocal relationship to develop between those groups and the model foreign governments. Later phases of policy would see such reciprocal relations arise, but not here.

The developments associated with phase one take on added significance when interpreted in the light of interest group theory. Up to a point, theory is employed in this discussion through the stress placed on patronage as informed by the group maintenance theory of Jack L. Walker and his colleagues at the University of Michigan.[1] Still, other theories are relevant as well in seeking a fuller understanding of this interesting period.

As a means of introduction, it is useful to consider the important shift occurring around the turn of the century in public attitudes toward aging and aged individuals. Historically, the elderly were expected to look after themselves, with possible assistance from family, church, and private charity.[2] Seniors at the time had essentially no sense of collective identity or shared consciousness. The inevitable decrements associated with advancing age were regarded not so much as problems as simple facts of life to be coped with individually as best one could.

Following 1900, however, a changing pattern of attitudes and economic circumstances in all three of the countries caused seniors to be considered in fresh light, and this shift would later have important implications for how elderly persons perceived themselves. And it appears that this shift was associated with a transformation of the elderly from a mere statistical category into what a leading political scientist, David B. Truman, has termed a "potential group."[3] The elderly had not yet achieved the level of interaction required to be defined as an interest group, but did now possess certain widespread, albeit weakly held, interests.[4] Elderly persons, unable at this point to act collectively on their own behalf, but nevertheless marked by a host of shared concerns and insecurities, became an object of altruism on the part of humanitarians of various types. The latter's concern was manifested in the formation of various committees and caucuses intended to address age-related problems:

1. Jack L. Walker, "The Origin and Maintenance of Interest Groups in America," *American Political Science Review* 77 (June 1983): 390–406; Jack L. Walker, *Mobilizing Interest Groups in America: Patrons, Professionals, and Social Movements* (Ann Arbor: University of Michigan Press, 1991).

2. W. Andrew Achenbaum, *Shades of Gray: Old Age, American Values, and Federal Policies since 1920* (Boston: Little, Brown, 1983), p. 39.

3. David B. Truman, *The Governmental Process* (New York: Knopf, 1951), p. 34.

4. Ibid., p. 114. In reference to the United States, W. Andrew Achenbaum points out that in the first two decades of the twentieth century, old age came to be recognized as a national problem. Yet it is apparent from his discussion that seniors did not at this point regard themselves as possessing shared attitudes that could serve as the basis for interaction. *Old Age in the New Land: The American Experience since 1790* (Baltimore: Johns Hopkins University Press, 1978).

the National Pensions Committee (NPC), the American Association for Old Age Security (AAOAS), the American Association for Labor Legislation (AALL), and the Moral and Social Reform Council (MSRC). Such group formation might appear logical at first glance, yet it nevertheless represents something of a conundrum from the standpoint of group theory, as expounded by Mancur Olson. According to Olson's "logic of collective action," humanitarian efforts of this type are inexplicable on any rational basis and instead must be considered as irrational.[5] The element of altruism or otherregardingness, inherent in pension reform collective effort, is alien to the notion of rational choice that lies at the core of Olson's logic, and it is therefore not surprising that Olson's writings should say almost nothing about interest groups of this type, save to acknowledge their existence.

Following the appearance in the middle 1960s of Olson's analysis, various theorists wrestled with its somber implications for the successful maintenance of altruistically based voluntary organizations. One of these, James Q. Wilson, in an important 1973 book essentially rejects Olson's rational-actor model, at least as a general explanation, and asserts instead that interest groups can form and maintain themselves on a wide variety of bases—with strictly rational motivation being but one, and not necessarily the most important. Thus, Wilsonian theory explicitly provides for altruistic, or purposive, incentives as one basis for organizational maintenance.[6]

Yet the mood among political scientists who treated this topic still more recently, especially during the 1980s, was more accepting of Olson's logic when coupled with modifications of his thought on certain particulars. One such theorist, Terry M. Moe, rejects the notion, implicit in Olson's work, that rational behavior is inconsistent with organizational participation based on political instincts and motivations. On the basis of both empirical evidence and abstract reasoning, Moe justifies the reintroduction of politics as a group incentive—a theme central to orthodox liberal notions of interest groups, but implicitly denied in the Olsonian rational-actor model.[7] Two other recent theorists, Russell Hardin and Fred M. Frohock, in separate works find less need basically to recast Olson's logic but instead argue that altruistic or purposive behavior should properly be looked upon as "extrarational," as Hardin puts it,[8] or as "intrinsic" (rather than extrinsic and rational), as does

---

5. Mancur Olson, *The Logic of Collective Action* (Cambridge: Harvard University Press, 1965), pp. 160–61.

6. James Q. Wilson, *Political Organizations* (New York: Basic Books, 1973), chap. 3 and passim.

7. Terry M. Moe, *The Organization of Interests: Incentives and the Internal Dynamics of Interest Groups* (Chicago: University of Chicago Press, 1980), p. 221.

8. Russell Hardin, *Collective Action* (Baltimore: Johns Hopkins University Press, 1982), p. 107.

Frohock.[9] Both these theorists agree with Moe, while departing from Olson, in finding a large potential for forming and maintaining interest groups on the basis of motives internal to the individual, altruism among them. For example, as one solution to the problem of "efficacy failure," Frohock writes that personal "internal rewards [can] provide a measure of support . . . that is traded off against efficacy."[10]

The theories mentioned here are of value in accounting for some otherwise-puzzling aspects of early pension-advocacy groups in the countries here under discussion. None of these groups found it possible to expand its base of members beyond an initially small size. This is partially explainable on the basis of Olson's logic, which regards selective benefits and coercion as the only bases upon which large, voluntary organizations can be maintained— neither of them being present, essentially, in any of these cases. Thus, the absence of these elements can serve as an explanation for these groups' failure to achieve large size.

Others among the theories presented here are also suggestive in this context. The politically active pensioner groups of the early twentieth century are illustrative of the enduring potential in democratic societies for the formation of groups of nonrationally motivated individuals. In line with the thought of writers such as Hardin and Frohock, the existence of such groups should not be considered as inexplicable, or aberrant. While direct evidence of this point is lacking, it is at least plausible that the early pensioner groups owed their existence in large part to (1) a shared awareness among altruistically inclined members and potential members of each other's existence and (2) "contractarian" instincts, to use Hardin's phrase, under which one such person's willingness to make a group contribution was enhanced by the knowledge that others were prepared similarly to contribute their fair share.[11]

Phase Two

One unexpected finding relating to phase two, but again explainable in light of theory, is the apparent disincentive effect of the newly enacted old age security legislation with respect to the mobilization of seniors. Instead of benefiting from the breakthrough legislation on old age security, the newly adopted legislation seems to have exerted more of an opposite interest group impact. Groups such as the Townsend movement in the United States and the National Conference on Old Age Pensions (NCOAP) in Britain, each with their

---

9. Fred M. Frohock, *Rational Association* (Syracuse, N.Y.: Syracuse University Press, 1987), p. 87.
10. Ibid.
11. Hardin, *Collective Action*, p. 105.

own preferred plan for increased government action, found themselves directly in competition with the newly introduced government plans and severely affected in the ensuing government and interest group competition.

One can generalize from this to suggest that a government's decision to enter a previously unoccupied field of social policy typically involves more than merely the authorization of public benefits and outlays of public funding. It also is likely to involve symbolic reassurances, whose purpose is to demonstrate that the problem that initially prompted the state intervention has now been addressed, and that any remaining program inadequacies or imperfections soon will be corrected. One indirect result of this, not intended by the sponsors, but nevertheless real, can consist in a lowering of the participation potential among the program beneficiaries, in this case senior citizens.[12]

Furthermore, as interpreted by Murray Edelman, such lowering of the potential for mass collective action is especially prone to occur in cases where the rhetoric of elective officials and lawmakers employs the "symbols of political quiescence."[13] Political rhetoric embodying both symbols of reassurance and symbols of quiescence was clearly present in the statements emanating from political elites following the initial adoption of old age pension legislation. Thus, for example, the 1936 U.S. Democratic party platform proclaims:

> *We hold this truth to be self-evident*—that government in a modern nation has certain inescapable obligations to its citizens. . . . These obligations, neglected through 12 years of the old leadership, have once more been recognized by American Government. Under the new leadership they will never be neglected. . . . We [Democrats] have built foundations for the security of those who are faced with the hazards of unemployment and old age. . . . On the foundation of the Social Security Act we are determined to erect a structure of economic security for all our people.

In short, given that the level of tangible pension benefits was at this point decidedly low, the high level of symbolic reassurance accompanying the 1935 Social Security Act tended to offset whatever organizational stimulus may have inhered in the newly enacted state benefit. In other words, any incentive

---

12. For a discussion of the symbolic strategy of dissuasion, involving the utilization of symbols to discourage supporters, see Roger W. Cobb and Charles D. Elder, *Participation in American Politics: The Dynamics of Agenda-building* (Boston: Allyn and Bacon, 1972), pp. 147–48.

13. Murray Edelman, *The Symbolic Uses of Politics* (Urbana: University of Illinois Press, 1985), pp. 42–43.

toward collective action implicit in this newly authorized government benefit was probably overwhelmed by the negative impacts—from the standpoint of interest group development—inherent in the accompanying rhetoric.

It is interesting in this context that the single successful example of age-group formation in phase two, namely the National Conference on Old Age Pensions (NCOP) in Britain (1916–26), took place in a country where the leading politicians seem not to have employed the kinds of rhetoric described earlier. Based on the statements appearing in British party manifestos during this period, as reported in chapter 6, it appears that party leaders for whatever reasons chose not to extol the existence of old age pension benefits, as provided for in the legislation of 1908.

Given the fragility at this time of nationally active pensioner organizations, the agenda-setting function, typically fulfilled by interest groups, was largely assumed by other political actors, especially career civil servants and elective officeholders. Civil servants were important by virtue of their near monopoly of specialized state pension knowledge, and capacity to focus on this field in single-minded manner. They ended up playing a critical role in the formulation of regulations relating to implementation of pension programs, and in advice-giving relating to proposed reforms of the existing system. And elective politicians also asserted themselves vigorously, doing so in the apparent belief that there was little risk, fiscal or political, attendant on their playing an active role. All of this can be interpreted in light of functionalist theory, which teaches that interest articulation must occur somewhere in the political system, and that while interest groups can be, and often are, important in assuming this function, other political actors are fully capable of doing so given certain conditions.[14]

Phase Three

From the standpoint of interest group theory, phase three can be interpreted as marking the point at which the elderly, having evolved from their earlier stage of potential, finally achieved a rate of interaction needed to qualify as an interest group, and also—to a more limited extent—as an organized group in the sense employed by David B. Truman.[15] The tendency for such newly formed groups to attain large size—and some, such as the American Association of Retired Persons (AARP) in the United States and Age Concern England, now became large by any standard—resulted in part because of their capacity to

---

14. Gabriel Almond and James S. Coleman, *Politics in the Developing Areas* (Princeton: Princeton University Press, 1960).

15. For discussion of the possible evolution from potential group to interest group to organization, see Truman, *Governmental Process*, p. 114.

offer selective incentives, or direct member services, in the manner empha-sized by Olson for the maintenance of large voluntary organizations.[16]

Olson's theory can be applied to phase three in other respects as well, but only on the basis of some modification. The prototypical phase three aging organization was the general membership type having broadly defined social policy goals. As previously mentioned, voluntary organizations of this type were reflective of the then-existing system's public pension schemes, which extended coverage to all, or nearly all, elderly persons, but whose benefit levels were still insufficient to protect adequately against the risk of economic insecurity, including especially the risk of poverty in old age. Olson's thought cannot be easily applied, in unmodified form, to the emergence of these aging-related voluntary organizations, given its rejection of shared interest as a basis for rationally inclined persons lending their support to large voluntary organizations. Yet it is the case that the interest groups here under discussion in fact did strongly emphasize senior citizens' and retirees' shared economic concerns. The present data are therefore supportive of Terry M. Moe's revised approach to membership, which basically accepts Olson's reasoning, but modifies it through an insistence upon the motivational significance of com-mon interests, even for large economic interest groups.[17]

The Uniqueness of Phase Four

The present, fourth phase of policy development was ushered in by a series of legislative and executive branch decisions whose general effect was to expand significantly the visibility of public pensions and other government benefits in aging. These events were associated in time with subsequent realignments of age-political arenas in each of the countries, including the tendency for exist-ing seniors' organizations to expand numerically and also in terms of re-sources. Many new groups now were formed. As demonstrated previously, the transition from phases three to four was facilitated by certain wider soci-etal trends: the general public's increased awareness of older people as a social presence, the expansion in the sheer number of elderly persons (both absolutely and as a proportion of total populations), and the growing recep-tivity to elderly voters on the part of party leaders and elective officeholders.

As mentioned in chapter 1, the apparent linkage between policy outputs in aging and interest group behavior has been noted from time to time by other observers in discussions devoted to particular countries and a particular period of public policy. The present study, in which this relationship is viewed in historical as well as cross-national perspective, enables one to broaden and

---

16. Olson, *Logic of Collective Action*.
17. Moe, *Organization of Interests*, p. 221.

deepen the existing level of understanding; the factors that have caused a unique pattern of interest group behavior at this time can be interpreted with increased clarity.

From the beginnings of phase one through the close of phase three, the fundamental problem facing age-advocacy voluntary organizations was essentially that of survival. Despite some variation across countries and across periods, it was generally the case that the danger of organizational bankruptcy during these years was never far from group leaders' thoughts. The actual rate of bankruptcy was fairly high, and the survivor groups were the exceptions, not the norm. In phase four, for the first time, sheer survival ceased to be such a central problem, and instead the challenges became those that are typical of stable organizations, mature in their outlooks. Even though a lack of relevant data renders it impossible to treat this topic with any certainty, one can plausibly speculate that, for example, the more highly politicized organizations—National Pensioners and Senior Citizens Federation (NP&SCF), Canada; National Council of Senior Citizens (NCSC), United States; and Pensioners' Voice, Britain—now must contend with the problem of boundary definition. By this I mean the need to preserve the groups' traditional uniqueness against threats posed by emergent rival groups, typically only recently politicized, but often enjoying a larger tangible resource base than themselves. Other types of organizations on aging must contend with their own peculiar problems and dilemmas. But again, sheer survival does not seem to be among them, at least not typically.

Expanding government outputs have been suggested as fundamental in this changed setting, serving to generate greatly increased senior citizens' awareness of aging benefits, and, indirectly, to augment the fund of available incentives, essential in attracting and maintaining group memberships. It is my impression that in the industrialized world generally the number and size of seniors' organizations have increased of late at a rate exceeding that for counterpart interest groups identified with other categories of the population or other areas of social concern. Assuming that to be the case, it is readily explainable on the basis of the sheer massiveness of government's impression on this area, as reflected in enlarged expenditure figures and in other ways, and the wide disparity between that impression and those made elsewhere.

The actions of government in phase four are interpretable in light of what has been termed the "social construction of reality." This concept has been richly developed on the basis of investigations conducted by several scholars, and two schools now exist concerning the manner in which society and reality are linked. In the view of one school, as expressed in separate writings by two analysts of aging policy, Carroll L. Estes and Peter Townsend, it is a process whereby society employs its potential to manufacture problems, to confuse both the public and the relevant clientele population, and finally to enhance the narrow interests of service organizations.[18] The second school employs the same terminology in a more neutral, less ideological spirit. Thus, David A. Rochefort develops what he terms the "social images perspective"—the images being viewed as socially determined,[19] and likewise Aaron Wildavsky speaks of how policy problems serve "to give affirmation to a particular conception of reality."[20] And of particular interest in this context are the insights of Charles D. Elder and Roger W. Cobb, who write jointly about the social definition of reality in regard to American politics generally,[21] as well as to U.S. policy on aging.[22]

The present findings can be usefully interpreted in a social images or social construction context, as defined by the second of the schools of thought more so than the first. The findings point to the potential inherent in government to not simply define what is real at a given point, but to redefine, over time, the nature of that reality. This study identifies four phases, the first involving influence exerted indirectly by foreign governments and the other three a direct shaping by domestic governments of what is meant by "aging" and "the aged." (One can reasonably anticipate that the future will see further such definitions and redefinitions.) With each such definition of the problem, a new political environment has been seen to emerge, its participant actors becoming significantly involved in shaping the stage next to follow. The membership appeals adopted, and the content of the policy agendas selected, are in large part predictable on the basis of the stage, or phase, existing at the time of a particular group's formation.

An Alternative Hypothesis

The phenomenon chiefly of interest in this study, namely the increase in the number and size of voluntary organizations for seniors that has occurred during the twentieth century, is open to varying interpretations. The increase

---

18. Carroll L. Estes, *The Aging Enterprise* (San Francisco: Jossey-Bass, 1979), pp. 6–10; Peter Townsend, "The Structured Dependency of the Elderly: A Creation of Social Policy in the Twentieth Century," *Ageing and Society* 1 (1981): 9.

19. David A. Rochefort, *American Social Welfare Policy: Dynamics of Formulation and Change* (Boulder, Colo.: Westview Press, 1986), chap. 1.

20. Aaron Wildavsky, *Speaking Truth to Power: The Art and Craft of Policy Analysis* (New Brunswick, N.J.: Transaction Books, 1987).

21. Cobb and Elder, *Participation in American Politics*, p. 172.

22. Charles D. Elder and Roger W. Cobb, "Agenda-building and the Politics of Aging," *Policy Studies Journal* 13 (September 1984): 116. See also Cobb and Elder, *Participation in American Politics*, p. 172; Wildavsky, *Speaking Truth to Power*.

has not gone unnoticed by previous observers, and one needs to take into account these alternative views as a means of comprehending more fully the viewpoint advanced in the present study.

An explanation commonly offered in the literature for the proliferation of interest groups on aging is one based on demographic trends. Such explanations typically begin by pointing out that in the late nineteenth century the number of persons aged sixty-five and above commenced a steady expansion in industrialized countries, both in absolute numbers and as a percentage of total populations. It is further observed that the late nineteenth and twentieth centuries witnessed a substantial increase in the number of elderly persons living in retirement, as opposed to full work-force participation; indeed, retirement now accounts for roughly one-fifth of the average person's life-span.[23]

The three countries here under investigation are consistent with the wider international pattern noted in the literature. In Canada, the proportion of persons sixty-five and above increased from 5.1 percent of the population in 1901 to 9.6 percent in 1981; in Britain, it rose over the same span of years from 4.7 percent of the total to 14.8 percent; and in the United States, it went from 4.1 percent of the whole in 1900 to 11.3 percent in 1980.[24]

Observers have then gone on to stress the apparent connection between the aging of populations, the trend toward retirement, and the efforts undertaken by political entrepreneurs ("seniors' organizers") to form voluntary organizations around aging issues. The view commonly taken is that the present-day existence of viable membership organizations of seniors, in addition to other organizations not primarily composed of seniors but sympathetic to their interests, can be directly linked to the large potential membership implicit in the demographic trends.[25]

Any thoughtful observer needs to bear in mind the increasing older and

---

23. C. G. Gifford, *Canada's Fighting Seniors* (Toronto: James Lorimer, 1990), chap. 1; William W. Lammers, *Public Policy and the Aging* (Washington, D.C.: Congressional Quarterly Press, 1983), chap. 1; Christine L. Day, *What Older Americans Think: Interest Groups and Aging Policy* (Princeton: Princeton University Press, 1990), pp. 17–18.

24. M. C. Urquard and K. A. Buckley, eds., *Historical Statistics of Canada*, 2d ed. (Ottawa: Statistics Canada, 1983); U.K. Central Statistical Office, *Annual Abstract of Statistics* (London: Her Majesty's Stationery Office, 1990); U.S. Bureau of the Census, *Historical Statistics of the United States: Colonial Times to 1970* (Washington, D.C.: Government Printing Office, 1975).

25. Gifford, for example, remarks,

We are just completing the first generation—the pioneer generation—of seniors sufficiently numerous to create movements and institutions required by this new factor (i.e., retirement) in our national life. . . . [T]he number of Canadian seniors has doubled during the lifetime of some of the leaders in this book. . . . As the years go by and the numbers of retired people increase, so will their political clout. (Gifford, *Canada's Fighting Seniors*, pp. 8–9)

retiree population as an influence on expansion in the number and scope of seniors' organizations. And yet I am reluctant entirely to accept this line of thought, which I consider to be suggestive in some ways, but misleading in others. It would seem that a satisfactory account of the formation and growth of interest groups of this type should offer an explanation for the tendency, pointed out in chapter 1, for such groups to form in clusters. Unfortunately, the demographic hypothesis is problematic in this regard. The relevant census data indicate that the increased number of seniors as a proportion of national totals has occurred fairly steadily, year by year and decade by decade. That being the case, it is difficult to understand why age-group formation has not been similarly steady.

Logic would suggest, moreover, that population aging should exert its greatest impact on age-group formation in the immediate aftermath of surges in the size of the sixty-five and above age cohort. Yet, census data indicate that the largest such surges in population aging have not in fact had this anticipated effect. The largest surges in the relative size of aging populations occurred during the first third of the twentieth century: in Canada, the aged in relative terms surged 45.6 percent over the thirty-year period 1911–41 (i.e., from 4.6 percent to 6.7 percent of total population); in Britain, the thirty-year time span beginning in 1900 saw an increase of 57.5 percent (i.e., from 4.7 percent to 7.4 percent of the national total); and in the United States, the 1900–30 period witnessed a 65.8 percent rise (i.e., from 4.1 percent to 6.8 percent). These large relative increases did not recur in subsequent years, even though the numbers of elderly persons continued to rise. Thus, in Canada, the fraction of persons sixty-five and above grew 25.6 percent over the thirty-year period 1951–81—a decline from the above-mentioned 45.6; in Britain, the elderly's share of total population rose 24.6 percent between 1950 and 1980—a decrease from the above-mentioned 57.5; and in the United States, the fraction represented by the same age grouping grew 39.5 percent from 1950 to 1980—down from the above figure of 65.8.[26] These numbers would lead one to expect, on the basis of purely demographic analysis, that the greatest waves of senior-group formation would have occurred in the earlier of the two periods, namely toward the end of, or immediately following, the first third of the century. Yet, as indicated earlier in this study, the largest increases in fact have occurred during the last third. In sum, the demographic hypothesis tends to over-predict interest group formation in the early part of the century, and to under-predict the rate for more recent decades.

None of this is intended to suggest that population aging is unimportant. What it does suggest is an apparent need to avoid an undue emphasis on

---

26. Urquard, *Historical Statistics of Canada*; U.S. Bureau of the Census, *Historical Statistics of the United States*; U.K. Central Statistical Office, *Annual Abstract of Statistics*.

demography, and to bear in mind other relevant dimensions. Of special interest in this connection are public policy outputs. Based on the evidence presented in this study, one can usefully conceptualize such outputs as intervening between various contextual factors, among them population aging and the large-scale retirement of persons over sixty-five, and the decisions arrived at by entrepreneurs/organizers to attempt seriously the formation of new interest organizations. Public policy outputs emerge as a necessary, though by no means sufficient, explanation for the waves of senior-group formation in the twentieth century, and as especially useful in explaining their timing.

Continuing Cross-National Contrasts

Having made clear the apparent significance from an age-policy standpoint of the various stages of policy evolution, one now can return to the point made earlier regarding the persistent contrasts among the three countries. What attributes may have distinguished each of these countries—not just at one given stage but at all stages? As previously suggested, such national characteristics deserve consideration even if they do not represent this study's most salient finding.

Britain

In the case of Britain, the political context of aging has been distinguished from the outset by a pronounced crystallization around London, the national capital. From the National Committee on Organized Labor, formed in the late nineteenth century, through the formation at the end of the 1960s of Age Concern England, London has served as the national center for pension activism, and of related aging politics.

Admittedly, exceptions to this pattern exist, most especially Pensioners' Voice (or National Federation of Retirement Pensions Association [NFRPA]), whose headquarters throughout almost its entire six decades of existence has been in the north of England—Blackburn, in Lancashire. Nevertheless, this may be less of an exception than it might appear. This organization was officially constituted at a meeting held in the late 1930s in central London, and its center of activity would remain in London for the next several months. The decision taken subsequently to relocate its base of operations to the North was largely fortuitous, stemming more from the disruptions associated with World War II than from any long-term plan or strategy. One should also point out that the relative remoteness of the headquarters has not been without its cost in terms of NFRPA's political influence. Even though the group for a time enjoyed something approaching a monopoly of pension advocacy in Parliament, the loss of that preeminence during the 1970s and 1980s was at least partially attributable to its physical remoteness from the center of British government. Upon close inspection, then, this case can serve as additional confirmation of the point made concerning London's unique importance.

The centrality of London most probably was a factor in the recent clustering of interest groups into various coalitions, the age coalition and the pension. Since regionalism is relatively less important in Britain than in the other two countries, British pensioner groups have sorted themselves out more along social class than on regional lines. As previously noted, the pension coalition has long displayed a pronounced working-class and lower middle-class coloration, whereas the age coalition, with its strong emphasis on social access and social service concerns, has been oriented more strongly toward the concerns of pensioners and retirees somewhat higher on the economic ladder. The fact that national voluntary organizations in both these coalitions are in most cases London-centered has obviously facilitated their coalescence.

Canada

The Canadian case is in some respects the polar opposite of the British. Even though both countries were heirs, traditionally, to the English poor law system, and notwithstanding Canada's inclusion until the 1920s as a dominion within the British Empire, the two nations have evolved in fundamentally different directions with respect to aging policy and age-political organizations. Canada's decentralized form of federalism, in which the ten provinces enjoy considerable autonomy, has strongly impacted seniors' organizations and other age-advocacy groups. It was not accidental that the first age-based seniors' organization in North America was in British Columbia, or that senior citizens coalesced first in various provincial federations before managing to establish even a tenuous presence in Ottawa. (On a research trip taken in the early 1980s pursuant to this study, I was astonished to discover that not a single Canadian seniors' organization then maintained an office in the national capital vicinity.)

The implications of decentralized federalism for Canada's political arena on aging, however, extend beyond the tendency toward weak interest group representation at the center. They include as well a tendency for seniors' organizations to be internally federalized, with representation based on provincial affiliation. The three largest nationally based seniors groups in Canada—Canadian Pensioners Concerned (CPC), NP&SCF, and One Voice Seniors Network—all elect their governing boards largely on the basis of provincial representation, and two of the largest seniors' organizations in Canada, namely Federation de l'Age d'Or due Quebec (FADOQ) and United Senior Citizens of Ontario, are both provincially based.

Such imbedding of regionalism in organizational structure is reflective of

Canada's tendency to assign age-program administrative functions chiefly to the provinces. As a leading observer notes, "The responsibilities and activities of provincial governments are much more extensive [in aging] than those of the federal government."[27] The Canadian public appears to be fully aware of this provincial tilt to their governmental system, and of the strong provincial role in age-benefits administration. Such awareness has evidently contributed to the larger scale and resource base typifying seniors' provincial federations, as compared to the resource scarcity typifying their counterparts at the federal level.

An argument can be made, however, that this imbalance in relative strength between groups operating at the two levels of government does not entirely square with present realities. Some of the more critically important age-related programs, including all the major ones in the field of income security (Canada/Quebec Pension Plan [CPP], Guaranteed Income Supplement [GIS], Old Age Security [OAS], and Spouses Allowance), fall within the constitutional jurisdiction of Ottawa, and it therefore appears that the traditional interest group weakness at the political center is problematic from a seniors' standpoint.

United States

If there has been any single feature that most distinguishes the American age-policy arena from its counterparts elsewhere, it would be its extraordinary proliferation of voluntary organizations. Such diversity of representation cannot be explained simply on the basis of the disparity in population (i.e., the fact that the United States exceeds Canada's population by a factor of ten and the British by a factor of four). Even when population is controlled, the pattern remains. Thus, for example, California's population is roughly half that of Britain and approximately equal to that of Canada as a whole, yet this state traditionally has had a larger number of aging-related interest groups than has either of those countries.[28] A more persuasive explanation would take into account the "multiple crack" character of American government, in which separation of powers in both national and state governments is combined with a federal union under which jurisdiction is constitutionally divided between national government and the states. These features encourage the formation of interest groups in all fields of public policy, since access denied at any one point often can be offset through access achieved elsewhere in the

---

27. Kenneth Kernaghan and Olivia Kuper, *Coordination in Canadian Governments: A Case Study in Aging Policy* (Toronto: Institute of Public Administration of Canada, 1983), p. 39.

28. Jackson K. Putnam, *Old-Age Politics in California: From Richardson to Reagan* (Stanford: Stanford University Press, 1970); Day, *What Older Americans Think*, pp. 20–22.

political system. Also contributing to the pattern has been the traditional American emphasis on voluntarism and the striving for solutions to social problems through collective action—an orientation already fully developed by the mid-nineteenth century, as is attested to by the early nineteenth century writings of Alexis de Tocqueville.[29]

Interest groups on aging could serve as an excellent example of this wider American tendency toward group participation and activism. Whether one is speaking of phase one, when the AAOAS competed with the Fraternal Order of Eagles and the AALL for the leadership of the early pension movement,[30] or of the present phase four, when age-active organizations in Washington, D.C., are dazzling in their variety, and when the AARP is perhaps the largest direct-membership organization in the country, the array of interest groups in this field has been consistently remarkable.

Such diversity is not just apparent from a distance, as viewed through a scholarly lens, but represents a visible reality for persons active in this field. For them, it has posed something of a problem. Given the plethora of American organizations on aging, they have found it necessary to establish coordinating councils where differing political priorities can be considered and potential conflicts ironed out before reaching the public arena. As earlier pointed out, these councils have been successful, but only up to a point, considering that differences of opinion among them from time to time still reach public attention. It is useful to point out that such councils are thus far a uniquely American phenomenon, given the absence of counterpart organizations in either Canada or Britain.

Larger Implications

The findings reported in this study point in several directions. In the section to follow their apparent wider implications are explored under the following four rubrics: (1) relevance for the comparative study of social policy, (2) patronage as an organizational resource, (3) nonpatronage groups' incentive systems, and (4) long-term threats to gray lobby stability and political influence.

Relevance for Comparative Policy Studies

The findings reported here contrast somewhat with the general pattern of social welfare studies to be found in the literature. Published writings in the

29. Alexis de Tocqueville, *Democracy in America*, translated by Henry Reeve, 2 vols. (New York: Vintage Books, 1958).

30. Henry J. Pratt, *The Gray Lobby* (Chicago: University of Chicago Press, 1976), chap. 1.

field of social security and aging have tended to particularize each country's policy history. Writings dealing with the United States, for example, typically emphasize that country's late adoption of its highly important Social Security Act in 1935—decades after the comparable enactments in most other industrial nations and despite the obvious economic capacity of the United States, from as far back as the turn of the century, to fund a national old age pension. Such writings strongly underscore the theme of America's uniqueness and exceptionalism.[31] Similarly, the literature on Britain stresses the features unique to that country, for example, Britain's embrace of the "subsistence principle," under which society is viewed as accepting, from as far back as the sixteenth century, an obligation to protect the "social minimum" and "poverty line" while at the same time maintaining the virtues of thrift and personal savings.[32] Still another country whose uniqueness has been emphasized in the literature is the Germany of Chancellor Otto von Bismarck. As more than one analyst observes, modern social insurance originated in Bismarckian Germany, where it was promoted by ministers of state and civil servants not as a progressive measure, but rather as an antisocialist device for building working-class support for the state.[33] The findings of this study, while in no sense refuting the theme of national exceptionalism, do suggest an alternative perspective. The stage-to-stage contrasts within any given country are found to be substantially more pronounced than the contrasts cross-nationally at any single stage. It is shown as well that at any given stage the three countries have been remarkably similar in regard to their prevailing age-political arenas. While certain continuing between-country contrasts are identified, it is the marked within-stage similarities that stand out most clearly, and that appear most suggestive in a wider policy studies context. The theme of national exceptionalism finds essentially no support in the present data.

Patronage and the Resource Base of Formed Groups

One of this study's more-intriguing findings relates to the conditions tending to facilitate interest group formation and survival. As shown, newly formed

---

31. Jill Quadragno, *The Transformation of Old Age Security: Class and Politics in the American Welfare State* (Chicago: University of Chicago Press, 1988), chap. 8 and passim; John B. Williamson, Linda Evans, and Lawrence A. Powell, *The Politics of Aging: Power and Policy* (Springfield, Ill.: Charles C. Thomas, 1982); Abraham Holtzman, *The Townsend Movement* (New York: Bookman Associates, 1963), chap. 1.

32. Richard Lee Deaton, *The Political Economy of Pensions: Power, Politics, and Social Change in Canada, Britain, and the United States* (Vancouver: University of British Columbia Press, 1989), p. 21. See also Bentley B. Gilbert, *British Social Policy, 1914–1939* (Ithaca: Cornell University Press, 1970).

33. See, for example, Arnold Heidenheimer, Hugh Heclo, and Carolyn Adams, *Comparative Public Policy: The Politics of Social Choice in Europe and America* (New York: St. Martin's Press, 1975), p. 193.

interest groups in this field have not always been successful; indeed, organizational bankruptcies have been fairly common. As previously mentioned,
Jack L. Walker and his University of Michigan colleagues significantly
enhanced the understanding of new group formation by documenting the
prevalence of outside patronage in the context of group formation, especially
at such groups' earliest, fledgling stage. In those terms, the present findings
offer some additional insights. In line with Walker's view, successful organizing ventures in aging have often relied at least partly on some form of outside
patronage.

Still, the present findings give reasons for caution, lest one overstate the
significance of patronage from an age-group standpoint. Having once survived beyond the early, fledgling stage, the further expansion of an organization is likely to be less and less dependent on the provision of outside subsidies, whether governmental or nongovernmental. While this study does not
probe deeply into the extent of patronage among the seniors' organizations,
various scraps of evidence from the three countries give rise to the suspicion
that subsidies from various patrons, even when continuing, are likely to be
seen as less and less critical. Governments' most substantial contributions to
these groups appear to consist less of patronage, in the final analysis, than of
other supportive elements, including legitimacy—accruing to the groups as
one by-product of governments' having declared aging to be a critically important field—and enlargement of the base of potential members—arising from
governments' indirect role in helping to expand senior citizens' collective
consciousness and group awareness.

The Self-generating Aging Organizations

Although patronage served as an element in the emergence and growth of
several of the organizations covered in this study, some important exceptions
to that pattern should not be overlooked or minimized. Certain interest
groups, of which the NP&SCF (in Canada), the NFRPA (in Britain), and
the Gray Panthers (United States), are perhaps the leading present-day examples, have evolved without apparent benefit of patronage from any source.
Relying heavily on volunteer labor for the performance of vital functions, and
with headquarters expenses kept low through an avoidance of office quarters
in some expensive national capital venue, these organizations have remained
free of dependency on established and well-funded benefactors. It is true that
the resulting organizational austerity has not been to the liking of all their
active members, as exemplified by the efforts on the part of some NP&SCF
leaders in the 1980s to qualify their group for funding from the Bronfman
foundation. Yet, the proved capacity of these groups to endure over time in
the absence of patronage should serve as a caution to any easy overgeneraliza-
tion regarding the necessity of that particular form of support.

There is some tendency for interest groups of this type to trace their origins back to campaigns that aimed to achieve expanded state pension benefits. Yet, their survival would not have been possible simply on the basis of member agreement with that or any other political objective. An additional element in their survival was their leaders' pronounced emphasis on the importance of the groups' local associations (in Britain), or provincial federations (in Canada), or networks (in the case of the Gray Panthers). Throughout their formative stages each of these organizations relied upon revenues generated out of chapter dues, making use of an agreed upon dues structure. Little if any effort was made at this time to attract support from directly contributing members who were not chapter affiliated. Such a structure enabled them to generate nationwide support based upon members' feelings of solidarity, mutual dependency, and face-to-face contacts. The members might receive little or nothing in the way of direct benefits from the national organization—essentially only an occasional newsletter or house organ—but the lack of such benefits evidently did not impede the sense of member loyalty, given the power of the local or provincial chapters to generate commitment and a sense of personal satisfaction.

Although this system obviously worked for many years, it has not proved so successful recently, under the conditions associated with phase four. In recent years, as their chapter or provincial structures have weakened, and as competition from other seniors' organizations has posed an increasing threat, these groups' national leaders have placed increasing emphasis on the need for support among directly contributing individuals. Other new avenues, likewise aimed at overcoming threats to the support base, also are being explored. It is not entirely clear at this writing whether these new strategies will prove adequate from an organizational-maintenance standpoint for any of the organizations mentioned here.

It is also interesting that among the numerous political organizations covered in this study not a single one proved capable of surviving over time in the absence of both substantial external patronage and a strong network of supportive local chapters. In other words, one or the other of these elements can be considered as essential to long-term group viability. And in a few cases, for example the NCSC (in the United States) and Age Concern England, both supportive elements were present in combination.

Speculations on the Future of Gray Lobbies

Differing views can be taken regarding the findings that emerge out of this study. Some observers may view the data as a basis for satisfaction, as evidencing liberal democracy's capacity to give voice to its citizenry in fresh, new ways, including the formation of new interest groups. Others may view the findings as offering no such basis for optimism. Instead, they would emphasize the point, made in this book's opening chapter, that the present system of representation displays a marked bias in favor of the higher-status, higher-income elderly, while inadequately representing their age peers at or near the bottom of the social scale, including especially racial minorities. Other interpretations, in a similarly normative vein, are also possible.

Rather than adopt either the optimistic or the pessimistic view, my own inclination is to consider the findings from a slightly more detached perspective. The level of state activity on aging over the course of the twentieth century, in each of the three countries, has followed a linear upward trend, starting from a low point in the second phase, and then rising to quite high levels of inflation-adjusted spending during the present, fourth phase of policy development. Assume that the analysis has succeeded in demonstrating a fundamental relationship in each of the cases between the level of prior state activity on aging and the subsequent scope and character of its age-based organizational development. Taking that for granted, the following interesting question presents itself: what consequences might ensue for the gray lobbies of Britain, Canada, and the United States if their national governments at some future point were to substantially scale back, and even possibly eliminate entirely, their present heavy involvement in aging, including possible drastic downsizing of existing programs in the fields of income security, social services, and health care?

I wish to emphasize that I am in no way personally supportive of any such drastic shift in governmental priorities. My purpose in raising the point is that it is not inconceivable or even necessarily highly improbable. Although a decade or more in the past it might have appeared idle to ponder the kind of policy shift suggested here, given the seeming invulnerability of existing old age security programs, such a sanguine view can no longer be taken as a given. Some recent rumblings have occurred, not just among the three countries here under discussion but more generally among the industrial democracies, indicative of an apparent decline in public support for existing old age benefits. Thus, a leading student of aging in Britain, Alan Walker, remarks of that country that "a significant shift has begun to occur in the longstanding consensus about the deprived status of elderly persons, and, to some extent, about their position as the most deserving of minority groups."[34] The 1983 proposal by the Thatcher government to abolish the State Earnings-related Pension System (SERPS), and to promote instead personal pensions, was widely viewed as reflective of a larger movement to shift responsibility from

---

34. Alan Walker, "Pensions and the Production of Poverty in Old Age," in Chris Phillipson and Alan Walker, eds., *Aging and Social Policy: A Critical Assessment* (Aldershot, England: Gower Publishing, 1986), p. 194.

the state to the individual. And nowhere was the effect of this apparent shift in the British mood more tangibly felt than among pensioner advocates, who are reported in a 1990 study as being "no longer able to command public attention."[35] Similarly, interviews conducted in the late 1980s in Washington, D.C., by Christine L. Day suggest that a similar change in political mood may also apply to the United States. She reports that the gray lobby's former defensive strength, as manifested in its capacity to veto unwanted changes in federal policy, is beginning to weaken in the face of budgetary constraints and a growing political backlash against the elderly's special status.[36]

None of this is meant to suggest that existing age-benefit programs, including old age pensions, stand in any immediate jeopardy. The 1980s were marked by several attempts by government leaders to scale back aging benefits, which were subsequently defeated following storms of protest. At a time when many other social welfare constituencies were suffering cuts in an effort to trim government deficits, spending on programs that benefit the elderly was largely protected, reflecting in part an awareness among policymakers that spending on the elderly is still more popular than social welfare spending generally.[37] Still, having said all this, it remains the case that past trends in this area ought not be taken as a sure guide to future events, and that successful attacks on aging programs cannot be entirely ruled out on the basis of present evidence.

What might be the impact of such a reversal of course by governments on the larger political context of aging? Several plausible answers to this question are possible. For some types of seniors' organizations, especially those with a reasonably large and stable resource base, it would probably have a stimulative effect, heightening their consciousness and enhancing their level of age political advocacy. Other groups might be little affected by any such diminishment of government involvement. Yet I imagine there would be other seniors' organizations that would be very negatively affected. What particular kinds of groups might that be true of?

The suggestion that certain kinds of seniors' organizations continue to be heavily dependent for their welfare upon the continuance of a positive attitude toward seniors on the part of government reflects more than the simple extension of this book's essential thesis to the effect that governmental programs tend to impact interest groups active in a given field, and that many groups

35. John Miles, "Towards Equality: How Pensions Campaigns Are Changing: A Study of the Greater London Pensioners Association, 1989–1990" (Master of Science in gerontology thesis, King's College, University of London, 1990), p. 23.

36. Day, *What Older Americans Think*, pp. 107–8.

37. Ibid., p. 104.

have arisen in part in the wake of the emergence of such a positive attitude. That is part of what is being suggested here, but it is not the only part, or even necessarily the most important. Additional support is provided by some analogous cases.

Some Possibly Analogous Cases

There may be no precise modern parallel to the hypothetical situation outlined here. Governments do not commonly choose to make large-scale and persistent commitments in a certain area of social welfare only to reverse course and withdraw from that field at a later point. Nevertheless, governments do occasionally abandon earlier ventures, and under such circumstances interest groups active in that field often have been adversely affected. In this regard, two cases, both drawn from the American experience, are interesting to contemplate as possible analogous cases.

The first is the American war on poverty of the 1960s. Briefly stated, this policy venture began in a series of smaller programs created during the early 1960s under President John F. Kennedy, which then culminated in the 1964 Equal Opportunity Act as enacted under Lyndon B. Johnson. The 1964 act authorized the creation of a new federal agency, the Office of Economic Opportunity, and provided for the expenditure of substantial new money in the poverty field. President Johnson's decision to reformulate as a war the package of poverty-targeted proposals that had been inherited from his predecessor was a brilliant political strategy, given that any nonmilitary metaphor probably would have failed to mobilize public opinion or would have aroused even more hostility among conservatives.[38]

Yet, while it aroused the sympathy of the nation, the war imagery at the same time heightened expectations, and this in the end proved fatal to a program that was to remain underfunded in the face of a massive social problem. At its peak in the late 1960s and early 1970s, the program amounted to several billions of dollars in expenditure and the employment of hundreds of workers in Community Action Programs (CAPs) and other local offices across the country. By 1972, the program was in deep political trouble, and the following year the Office of Economic Opportunity was dismantled. The war at this point was essentially called off.

This eight-year effort by the federal government was associated with a flurry of interest group formation. Based on the interest groups listed under the antipoverty heading in the *Encyclopedia of Associations*, the number of

---

38. Michael B. Katz, *The Undeserving Poor: From the War on Poverty to the War on Welfare* (New York: Pantheon Books, 1989), p. 90.

such groups at the national level increased steadily during the 1960s and early 1970s, reaching a peak of nineteen in 1974, yet by 1990, with government legitimation in this field no longer forthcoming, their number had declined to fourteen. There was also an obvious qualitative change over this sixteen-year period in regard to the types of voluntary organizations newly established. In contrast to the militant and activist organizations characteristic of the 1960s, as suggested by the words employed in their names (*corps*, *task force*, and *center*), the more recent 1990 listing is suggestive of groups with essentially social service and philanthropic orientations, given the common use at this time of key words such as *association*, *fund*, and *foundation*. The war metaphor, highly visible in the earlier organizational names, is wholly absent from the more recent set.[39]

The potential inherent in all this for interest group formation and maintenance is nicely illustrated by the case of the National Welfare Rights Organization (NWRO). Formed in 1966 in the wake of recently enacted antipoverty legislation and the reinvigoration of the civil rights movement, in which the NWRO founder, George Wiley, had been an activist, this movement flourished for as long as federal patronage and the larger sense of federal legitimacy was available. But as these waned, NWRO likewise paled; Wiley quit the group in 1972 and his organization was finally disbanded in 1974 when no longer able to pay its bills. One analyst concludes that the decline and demise of NWRO was traceable to three factors: the decline in the welfare explosion of the late 1960s, the dismantlement of the Office of Economic Opportunity, and wider political developments, especially the election of Richard Nixon with his strong antipathy to the existing poverty program and close association with conservative intellectuals.[40]

The second possible analogy that is useful to consider is the determination of Ronald Reagan's administration, in the early 1980s, to reduce the influence of interest groups on American political life, especially as manifested in the efforts of liberal interest groups and activists to expand government spending. As argued persuasively in an essay by Harold Wolman and Fred Teitelbaum,[41] the Reagan White House sought to achieve such reduction in unwanted influence through a three-pronged campaign that included (1) the

---

39. *Encyclopedia of Associations* (Detroit: Gale Publishing Co.): 9th ed. (1975), 25th ed. (1990). The figure of nineteen given for 1975 was up marginally from 1973, when the total was eighteen (8th ed., [1973]).

40. David Street, George T. Martin, Jr., and Laura Kramer Gordon, *The Welfare Industry: Functionaries and Recipients in Public Aid* (Beverly Hills, Calif.: Sage Publications, 1979), p. 167.

41. Harold Wolman and Fred Teitelbaum, "Interest Groups and the Reagan Presidency," in Lester M. Salamon and Michael S. Lund, eds., *The Reagan Presidency and the Governing of America* (Washington, D.C.: Urban Institute Press, 1984), pp. 297–329.

decentralization of programs from the federal to the state levels, thereby reducing the importance of Washington, D.C., where liberal-oriented groups were well positioned and influential, (2) direct attacks made on the receipt of federal funding by groups identified with liberal causes ("defunding the left"), and (3) the exercise of fiscal discipline whereby existing federal programs in the domestic policy sphere would be reduced substantially in size. (The final reduction for fiscal year 1982 was a substantial $31.6 billion.) All this, it was hoped, would force the liberal groups into a new, redistributive, policy arena where their chances of achieving favorable policy outcomes were substantially lower than was true of the old distributive arena to which they were accustomed.

There can be little question that these several maneuvers had roughly their intended impact. Wolman and Teitelbaum, although cautious in projecting the possible long-term impacts of the White House actions, are explicit that in the short run "the influence of spending-oriented special-interest groups has indeed been diminished, primarily as a result of political support for overall budget constraint."[42] Among the three factors designed to reduce the liberal groups' power and influence, the most devastating, perhaps, was the last, namely fiscal discipline, since it adversely affected all the liberal "cause groups." Of lesser consequence were the first and second of the factors mentioned. Thus, the cutoff in federal patronage to interest groups (i.e., the "defunding of the left") had but modest effects, given that a majority of such human resources–related groups had not been in receipt of significant governmental funding in the first place. And the strategy of decentralizing programs to the state level was thwarted by a variety of forces.[43]

Therefore, were the preceding cases in fact analogous to the current circumstance of senior citizen organizations? Are the latter as vulnerable to the vicissitudes of changing public policy outputs as was true of the NWRO and the liberal interest groups targeted by the Reagan administration? The answer would appear to be a qualified no. It is true that any substantial reductions in government pensions, and in other aging-related public programs, would adversely affect a certain category of group. Most likely to be affected would be those of sharply defined membership, whose modest self-generated resources have forced a heavy reliance on government subsidies and largess. These might include, for example, ones focused upon various marginal categories of elderly persons: racial minorities, women, gays and lesbians, and native peoples. On the other hand, such reductions in strength would likely be offset by increased potency elsewhere, especially in a renewed sense of collective consciousness and political commitment among the

---

42. Ibid., p. 329.
43. Ibid., pp. 315–16.

larger, more broadly based, seniors' organizations, many of them not heavily government dependent. Adversity obviously can be a breeder of renewed strength.

Yet a more fundamental question remains: what is the likelihood that governments will carry through, or indeed even contemplate, large-scale changes in their existing social insurance and other age-benefit programs? The answer, in my opinion, is that such likelihood is remote. From a political standpoint, it is difficult to imagine that the general public, in any of the three countries here discussed, would tolerate substantial reductions in the real value of its public pension. Conversely, existing budgetary constraints, related to soaring national deficits, make improbable any largely age-benefit boosts, at least not in the near term. That being so, the possibly analogous cases mentioned here appear as not truly analogous. The wholesale dismantling of programs, which was the eventual fate of the U.S. war on poverty, or direct attacks by public officials upon interest groups on the model of the actions taken by the early Reagan administration are highly improbable in the context of securely established and highly popular domestic programs—public pensions being a leading example.

What this amounts to in the final analysis is that the century-long connection demonstrated in this study between the content of government programs and the subsequent formation and maintenance of interest groups may now no longer apply. Governments can be expected to remain as an important source of legitimation for seniors' organizations, and government benefits will likely continue as an indirect source of age-organizational incentives. Yet this may cease to have much practical significance. Of greater significance will be the fact that changes in government old age security policy, involving either increased or decreased benefits, will most probably occur within a fairly narrow range—too narrow to impact interest groups to any marked extent. As the present phase four of policy is replaced, as surely it will be, by a subsequent phase five, one can anticipate a decoupling of old age security programs from interest group formation and maintenance. The future will likely see new interest groups formed and existing groups to some extent transformed. Yet the apparent source of such change most probably will be less obviously governmental. With increasing resources and capacity to recruit needed personnel, interest groups on aging appear to be entering upon an era of enlarged autonomy and independence. Government can be expected to continue as a major target of group activity but, as compared to the past, will likely prove less a source, directly or indirectly, of organizational sustenance.

Bibliography

Abrams, M., and B. Robinson. *Forty-six National Leaders Speak Out on Options for Older Americans*. Washington, D.C.: NRTA/AARP, 1971.

Achenbaum, W. Andrew. *Old Age in the New Land: The American Experience since 1790*. Baltimore: Johns Hopkins University Press, 1978.

———. *Shades of Gray: Old Age, American Values, and Federal Policies since 1920*. Boston: Little, Brown, 1983.

———. *Social Security: Visions and Revisions*. New York: Cambridge University Press, 1986.

Almond, Gabriel, and James S. Coleman. *Politics in the Developing Areas*. Princeton: Princeton University Press, 1960.

Altmeyer, Arthur. *The Formative Years of Social Security*. Madison: University of Wisconsin Press, 1966.

Ball, Robert M. "The Original Understanding on Social Security: Implications for Later Developments." In Theodore R. Marmor and Jerry L. Mashaw, eds., *Social Security: Beyond the Rhetoric of Crisis*, 17–40. Princeton: Princeton University Press, 1988.

Banting, K. G. *The Welfare State and Canadian Federalism*. Kingston: McGill-Queens University Press, 1982.

Beer, Samuel. *Modern British Politics: A Study in Politics and Pressure Groups*. London: Faber and Faber, 1965.

Bell, Daniel. *Marxian Socialism in the United States*. Princeton: Princeton University Press, 1967.

Bercuson, David, J. L. Granatstein, and Walter R. Young. *Sacred Trust? Brian Mulroney and the Conservative Party in Power*. Toronto: Doubleday, 1986.

Berger, Victor L. *Broadsides*. Milwaukee: Social Democratic Publishing Company, 1913.

Beveridge, William. *Social Insurance and Allied Services*. London: His Majesty's Stationery Office, 1942.

———. *Full Employment in a Free Society*. London: George Allen and Unwin, 1944.

Binstock, Robert. "Interest-Group Liberalism and the Politics of Aging." *Gerontologist* 12 (1972): 265–80.

———. "Aging and the Future of American Politics." In Frederick Eisele, ed., "The Political Consequences of Aging" (special issue). *Annals of the American Academy of Political and Social Science* 415 (September 1974): 199–212.

———. "The Aged as Scapegoat." *Gerontologist* 23 (1983): 136–43.

Birtles, J. C. *The Ties That Bind: Being the Story of the Pensions Movement in Britain*. Blackburn, England: NFOAPA, n.d. (available in NFOAPA archives, Blackburn, England).

Blaikie, Andrew. "The Emerging Political Power of the Elderly in Britain, 1908–1948." *Ageing and Society* 10 (1990): 17–39.

Block, Fred. "The Ruling Class Does Not Rule: Notes on the Marxist Theory of the State." *Socialist Revolution* 33 (May–June 1977): 6–28.

Bogdanor, Vernon. *The Age of Affluence, 1951–1964*. London: Macmillan, 1970.

Bowen, William G., and T. Aldrich Finegan. *The Economics of Labor Force Participation*. Princeton: Princeton University Press, 1969.

Brennan, E. J. T. *Education for Efficiency: The Contribution of Sydney and Beatrice Webb*. London: Athlone Press, 1975.

Brinkley, Alan. *Voices of Protest: Huey Long, Father Coughlin, and the Great Depression*. New York: Vintage Books, 1983.

Brown, J. Douglas. *The Genesis of the American Social Security System*. Princeton: Industrial Relations Section, Princeton University, 1969.

Bruce, Maurice. *The Coming of the Welfare State*. London: B. T. Batsford, 1961.

———. *The Rise of the Welfare State: English Social Policy, 1601–1971*. London: Weidenfeld and Nicholson, 1973.

Bryan, Ingrid A. *Economic Policies in Canada*. 2d ed. Toronto: Butterworths, 1986.

Bryden, Kenneth. *Old Age Pensions and Policy-making in Canada*. Montreal: McGill-Queens University Press, 1974.

Cairns, Alan. "The Governments and Societies of Canadian Federalism." *Canadian Journal of Political Science* 10, no. 4 (December 1977): 695–725.

Canada Department of National Health and Welfare. *Reports of the Administration of Old Age and Blind Persons in Canada, Fiscal Years Ended March 31, 1948 to 1952*. Ottawa: Queens Printer, 1952.

———. *Historical Statistics on Old Age Security*: Ottawa: Health and Welfare Canada, December 1986.

Canada, Statistics Canada. *Population*. Vol. 1. Ninth Census of Canada. Ottawa: Queens Printer, 1951.

Canadian Directory of Foundations. Toronto: Canadian Center for Philanthropy, 1989.

Castles, Francis G., and R. D. McKinlay. "Public Welfare Provision, Scandinavia, and the Sheer Futility of the Sociological Approach to Politics." *British Journal of Political Science* 9 (1979): 157–71.

Cates, Jerry R. *Insuring Inequality: Administrative Leadership in Social Security, 1935–1954*. Ann Arbor: University of Michigan Press, 1983.

Chambers, Clarke. *Seedtime of Reform: American Social Service and Social Action, 1918–1933*. Minneapolis: University of Minnesota Press, 1963.

Chester, D. M., and F. M. G. Willson. *The Organization of British Central Government, 1914–1956*. London: George Allen and Unwin, 1957.

Clark, Robert L. "Reply [to Ken Judge]." *Gerontologist* 22 (1982): 131–33.

Clark, Robert L., and John A. Menefree. "Federal Expenditures for the Elderly: Past and Future." *Gerontologist* 21 (1981): 132–37.

Clarke, Richard. "The Number and Size of Government Departments." *Political Quarterly* 43, no. 2 (April–June, 1972): 169–86.

Cobb, Roger W., and Charles D. Elder. *Participation in American Politics: The Dynamics of Agenda-building*. Boston: Allyn and Bacon, 1972.

Collier, David, and Richard Messick. "Prerequisites versus Diffusion: Testing Alternative Explanations of Social Security Adoption." *American Political Science Review* 69 (1975): 1299–1315.

Craig, F. W. S. *British Election Manifestos, 1900–1974.* London: Macmillan, 1974.

Creedy, John. "Comments on Chapter 4." In Michael Fogarty, ed., *Retirement Policy: The Next Fifty Years,* 96–99. London: Heineman, 1982.

Cross, M. S. *The Decline of a Good Idea.* Toronto: New Hogtown Press, 1974.

Day, Christine L. *What Older Americans Think: Interest Groups and Aging Policy.* Princeton: Princeton University Press, 1990.

Deakin, Nicholas. *The Politics of Welfare.* London: Methuen, 1987.

Dearing, Mary R. *Veterans in Politics: The Story of the G. A. R.* Baton Rouge: Louisiana State University Press, 1952.

Deaton, Richard Lee. *The Political Economy of Pensions: Power, Politics, and Social Change in Canada, Britain, and the United States.* Vancouver: University of British Columbia Press, 1989.

Demkovich, Linda E. "There's a New Kick in the Step of Senior Citizen Lobbies." *National Journal,* October 2, 1976, 1382–89.

Derthick, Martha. *Policymaking for Social Security.* Washington, D.C.: Brookings Institution, 1979.

Directory of British Associations. Beckenham, England: CBD Research, annual.

Dobelstein, Andrew W. *Serving Older Adults: Policy, Programs, and Professional Activities.* Englewood Cliffs, N.J.: Prentice-Hall, 1985.

Dugger, Ronnie. *On Reagan: The Man and His Presidency.* New York: McGraw-Hill, 1983.

Edelman, Murray. *The Symbolic Uses of Politics.* Urbana: University of Illinois Press, 1985.

Elder, Charles D., and Roger W. Cobb. "Agenda-building and the Politics of Aging." *Policy Studies Journal* 13 (1984): 115–30.

Elkin, Stephen. *City and Regime in the American Republic.* Chicago: University of Chicago Press, 1987.

Encyclopedia of Associations, 1990. 9th ed. Detroit: Gale, 1990.

Epstein, Abraham. *Facing Old Age: A Study of Old Age Dependency in the United States and Old Age Pensions.* New York: Knopf, 1922.

———. *Insecurity, a Challenge to America: A Study of Social Insurance in the United States and Abroad.* 2d rev. ed. New York: Random House, 1938.

Estes, Carroll L. *The Aging Enterprise.* San Francisco: Jossey-Bass, 1979.

Foner, Philip S. *History of the Labor Movement in the United States.* Vol. 3. New York: International Publishers, 1964.

Ford, Laura C. "The Implications of the Age Discrimination in Employment Act Amendments of 1978 for Colleges and Universities." *Journal of College and University Law* 5 (1978–79): 161–209.

Freeman, Jo. *The Politics of the Women's Liberation Movement.* New York: W. W. Norton, 1975.

Friesen, Gerald. *The Canadian Prairies: A History.* Toronto: University of Toronto Press, 1984.

Frohock, Fred M. *Rational Association*. Syracuse, N.Y.: Syracuse University Press, 1987.

Gais, Thomas L., Mark A. Peterson, and Jack L. Walker. "Interest Groups, Iron Triangles, and Representative Institutions in American National Government." *British Journal of Political Science* 14, pt. 2 (April 1984): 161–85.

Galbraith, John Kenneth. *The Affluent Society*. Boston: Houghton Mifflin, 1958.

Gifford, C. G. *Canada's Fighting Seniors*. Toronto: James Lorimer, 1990.

Gilbert, Bentley B. *British Social Policy, 1914–1939*. Ithaca: Cornell University Press, 1970.

Gilder, George. *Wealth and Poverty*. New York: Basic Books, 1981.

Glazer, Nathan. "The Social Policy of the Reagan Administration." In D. Lee Bawden, ed., *The Social Contract Revisited: Aims and Outcomes of President Reagan's Social Welfare Policy*, 221–40. Washington, D.C.: Urban Institute Press, 1984.

"Gray Panthers' First Decade." *Gray Panther Network*, July–August, 1980, 1–2.

Greenwald, Carol S. *Group Power: Lobbying and Public Policy*. New York: Praeger, 1977.

Guest, Dennis. *The Emergence of Social Security in Canada*. Vancouver: University of British Columbia Press, 1980.

Hardin, Russell. *Collective Action*. Baltimore: Johns Hopkins University Press, 1982.

Harris, Richard. *A Sacred Trust*. New York: New American Library, 1966.

Heclo, Hugh. *Modern Social Politics in Britain and Sweden*. New Haven: Yale University Press, 1974.

Heidenheimer, Arnold, Hugh Heclo, and Carolyn Adams. *Comparative Public Policy: The Politics of Social Choice in Europe and America*. New York: St. Martin's Press, 1975.

Hobman, David. "Aging, Self-help, and Political Action." In Frank Glendenning, ed., *Self-help and the Over 60s* (a report of a seminar arranged by the Department of Adult Education, University of Keele), 9–26. Stoke-on-Trent, England: Beth Johnson Foundation, 1978.

Hofstadter, Richard. *Social Darwinism in American Thought*. New York: George Braziller, 1944.

Holtzman, Abraham. *The Townsend Movement*. New York: Bookman Associates, 1963.

Hudson, Kenneth. *Help the Aged: Twenty Years of Experiment and Achievement*. London: Bodley Head, 1982.

Hudson, Robert B. "The 'Graying' of the Federal Budget and Its Consequences for Old-Age Policy." *Gerontologist* 18, no. 5 (October 1978): 428–40 (article reprinted in Robert B. Hudson, ed., *The Aging in Politics: Process and Policy*, 261–80. Springfield, Ill.: Charles C. Thomas, 1981).

Hudson, Robert B., and John Strate. "Aging and Political Systems." In Robert Binstock and Ethel P. Shanas, eds., *Handbook of Aging and the Social Sciences,* 2d ed., 554–85. New York: Van Nostrand Reinhold, 1985.

Humphreys, Noel A. "Old Age Pensions in the United Kingdom." *Journal of the Royal Statistical Society* 74 (December 1910): 71–73.

Jacobs, Bruce. "Aging and Politics." In Robert Binstock and Linda K. George, eds.,

Handbook of Aging and the Social Sciences 3d ed. New York: Academic Press, 1990.

Jacobs, Ruth H., and Beth Hess. "Panther Power: Symbols and Substance." *Long-Term Care and Health Services Administration Quarterly* 2 (Fall 1978): 238–44.

Johnson, Bruce. *National Party Platforms*. 2d ed. Urbana: University of Illinois Press, 1978.

Jones, Greta. *Social Darwinism in English Thought*. Sussex, England: Harvester Press, 1980.

Jordan, A. G., and J. J. Richardson. *British Politics and the Policy Process: An Arena Approach*. London: Allen and Unwin, 1987.

———. *Government and Pressure Groups in Britain*. Oxford and New York: Oxford University Press, 1987.

Judge, Ken. "State Pensions and the Growth of Social Welfare Expenditure." *Journal of Social Policy* 10, no. 4 (1981): 503–30.

———. "Federal Expenditures for the Elderly: A Different Interpretation of the Past." *Gerontologist* 22, no. 2 (1982): 129–31.

Katz, Michael B. *In the Shadow of the Poorhouse: A Social History of Welfare in America*. New York: Basic Books, 1986.

———. *The Undeserving Poor: From the War on Poverty to the War on Welfare*. New York: Pantheon Books, 1989.

Kernaghan, Kenneth, and Olivia Kuper. *Coordination in Canadian Governments: A Case Study in Aging Policy*. Toronto: Institute of Public Administration of Canada, 1983.

Krieger, Joel. *Reagan, Thatcher, and the Politics of Decline*. Cambridge, England: Polity Press, 1986.

Lammers, William W. *Public Policy and the Aging*. Washington, D.C.: Congressional Quarterly Press, 1983.

Lehman, Christopher. "Patterns in Policy Development: Social Security in the United States and Canada." *Public Policy* 25, no. 2 (1977): 261–91.

Leotta, Louis. "Abraham Epstein and the Movement for Old Age Security." *Labor History* 16, no. 3 (1975): 359–77.

Light, Paul. *Artful Work: The Politics of Social Security Reform*. New York: Random House, 1985.

Lijphart, Arend. "Consociational Democracy." *World Politics* 21 (1969): 207–25.

Logan, H. A. *Trade Unions in Canada*. Toronto: Macmillan, 1948.

Lowi, Theodore. *The End of Liberalism: Ideology, Policy, and the Crisis of Public Authority*. New York: W. W. Norton, 1969.

Lubove, Roy. *The Struggle for Social Security*. Cambridge: Harvard University Press, 1968.

McKee, William Finley. "The Attitude of the Federal Council of the Churches of Christ in America to the New Deal: A Study in Social Christianity." M.A. thesis (history), University of Wisconsin, 1954 (available in University of Wisconsin Memorial Library, Madison).

McNaught, Kenneth. *A Prophet in Politics: A Biography of J. S. Woodsworth*. Toronto: University of Toronto Press, 1959.

Marmor, Theodore R. *The Politics of Medicare*. Chicago: Aldine, 1973.

Means, Robin, and Randall Smith. *The Development of Welfare Services for Elderly People*. London: Croom Helm, 1985.

Messinger, Hans, and Frank Fedyk. "The Impact of Government Income Transfers on Poverty in Canada." Paper delivered at the annual meeting of the Canadian Economics Association, June 1988 (available from the Department of National Health and Welfare, Ottawa).

Midwinter, Eric. "Commentary: Policies on Aging." In *Annual Report: Center for Policy on Aging*, 7–15. London: CAP, 1988.

Miles, John. "Towards Equality: How Pensions Campaigns Are Changing: A Study of the Greater London Pensioners Association, 1989–1990." Master of Science in gerontology thesis, King's College, University of London, 1990.

Mitchell, B. R., and P. Deane. *Abstract of British Historical Statistics*. Cambridge: Cambridge University Press, 1962.

Moe, Terry M. *The Organization of Interests: Incentives and the Internal Dynamics of Interest Groups*. Chicago: University of Chicago Press, 1980.

Murray, Charles. *Losing Ground: American Social Welfare Policy, 1950–1980*. New York: Basic Books, 1984.

Myers, George C. "The Demography of Aging." In Robert Binstock and Linda K. George, eds., *Handbook of Aging and the Social Sciences*, 3d ed., 19–44. New York: Academic Press, 1990.

Nathan, Richard P. *The Plot That Failed: Nixon and the Administrative Presidency*. New York: John Wiley, 1975.

National Pensioners and Senior Citizens Federation. *Annual Convention Report* [for convention held at Niagara Falls, Ontario]. Toronto: NP&SCF, 1988.

New Democratic Party. *Policy Resolutions Passed by Plenary Session, 1961–1986*. Mimeo (on file at National Library of Canada, Ottawa).

———. *1987 Policy Resolutions Supplement*. Mimeo (on file at National Library of Canada, Ottawa).

NFOAPA. *Our Fight for Your Pension*. Blackburn, England: NFOAPA, n.d. [circa 1958].

———. *What Do We Get Out of It?* Blackburn, England: NFOAPA, n.d. [circa 1975].

———. "Report of the General Secretary." *Proceedings of the Thirty-eighth Conference*. Blackburn, England: NFOAPA, 1977.

———. "Report of the Publicity Officer." *Proceedings of the Forty-first Annual Conference*. Blackburn, England: NFOAPA, 1980.

Nordlinger, Eric A. *On the Autonomy of the Democratic State*. Cambridge: Harvard University Press, 1981.

Novack, Janet. "Strength from Its Gray Roots." *Forbes Magazine*, November 25, 1991, 89–94.

O'Donnell, Helen Ann Nancy. "A Diagnosis by Ideology: Ideological Perspectives on the Formation of Pension Policy in Canada." Ph.D. dissertation, McMaster University, Hamilton, Canada, 1984.

Ogus, A. I. "Great Britain." In Peter A. Kohler and Hans Zacher, eds., *The Evolution of Social Insurance, 1881–1981*. London: Francis Pinter, 1982.

O'Higgins, Michael. "Public/Private Interaction and Pension Provision." In Martin Rein and Lee Rainwater, eds., *Public/Private Interplay in Social Protection*, 99–148. Armonk, N.Y.: M. E. Sharpe, 1986. 99–148.

Olson, Mancur. *The Logic of Collective Action*. Cambridge: Harvard University Press, 1965.

One Cause (pamphlet). London: Age Concern, Help the Aged, Center for Policy on Aging, n.d. [circa 1987].

Pateman, Carol. "The Civic Culture, a Philosophical Critique." In Gabriel Almond and Sidney Verba, eds., *The Civic Culture Revisited*, 57–102. Boston: Little, Brown, 1980.

Phillipson, C. *Capitalism and the Construction of Old Age*. London: Macmillan, 1982.

Pinner, Frank A., Paul Jacobs, and Philip Selznick. *Old Age and Political Behavior: A Case Study*. Berkeley: University of California Press, 1959.

Piven, Francis Fox, and Richard A. Cloward. *Regulating the Poor: The Functions of Public Welfare*. New York: Vintage Books, 1971.

Plant, Raymond. "The Resurgence of Ideology." In Henry Drucker, ed., *Developments in British Politics*, 7–26. London: Macmillan, 1985.

Pratt, Henry J. *The Liberalization of American Protestantism: A Case Study in Complex Organizations*. Detroit: Wayne State University Press, 1972.

———. *The Gray Lobby*. Chicago: University of Chicago Press, 1976.

———. "Symbolic Politics and White House Conferences on Aging." *Society* 15, no. 5 (July–August 1978): 67–72.

———. "The 'Gray Lobby' Revisited." *National Forum: The Phi Kappa Phi Journal* 62, no. 4 (Fall 1982): 31–33.

———. "National Interest Groups among the Elderly: Consolidation and Constraint." In William P. Browne and Laura Olson, eds., *Aging and Public Policy: The Politics of Growing Old in America*, 145–80. Westport, Conn.: Greenwood Press, 1983.

———. "Aging Policy and Process in the Canadian Federal Government." *Canadian Public Administration* 30, no. 1 (Spring 1987): 57–75.

———. "Uncapping Mandatory Retirement: The Lobbyists' Influence." In Karen C. Holden and W. Lee Hansen, eds., *The End of Mandatory Retirement: Effects on Higher Education*, New Directions for Higher Education Series, no. 65, 15–32. San Francisco: Jossey-Bass, 1989.

Presthus, Robert. *Elite Accommodation in Canadian Politics*. Toronto: Macmillan, 1975.

Putnam, Jackson K. *Old-Age Politics in California: From Richardson to Reagan*. Stanford: Stanford University Press, 1970.

Quadragno, Jill. *The Transformation of Old Age Security: Class and Politics in the American Welfare State*. Chicago: University of Chicago Press, 1988.

Rich, Bennett M., and Martha Baum. *The Aging: A Guide to Public Policy*. Pittsburgh: University of Pittsburgh Press, 1984.

Ripley, Randall B., and Grace A. Franklin. *Congress, the Bureaucracy, and Public Policy*. 4th ed. Chicago: Dorsey Press, 1987.

Rochefort, David A. *American Social Welfare Policy: Dynamics of Formulation and Change*. Boulder, Colo.: Westview Press, 1986.

Rovner, Julie. "Catastrophic-Costs Conferees Irked by Lobby Assaults." *Congressional Quarterly Weekly Report* 46 (March 26, 1988): 777, 780.

Rubinow, Isaac M. *Social Insurance, with Special Reference to American Conditions*. New York: Henry Holt, 1913.

Schlabach, Theron F. *Edwin E. Witte: Cautious Reformer*. Madison: Wisconsin State Historical Society, 1969.

Schwartz, John E. *America's Hidden Success: A Reassessment of Twenty Years of Public Policy*. New York: W. W. Norton, 1983.

Sears, Val. "Gray Power: Coming of Age." *Toronto Star* June 15, 1985, B1.

Senior Citizens' Provincial Council. *A Short History of Senior Citizens Organizations in Saskatchewan*. Regina, Saskatchewan: Senior Citizens' Provincial Council, 1981.

Shenfield, B. E. *Social Policies for Old Age*. London: Routledge and Kegan Paul, 1957.

Skocpol, Theda. *States and Social Revolutions: A Comparative Analysis of France, Russia, and China*. Cambridge: Harvard University Press, 1979.

Skocpol, Theda, and Ann Shola Orloff. "Why Not Equal Protection? Explaining the Politics of Public Social Spending in Britain, 1900–1911, and the United States, 1880s-1920." *American Sociological Review* 49 (December 1984): 726–50.

Street, David, George T. Martin, Jr., and Laura Kramer Gordon. *The Welfare Industry: Functionaries and Recipients in Public Aid*. Beverly Hills, Calif.: Sage Publications, 1979.

Thane, Pat. "Non-Contributory versus Insurance Pensions, 1878–1908." In Pat Thane, ed., *The Origins of British Social Policy*, 84–106. London: Croom Helm, 1978.

———. "The Working Class and State 'Welfare' in Britain, 1880–1914." *Historical Journal* 27, no. 4 (1984): 877–900.

Titmuss, Richard M. *Social Policy: An Introduction*. New York: Pantheon Books, 1974.

Tocqueville, Alexis de. *Democracy in America*. Translated by Henry Reeve. 2 vols. New York: Vintage Books, 1958.

Trattner, Walter I. *From Poor Law to Welfare State: A History of Social Welfare in America*. New York: Free Press, 1974.

Trimblinger, Ellen Kay. "State Power and Modes of Production: The Implications of the Japanese Transition to Capitalism." *Insurgent Sociologist* 7 (Spring 1977): 85–98.

Truman, David B. *The Governmental Process*. New York: Knopf, 1951.

TUC. Social Insurance and Industrial Welfare Department. *Pension Committee Survey Report*. London: TUC, August 1987.

U.K. Central Statistical Office. *Annual Abstract of Statistics*. London: Her Majesty's Stationery Office, 1990.

U.K. Government Actuary's Department. "Population and Pension Costs." Background paper prepared for *Reform of Social Security: Programme for Change*, Annex B. London: Her Majesty's Stationery Office, 1985.

U.K. Parliamentary Papers. *Report of the Royal Commission on the Aged Poor.* 14 (Command 7684). London: Her Majesty's Stationery Office, 1895.

U.K. Secretary of State for Social Services. *Reform of Social Security, Background Papers* 3, no. 1. London: Her Majesty's Stationery Office, 1985.

U. S. Bureau of the Census. *Historical Statistics of the United States: Colonial Times to 1970.* Washington, D.C.: Government Printing Office, 1975.

———. *Statistical Abstract of the United States, 1989.* Washington, D.C.: Government Printing Office, 1989.

———. *Statistical Abstract of the United States, 1990.* Washington, D.C.: Government Printing Office, 1990.

U.S. Congress. House. Committee on Ways and Means. *Social Security Act Amendments of 1949* (Hearings on H.R. 2893). 81st Cong., 1st and 2d sess., pt. 2, 1949.

U.S. Congress. House. Committee on the Budget. *Hearings before the Task Force on Income Security.* 100th Cong., 1st sess., 1987.

U.S. Congress. Senate. Special Committee on the Aging. *Developments in Aging 1972 and January–March 1973.* 93d Cong., 1st sess., 1973.

U.S. Department of Health and Human Services. *Income and Resources of the Population 65 and Over.* Washington, D.C.: Department of Health and Human Services, September 1986.

U.S. White House Conference on Aging. *Section Recommendations on Employment and Retirement.* Washington, D.C.: Government Printing Office, 1971.

Urquard, M. C., and K. A. Buckley, eds. *Historical Statistics of Canada.* 2d ed. Ottawa: Statistics Canada, 1983.

Vinyard, Dale. "White House Conferences and the Aged." *Social Service Review* 53 (December 1979): 655–71.

———. "Political Rhetoric and the Elderly." Occasional Paper, Department of Political Science, Wayne State University, 1981.

Walker, Alan. "Pensions and the Production of Poverty in Old Age." In Chris Phillipson and Alan Walker, eds., *Aging and Social Policy: A Critical Assessment*, 184–216. Aldershot, England: Gower Publishing, 1986.

Walker, Jack L. "The Origins and Maintenance of Interest Groups in America." *American Political Science Review* 77, no. 2 (June 1983): 390–406.

———. *Mobilizing Interest Groups in America: Patrons, Professionals, and Social Movements.* Ann Arbor: University of Michigan Press, 1991.

Wildavsky, Aaron. *Speaking Truth to Power: The Art and Craft of Policy Analysis.* New Brunswick, N.J.: Transaction Books, 1987.

Wilensky, Harold. *The Welfare State and Equality: Structural and Ideological Roots of Public Expenditure.* Berkeley: University of California Press, 1971.

Williams, P. M. (Thane). "The Development of Old Age Pensions in the U.K., 1878–1925." Ph.D. diss., University of London, 1970.

Williamson, John B., Linda Evans, and Lawrence A. Powell. *The Politics of Aging: Power and Policy.* Springfield, Ill.: Charles C. Thomas, 1982.

Williamson, John B., Judith A. Shindul, and Linda Evans. *Aging and Public Policy.* Springfield, Ill.: Charles C. Thomas, 1985.

Wilson, James Q. *Political Organizations.* New York: Basic Books, 1973.

Witte, Edwin E. *The Development of the Social Security Act.* Madison: University of Wisconsin Press, 1963.

Wolfinger, Raymond A., and Stephen Rosenstone. *Who Votes?* New Haven: Yale University Press, 1980.

Wolman, Harold, and Fred Teitelbaum. "Interest Groups and the Reagan Presidency." In Lester M. Salamon and Michael S. Lund, *The Reagan Presidency and the Governing of America*, 297–329. Washington, D.C.: Urban Institute Press, 1984.

Young, Walter R. *Anatomy of a Party: The National CCF, 1932–1961.* Toronto: University of Toronto Press, 1969.

Zeigler, L. Harmon, and Wayne Peak. *Interest Groups in American Politics.* 2d ed. Englewood Cliffs, N.J.: Prentice-Hall, 1972.

Index

Abrams, M., 187
Achenbaum, W. Andrew, 5, 25, 49, 72, 83, 202
Adams, Carolyn, 216
Administration on Aging (AOA), 177–78
Age Concern England, 91, 130–35
Aging organizations, present-day importance, 1–4; clustering tendency of, 4–8; state-centered approach toward, 8–13; patronage in formation of, 13–14; impact of public policy on, 15; importance compared to other actors, 16–17; difficulty in forming following early pension enactments, 62–63; maintenance theory applied to, 201–12
Aging policy, distinguishing features, 15–16
All Party Pensions Group, 133
Almond, Gabriel, 206
Altmeyer, Arthur, 55–56, 68
American Association for Labor Legislation (AALL), 42, 59–60, 203, 215
American Association for Old Age Security (AAOAS), 43, 59–60, 203, 215
American Association for Social Security (AASS), 43, 59–60, 215
American Association of Retired Persons (AARP), exceptional in size terms, 1, 206, 215; formed in cluster with other groups, 6; early recipient of NRTA patronage, 84; initial low Capitol Hill visibility, 85, 102; pointed to enviously by pension activ-

ist in Britain, 132; formation date compared to other groups, 179, 180; significance of headquarters locale, 181, 182–83; active on behalf of nonmandatory retirement, 186–90; role in Medicare Catastrophic Coverage struggle, 193–99
American Federation of Labor (AFL), 44–45, 198
Andrews, John B., 59
Andrus, Ethel Percy, 186
Area Agencies on Aging (AAA), 177

B'nai B'rith, 46
Ball, Robert M., 75, 81, 82
Banting, K. G., 147
Baum, Martha, 179
Beer, Samuel, 93
Bell, Daniel, 47
Bercuson, David, 105, 108
Berger, Victor L., 47
Beveridge, William, 86, 118–20
Binstock, Robert, 1, 14, 84, 109
Birtles, J. C., 89
Bismarck, Otto von, 216
Blackley, Canon William L., 32–33
Blaikie, Andrew, 64, 90
Block, Fred, 11
Bodganor, Vernon, 105
Booth, Charles, 33
Bowen, William G., 83
Brennan, E. J. T., 24
Brinkley, Alan, 61
Britain, early pension developments, 31–36; early means-tested programs in, 56–58; phase two group forma-